Dale Peck was born on Long Island and raised in Kansas. He is
the author of the highly acclaimed books *Now It's Time to Say
Goodbye*, *The Law of Enclosures* and *Fucking Martin*.

BOOKS BY DALE PECK

Fucking Martin
The Law of Enclosures
Now It's Time to Say Goodbye

What We Lost

A Story of My Father's Childhood

DALE PECK

Granta Books
London

Granta Publications, 2/3 Hanover Yard, Noel Road, London N1 8BE

First published in Great Britain by Granta Books 2004
First published in the US by Houghton Mifflin Company 2003

A CIP catalogue record for this book is available from the British Library.

1 3 5 7 9 10 8 6 4 2

Printed and bound in Italy by
Legoprint

This book is for my father and Gloria Hull,

and for Paul Hamann,
who set me on the road that led to them.

———

And for M.S., and a loss I could never render in words.

It is not just
that a man be given what he throws away.

—Dante, *Inferno*

PART 1

1

THE OLD MAN has an odor like a force field. He wakes the boy before dawn. Quiet, he says, and underneath his black coat his kitchen whites reek of cabbage, stewed meat, spoiled milk. We don't want to get your mother up.

The old man's clothes stink of institutional food but it is his breath, wet and sickly sweet, that leaves a weight on the boy's cheek like his sisters' hairspray when they shoo him from the bathroom. Reluctantly he edges out of bed. Like the old man, he wears his work clothes, jeans, undershirt, brown corduroy jacket—everything but shoes. He shivers in his socks and watches in the half light as the pillowcase is stripped from his pillow and filled with clothes from the dresser, trying to warm his thin chest with thin arms and the thinner sleeves of his jacket.

That's Jimmy's shirt.

The old man claps him in the stomach with a pair of boots.

You shut up and put these on.

The boots are cold and damp and pinch the boy's feet as he squeezes into them, and as he knots the laces he watches Lance's drawers and Jimmy's football jersey disappear into the pillowcase.

But Dad.

Sshh!

The old man stuffs a pair of jeans into the sack.

But Dad. Those are Duke's.

The old man looks at the shock of blond hair on the far side of the bed, and when he turns to the boy the empty bottles in his pockets rattle and the boy can smell what was in them too.

3

You won't have to worry about that bastard no more, the old man says, breath lighting up the air like sparked acetylene. Not where you're going.

If any of the boys has awakened he gives no sign. Already Lance is hugging the extra inches of blanket where the boy had lain, and Jimmy, slotted into the crease between the pushed-together mattresses, seems folded along his spine like a blade of grass. At the far end of the bed Duke lies with his back to his dark-haired brothers, the stiff collar of his houndstooth coat sticking out beyond the blanket. A few inches beyond Duke's nose the rope-hung sheet dividing the boys' bed from their sisters' puckers in a draft, but Duke never goes to sleep without making sure the holes on the girls' half of the curtain are covered by solid patches on the boys', and so the boy can catch no glimpse of Lois or Edi or Joanie as he is surfed out of the room by the old man's frozen spittle. All he glimpses in the gap between curtain and floor is a banana peel and two apple cores, and his stomach rumbles and he wants to check his jacket to see if his siblings have left him any food. But the old man is nudging him, Faster, faster, and the boy has to use both hands to descend the ladder's steep rungs. Down below, the quilts fencing off his parents' bed are drawn tight as tent flaps, and although his mother's snores vibrate through tattered layers of cotton batting both she and the baby, Gregory, tucked in his crib beside her, remain invisible.

The boy pauses at the stovepipe and its single coal of heat in the hopes of warming his stiff boots, but the old man steps on his heels.

Hurry it up, he whispers, clouting him on the back of the head with the sack. Unless you feel the need for a goodbye kiss from your ma.

Outside the air is cold and wet and, low down—down around his knees—gauzy with dawn vapors, and underneath the vapors the frozen grass breaks beneath the boy's boots with a sound like ice chewed behind closed lips. His ice-cold boots mash his toes, but it's not until they've walked through their yard and the Slovak's that a space opens up between two ribbons of mist and the boy sees that the

4

boots are pinching his feet not because they're cold or wet but because the old man has handed him Jimmy's instead of his own. They *had* been the boy's, up until about three months ago, but even though Jimmy is two years older and two inches taller than the boy, his feet have been a size smaller than the boy's since he was eight years old, and just before Thanksgiving the boy had traded Jimmy his shoes for the pants he's wearing now. The pants are a little long on him, a little loose in the waist, the outgrown boots squeeze his feet like a huckster's handshake. But when he turns back toward the house there is the old man, hissing,

C'mon, c'mon, hurry it up. It's late enough already.

All around them the dark round shapes of their neighbors' cars loom out of the fog like low-tide boulders, and down at the end of the block the cab of the old man's flatbed truck rises above them, a breaching whale. The cab is white, or was white; it's barnacled with flecked rust now, a lacy caul of condensation veils the windscreen. The boy stares at the soft-skull shape of it as he minces down the block, not quite understanding why the sight is confusing, unsettling even. Then:

Hey Dad. Why'd you park all the way—

The old man cuts him off with another Sshh! and then, when the driver's side door breaks open from the cab with the same sound the shade tree made when it fell in front of the garage three winters ago, the boy suddenly realizes how quiet their street is, and the streets beyond theirs. Seatsprings creak and whine like the grade school orchestra as the old man settles into the cab, the pillowcase rustles audibly as the boy takes it from him and drops it to his lap. Then glass clinks as the old man opens his coat and pulls what looks like an empty bottle from a pocket in the lining, and when he arches his head back to suck whatever imagined vapor lingers in the brown glass the sound that comes from his loose dentures is the same sound that Gregory makes when his mother puts a bottle to his toothless lips. And all of these noises are as familiar to the boy as the thinning strands of the old man's hair, his winter-burned scalp, the globe of bone beneath the skin, but just as the half light shadows the old man's features, deepening and obscuring them, the morning hush seems to amplify the noises in the cab, giving them the ominous sharpness of a movie soundtrack. And there is a hardness to the old man's eyes as well, slitted into the ravines of his slack stubbled cheeks, a glint Duke once said always came about nine months before another baby. The boy can't remember if Duke had said that before or after the old man whipped him.

The old man throws the empty bottle with the others at the boy's feet and straightens behind the wheel. His left and right hands work choke and key with the resigned rhythm of a chain gang, and after three rounds the engine turns over once, twice, then chugs into life with a lifelong smoker's cough, and the boy remembers something else Duke had said about the old man. The old man, Duke said, used to smoke like everyone else, but he gave it up when one time his breath was so strong his burps caught fire, and he pointed to the charred leather above the driver's seat as proof. Sitting in the cab now, it is easy to believe Duke's story. Everything about the truck is animated as a carnival, from the trampolining seat to the pneumatic sigh of the clutch to the spindly stick of the gearshift, which the old man manipulates as though it were a cross between a magic wand and a knob-headed cane. Down around the boy's throbbing feet the glass bottles tinkle their accompaniment and up above are the old man's fiercely focused eyes, and the boy is so distracted by all this drama that he nearly forgets to take a last look at his house. By the time he turns all he sees are the empty panes of glass in the garage door that the shade tree smashed when it fell. The black rectangles gape like lost teeth amid the frosted white panes, like pages ripped from a book or tombstones stolen from a graveyard, and for some reason the sight of them fills the boy with a sense of loss and dread. Then there is just the shade tree, dead now, leafless and twigless but otherwise intact, and still blocking the garage door as it has for the past three years.

Brentwood, Long Island, 1956. The most important local industry might not be the Entenmann's factory but it is to a boy of twelve, almost thirteen, and as the truck rattles down Fifth Avenue the boy cracks open the triangular front window in his door and presses his nose to it as he always does. It is too cold and the factory is six blocks away and the boy can smell little more than a ghost of sugar on the wet air, but in his mind the street is doughy as a country kitchen, and as he inhales he pretends he can sort the different odors of crumb and glazed and chocolate-covered donuts from an imaginary baker's hash of heat and wheat and yeast. The sharp vanilla edge of angel food cake or the cherry tinge of frosted Danish or his favorite, the soft almost wet odor of all-butter French loaf. He likes it for the name even more than the taste—a loaf they call it, like bread, when it is sweeter than any cake. In fact he has eaten it so few times the taste is a memory trapped in his head in a space apart from his tongue, but whenever he stocks the pastries section of Slaussen's Market his nostrils flare as if they can smell the brick-sized loaves through waxed cardboard and cellophane.

It's when they pass Slaussen's that the boy realizes they're headed for the Southern State. Big white signs fill the store's dark windows. PORK CHOPS 19¢/LB! IDAHO POTATOES, PERFECT FOR BAKING! ORDER YOUR XMAS TURKEY NOW! The boy turns his head to stare at this last notice as they drive by. It's the second week of January and the disjunction tickles his mind, but only faintly, like the flavor of all-butter French loaf. But then he remembers something else.

Will I be back for work?

The way the old man operates the truck reminds the boy of a puppet show. He is all elbows and knees, jerks and lunges and rapid glances to left and right, and he doesn't spare an eye for the boy when he answers him.

Close your window, he says. And then: What time do you clock in?

I go in after school.

The old man turns right onto Spur Drive North without slowing, drops the truck into second in an attempt to maintain speed up the on-ramp. The tires squeal around the corner and the truck bucks as though running over a body when the old man downshifts, and then the ancient engine hauls the truck up the incline like a man pulling a sled by a rope.

What time do you clock in?

The boy doesn't answer. Instead he watches the road, not afraid, only mildly curious, as the truck slides across both lanes of the parkway and drops two tires into the center median before the old man steadies its course. The old man has gone into the median so many times that the older boys refer to the strip of grass as the Lloyd Parkway, and one time, according to Duke, the old man went all the way over to the eastbound lane and was halfway to work before he realized it. Now he continues half-on and half-off the road for another quarter mile before jerking the truck back into the left lane.

Did you close your window?

The boy looks up. The old man is using the end of his sleeve to rub something, dust or frost, off a gauge on the dash, and when he's finished he squints at the gauge and then he says, You won't be going into Slaussen's tonight. He looks down at the boy and lets the big wheel go slack in his hands. Where you're going you'll wish sacks of potatoes was all you had to haul around. Shit, boy, he says, that's what you'll be carting soon. Wheelbarrels full of—

The crunch of median gravel under the left front tire brings his attention back to the road. The steering wheel is as big as a pizza and twirls like one too, as the old man wrestles the truck onto the roadway.

Did you close your window?

The boy ignores him. The truck's heater has been broken since before he can remember and it will make no difference if the vent window is open or closed. If they drive long enough the engine's heat might pulse through the dash and if it does he will close the window, but at this point, despite the sack of clothes he has buried his hands in for warmth, he doesn't believe they will be on the road very long. And besides, the pillowcase is tiny, almost empty. Only one change

8

of clothes, even if none of them fit him. But at least they won't hurt him, like Jimmy's shoes.

Already the fog has thinned, skulking in the median as if afraid of the big truck, but no other cars are on the road; and as they drive the pain in the boy's feet changes. The sharp pinching in his toes dissipates slightly, becomes a general ache he feels throughout his feet, less strong but more pervasive, and he is trying to decide if this is more or less bearable than the initial pinching when the old man veers toward the exit for Dix Hills.

The boy relaxes then. Even though he doesn't know the names of these streets he knows the rhythms of the starts and stops and turns through them, can feel the rightness or wrongness of the truck's movement in his belly—indeed, he's been feeling it since his time in his mother's. Both his parents are employed at Pilgrim State Mental Hospital, and before the boy started school he stayed at the enormous hospital's daycare facility, which he remembers as a place of lights so bright he could never find Jimmy and his sisters—Duke was already in school by then, and Lance wasn't born until after the boy started going to Brentwood Elementary. Then, not long after he left daycare, the boy's mother began sending him with the old man when he went to pick up his paycheck Friday afternoons, because most of the bars the old man frequents won't let him bring the boy in with him and, during the winter at least, the old man doesn't make the boy sit out in the truck for more than a half hour or two. And even though it is Saturday morning and the old man should have collected his paycheck yesterday, the boy isn't all that troubled. He simply assumes they're en route to another of the old man's errands: helping the hospital's dairyman unload crates of eggs onto the back of their truck, or taking out the kitchen trash, which just happens to contain a couple gunnysacks of potatoes or waxed cardboard boxes of broccoli still tightly packed in ice. He ignores the pillowcase in his hands, the glint in the old man's eyes. The old man is twitchy but repetitive, he reminds himself—a broken record, Duke calls him, stuck in a groove. If his actions sometimes appear random, it is only the contained chaos of one marble clicking off another in the schoolyard, willy-nilly inside the tiny chalk circle but easily predictable within the broad scheme of things. Eventually everything will become clear, if not immediately then at some not-too-distant point.

The looming crooked edifice of the hospital is just visible in the distance when the old man eases the truck down a dark narrow alleyway, seemingly forgetting to brake until the nose of the truck is inches from the sooty bricks of the alley's terminal wall. Now the boy understands what's going on. This is the Jew's back door, and the old man comes here with almost the same regularity as he goes to the payroll office at the hospital a mile down the road. The boy only takes the time to loosen the laces on his boots before pressing his ear to the open window—his left ear, so he can turn and face the scene taking place at the back of the truck. Through the window he hears the old man's muttered curses, the soft thud of his fist on the gray metal door.

Come on, come on, he growls, drag your lazy ass out of bed, come on!

This goes on for several minutes until finally there is a muffled voice from beyond the door.

All right, all right, enough with the pounding, all right!

The Jew is shaped liked a candy Easter egg stood up on end: oval on one side just like a regular egg but flat on the other. This morning his big stomach pushes his white shirt and black pants out of a bathrobe instead of the lab coat he normally wears, and in place of his black skullcap a handkerchief is draped over the bald wrinkles of his head. Both the handkerchief and the hand that holds it in place are as stained as the old man's kitchen uniform.

Floyd, he says, getting the old man's name wrong as he always does, we don't normally see you this early. Not an emergency I hope.

This is the part the boy is fascinated by: the part where the old man fakes a cough. He must summon a breath for it, and when he does manage to force out a sputter it's hardly louder than the wheeze of a punctured tire. His face contorts in pain and both his hands clutch not at his lungs but at his belly.

Ah jeez Doc, the old man says with ragged breath. I'm feeling pretty bad. What fascinates the boy is the fact that this both is and is not a lie.

A pity, a pity. And too early to see your physician I'm sure.

Still at the country club. The old man tries to soothe his grimace into a grin. Probably on the golf course right now.

The morning light barely penetrates the high-walled alley, but the Jew doesn't bat an eye at this ill-timed delivery of the old man's line.

No matter. We'll send you home with something that'll fix you right as rainbows.

He closes the door in the old man's face, offering a brief glimpse of his white-cloaked back — from shoulders to heels as flat as a tabletop after the dishes have been cleared away. The old man stamps his feet impatiently but it's only a few minutes before the Jew returns. The handkerchief flies off his head when he opens the door and he grabs for it with one doughy hand, misses, then lets the hand sit there as if embarrassed to be bareheaded in the presence of a customer. The boy thinks the Jew's wrinkled skull is as ugly as a shrimp's mottled front end — he's seen those too, at Slaussen's, thousands of them as gray and slimy as the ash pail when Duke takes a leak into it — and then, one hand still covering his head, the Jew holds out a small white bag weighed down by heavy round shapes.

I have taken the liberty of prescribing seven. Two tablespoons three times a day. They should see you through the week, but if they don't.

He leaves the sentence unfinished.

The old man scrabbles through his pockets. The first produces an empty bottle and the second produces another, but finally he finds a wad of bills and extracts some and gives them to the Jew. The Jew puts them in a pocket of his robe without counting them and hands the bag to the old man. The boy knows from Duke how greedy Jews are, but Duke has also told him that the old man is even more desperate than the Jew is greedy, and the Jew knows this too. The Jew knows that the old man will not shortchange him because then the old man will not be able to get his prescriptions renewed anymore.

11

The boy knows all this in the same way his stomach knows the twists and turns of the streets that lead to this alley and his head knows the taste of all-butter French loaf. He knows that the bottles in the bag contain a cough medicine whose primary ingredient is corn syrup and whose active ingredient is turpenhydrate, an explosive word whose size and syllables slot it in the boy's head somewhere between peroxide and nitroglycerin, and he knows too that it is the combination of these two ingredients, corn syrup and turpenhydrate, that makes the old man's breath smell as sour as eggnog left on the counter overnight.

And your son. The boy sees the Jew's eyes glance toward the cab. He is well I hope.

He's fine, he's fine. My boy's fine.

Your firstborn, no? Your eldest?

The boy knows the Jew has seen Duke and Jimmy—his mother had sent both of them in turn to guard the old man's paycheck—and now he knows the Jew is aware of this other thing as well, less the family secret than the family shame.

The old man turns and looks in the boy's direction, but if he sees him his face doesn't register it.

The boy's fine. We're going to see his uncle Upstate.

A trip to the country! the Jew calls out to the old man, already heading back to his side of the truck. A weekend adventure! All best wishes for a speedy recovery and safe return. Just before the old man climbs in the cab, the Jew makes a clucking sound with his tongue. Such a young man, he says, and then both truck and pharmacy doors slam closed at the same time.

The old man takes one of the bottles from the white bag and drinks it, and then he casts around the truck until his eyes light on the pillowcase filled with the boy's brothers' clothes. The finger that points to it wavers like the needle of a cheap compass, and the boy doesn't hand it to him but instead pushes it across the seat. With the persistence of a chicken scratching for corn the old man attempts to separate one side of the open end of the pillowcase from another, scraping and clawing until a hooked finger manages to pull the sack open. The old man scrunches up the white bag as tight as it will go and then rolls the bag into Duke's jeans and stuffs the jeans back into the sack and pushes it toward the boy. But the boy is still hearing the Jew's last words. *Such a young man.* For a moment he'd thought the Jew was talking about him—he'd felt almost grown up. But as he watches the old man's balding but babyish face, his purple tongue clamped between yellow dentures as he concentrates on his task, he realizes the Jew was referring to his father.

Guard this with your life. One of these breaks, it'll be your head.

The boy holds the bag for a moment, then drops it to the floor of the truck and puts one of his feet on it. Even that small pressure hurts his foot and, briefly, the boy thinks about smashing the old man's medicine with the heel of Jimmy's shoe. But the morning's balance is already fragile, and he doesn't want to risk sending it over the edge to someplace new. Someplace he has never been.

No matter how many times the old man does it the boy can never believe he will be able to back out of the alleyway. It's as if all the benevolence providence denies him in every other area of his life is trapped in this brick-and-mortar gulch, and no matter how many medians or telephone poles or dogs the old man runs into or over he is always able to back the truck out of the Jew's alley as easily as if he were parked on a conveyor belt. He doesn't even turn around—does it all with mirrors—nor does he pause at the exit, and more than once cars have veered around the truck as it catapults from the alley's blessed sanctum. But the roads are clear this morning, of cars and fog too, which seems to have burned off in the few minutes it took the old man to renew his prescription. The sun has cleared the horizon and ascends the convex surface of the sky and the boy turns and watches it through the warped glass of the cab's rear window. If the boy tilts his head the irregularities in the glass distort the rising sun into a sliver, a pinhole, an orange portal with pulsating, beckoning edges, and he toys with the shape as the truck rattles toward the parkway, not turning around until, with a sickening lurch, the truck veers right when it should veer left. Although the boy doesn't know his compass points—knows only that eastbound and westbound lanes lead toward home and away, that south shore and north shore mark the poles of a socioeconomic axis whose bottom end his family occupies—he does know that a right turn means they are heading beyond Dix Hills. He has never gone beyond Dix Hills before.

Quickly, he faces forward in his seat. All he can think to do is chart their progress by the signs that dot the road, so that when the old man pulls onto a side street for his inevitable nap the boy will be able to tell him where they are when he wakes up, which way they came from and how to get back home. But even though the old man's head nods every once in a while he doesn't stop driving, and each road he turns onto seems bigger than the last. The Southern State to the Long Island Expressway and the Long Island Expressway to the Clear View Expressway and the Clear View to the Throg's Neck Something, the Throg's Neck Bridge the boy sees when the road lifts off the ground and floats across an expanse of water, and after the Throg's Neck comes the Cross Something or Other, the boy doesn't see what they are crossing because by then the road is studded with signs, too many for him to read, too many for him to keep track of. Mother Mary Dolorosa Welcomes All, as does Riccio's Italian Restaurant—Family Style! The Utopia Estates Promise A New Beginning and Kaufmann Bros. Storage Keeps Your Dreams Safe and the Maritime Academy Provides Hope For Tomorrow but right now the boy has no dreams and he has no hope because he's lost track of their route, and at some point he's lost his feet too, which have gone numb in their too-tight shoes. It is an empty yet heavy sensation, in its way much more compelling than the pain that had been there before, or the hunger gnawing at his gut. He had to work last night and so hasn't eaten since lunch yesterday, but he is so used to being hungry that he almost doesn't notice it, what with his feet and what's going on outside the truck.

Over the course of several hours the buildings have gotten bigger and more numerous but now they're smaller again, thinning out until finally they're so sparse they seem to mark the space between parcels of property rather than the other way around. Indeed, the land has an unfamiliar, unsettling sprawl here. On Long Island the water's boundary is always palpable, even when it's not visible — you can feel it in the horizon's abrupt drop-off. But here the land stretches out in all directions, leaving the boy with the disturbing impression that they could keep driving forever. And then there are the mountains. The only mountains the boy has ever heard of are the ones the old man is always going on about, the mountains of his childhood. Those verdant slopes were green and crisscrossed by babbling brooks and sweet clean streams, and some quality of the old man's words had always led the boy to picture them as curved and comely, nature's pinup stretched on one hip across the horizon. Whereas these mounds are jagged as cookie dough: their leafless forests are as ugly as January Christmas trees heaped on the curb, their snowcaps ash colored. Even their massive rock faces seem smeared across them, like Lance's cheeks after he eats a slice of chocolate cake. The combination of the land's sprawl and the lumpy protrusions, in such stark contrast to the old man's drunken rambles about his youth in the country, give the boy the idea that he is being driven into a past that isn't as rosy as the old man would have him believe. For a long time the truck runs along an enormous river though, and the boy is fascinated by the two frozen shelves that stick out from either shore and the ice-chunked strip of ice-blue water between. The glacial shelves look like teeth to the boy, cartoon teeth breaking apart after biting on a rock hidden in blueberry pie, and the boy laughs quietly to himself when he imagines the river being fitted for dentures like the old man. A trip to the country, he reminds himself, attempting to relax again. A weekend adventure.

Hey Dad. How old are you?

The old man doesn't answer, but a moment later his foot taps out a rhythm. Da-da-DA-da, da-da-DA-da. He taps with his right foot, the foot on the gas pedal, and on the third DA the truck surges forward with a grunt.

Dad.

The old man turns. Twice he has had the boy pull a bottle of cough syrup from the pillowcase — as many times as they have stopped to gas up the truck—and the medicine has pinked his pallid cheeks. He examines the boy as if checking for something then turns back to the road.

My own boy. My own and oldest boy.

The boy repeats his question.

My oldest boy, the old man says, louder now. Not like that bastard. Not like that bastard Duke. The old man does something with the truck's levers and pedals. The boy doesn't feel any difference in the truck's motion but the old man pats the dash with the flat of his hand. That's a good girl, he says. That's my baby. He sits up straighter. Not like that bastard Jimmy neither. Jimmy *Dundas* and Duke *Enlow*, he says, looking down at the boy. Jimmy Dundas and Duke Enlow and Dale *Peck*. Son of Lloyd *Peck*. My firstborn. My old and ownliest boy.

How old are you, Dad?

K-K-Katie, beautiful Katie, you're the only g-g-girl that I adore!

The old man rocks the wheel like a cradle and the truck meanders from lane to lane until a horn blares from somewhere below the cab and a car appears from the right shoulder and speeds ahead of the truck, still honking.

When the moon shines over the cowshed, I'll be waiting by the k-k-kitchen door!

How old were you when I was born?

Suddenly the old man turns to the boy, leaning so far over that the truck lists to the right. He makes a sucking noise on his dentures like a child with a lollipop and then, in a confidential insinuating voice, he says, I owe my troubles to a savage wife. He nods, sucks on his dentures, nods again. She's a whore, son. Your mother is a whore.

The boy takes hold of the steering wheel, righting it, and as wheel and truck rotate to the left the old man does too, until he is sitting up again. But he is still staring at the boy.

They tell you to stay away from whores but they never tell you why. They screw like pros, that's why. Your ma can screw with the best of em. That's how they get you. That's how she got me. She screwed me like a pro. She had two bastard children and a nose like

Jimmy Durante and a better man than me wouldn't've gone near her with a ten-inch pole, but she could swing pussy like a pro and I'm just a drunk and she got me fair and square. But I love my son. My firstborn son. Dale *Peck*. Firstborn son of Lloyd. I wouldn't let no whore take you away from me, no sir I wouldn't. Not again.

Up until the end the boy has been ignoring him. He has heard all of this before, either firsthand or secondhand. There is no place in their house that is more than a curtain away from any other and his parents have had this conversation too many times to count. But neither of them has ever said this last thing. Neither has ever said Not again.

What do you mean, Dad?

The old man makes a face, mouths an Oops, turns back to the road.

Not again, Dad?

Pedals, lever, pedals again. Then:

I'm a drunk, son. You know I'm a drunk. But never let it be said I let some whore take away my oldest child. My firstborn son. Never let anyone tell you that.

Dad?

I'm forty-two, the old man says. I was twenty-nine when you were born. I was just out of high school.

Dad?

Suddenly the old man's voice changes again. The strength is gone, replaced by a plaintive whine. I thought I told you to close your window. His hand on the boy's head is not quite a slap. Come on, come on now, hurry it up.

The window has been closed for several hours, and the boy reaches instead for the pillowcase on the floor.

Come on, come on, I don't got all day.

The boy hurries. Though he has never been afraid of the old man he has seen what happens to him when he doesn't get his syrup, and he doesn't want it to happen while the truck is in motion. He has to hold the wheel while the old man drinks bent down below the dashboard. He holds the wheel with his right hand and he watches not the road but the old man. Ten months later he will remember the old man's pose when he sees a week-old calf bend down on his forelegs and crane his neck up to drink from his mother's udder. The sinking and rising at the same time, the blissful expression in the eyes. Mother's milk, witch's brew. He will beat the calf off with a stick and hook his mother to a milking machine where she belongs.

The old man wipes his mouth when he finishes the bottle, and then he licks the back of his hand. The boy knows there is no use talking to the old man right after he has had his drink, but the stale sugary smell of the open bottle has reminded him of his own hunger. He puts his hands in his pockets and then on through, roots around in the hollow lining of his jacket to see if there is any food left. Last winter the old man had brought the big kids, Duke, Jimmy, Dale, Joanie, and Edi, on a field trip to the hospital's kitchen, where he'd instructed them to stuff the sleeves of their coats with any vegetable they could fit down them—it took Edi a week to shake all the papery garlic shavings out of her coat, and the smell lingered for months afterward. When the boy got the job at Slaussen's he'd done the old man one better, he thought, by having Joanie slit open the seams of his pockets so he could conceal his own contraband inside his jacket lining. He passes over the staples in favor of apples, bananas, whatever citrus fruit comes off the truck from Florida, but by the time he gets in at eleven from his after-school shift he is usually so tired he goes to bed immediately, and his brothers and sisters take the fruit while he's asleep—everyone except Duke, who refused to go along with the old man's plan at the hospital, and who won't eat the boy's food either. Today he finds only three grapes rolling around in his jacket lining. He knows that Joanie will have saved something for him, but Joanie is at home with the rest of his sisters and brothers.

The boy rolls a grape between thumb and forefinger, warming it up like a marble before he shoots it.

What did you mean just now, Dad? Not again?

The old man purses his lips and shakes his head. Uh-uh, he says through clenched teeth and closed lips, *nnhh-nnhh*, and then he opens them. I want you to mind your Uncle Wallace. Your Uncle

Wallace is my brother and a good man. A better man than I am. I want you to mind what he says.

Dad?

She was going to send you to military school. But I said no. I said not my firstborn son. I said she could send one of her bastard children to military school but not the firstborn son of Lloyd Peck could she send to military school. No sir. *Not again.*

The boy doesn't know what military school is, although he has heard the term used by his parents and has ridden past the gate to the LaSalle Military Academy on Sunrise Highway more than once. He goes to Brentwood Elementary, or at least he does on those days when he isn't suspended for betting on marbles in the schoolyard or getting beat up by boys who call his mother a whore and spit on his shoes. He is small for his age, the tiny son of a tiny man, and he doesn't know who his Uncle Wallace is though he has heard that name too. He is almost thirteen years old and he is not afraid of anything except the unknown, but he knows so little that in order to keep from being terrified all the time he has long since ceased believing in anything except what's in front of him, and right now what's in front of him is a cracked dashboard and a dirty windshield and an empty narrow road, gray, lined by shallow ditches, and disappearing over a hill the boy has to will himself to believe is not a cliff. He eats the three grapes, pretending each is an all-butter French loaf, and he spits the seeds on the floor one by one, and although he doesn't aim each seed still manages to ding off an empty apothecary bottle. When a burp bursts from the old man's mouth the boy sees it as a ball of flame, but what it burns up he's not sure. He looks at the blackened leather above the old man's head and then he closes his eyes as if they've been stung by smoke.

I'm forty-two years old, son. I'm a young man. But I'm old enough to be your father.

He must fall asleep then because when he opens his eyes the truck is stopped and the old man is not in the cab. He assumes they've stopped for gas until he sees a gnarled branch above the windshield like a jab of brown lightning and he sits up. To his right a row of leafless trees stretches up the side of a hill and to his left there is a white house, small and rectangular, its tiny second-story windows the shape of dominoes laid on their sides. Before he gets out of the cab he grabs the pillowcase containing his brothers' clothes and the old man's medicine, and the first thing he does is fall flat on his face because he can't feel his feet. Still half asleep, he sits on the crust of snow that covers the ground like stale cake frosting and takes off Jimmy's shoes. The ground is cold and hard beneath his bottom but the bottoms of his feet feel nothing at all, and, teetering, rudderless, he stands up and floats around the truck in his socks, the pillowcase less ballast than slack sail hanging down his back. A pitted two-track driveway runs around the house and up the hill toward a pair of barns and a tall round building that the boy recognizes instinctively as a silo even though it reminds him of a castle tower. At the foot of the silo he sees the old man talking to another man. Like the old man, this stranger is short and thin and has only half a dozen strands of hair slicked flat to his skull, but unlike the old man he stands absolutely still, one hand holding a pitchfork lightly but firmly, tines down, and a cap on the ground between the two men, bottom up like a busker's. The only thing that moves is his head, which shakes every once in a while, back and forth: no. The old man's legs are wobbling and his arms are flapping in the air, and as he wobbles toward them the boy is reminded of a seagull he saw once in the bay. The seagull's legs were trapped in a fishing net, and every time it flapped its wings its orange legs would lift out of the water trailing weed-draped mesh. Over and over the bird's legs had shaken like the old man's with its efforts to free itself but each time, exhausted, it splashed down again.

The old man and the stranger are still a good twenty yards away when the old man turns and reels toward the boy. His legs and arms make motions like the spokes of a rimless wheel, and he is shouting,

I won't let her send him away! Not my boy! Not my firstborn son! *Not again!*

He jerks right past the boy without seeming to see him, his doddering gait half step and half slide on the slick grade, and it seems pure chance that one of his flailing hands catches hold of the door handle, a veritable miracle that he is able to crack it open. The shotgun sound is like an echo of itself in the quiet air, and the boy whips his head from side to side as if he can find the original source. He is in the back of the house now. From this angle he sees that it is actually L-shaped. He can't see the farmhouse across the street, the mountain twenty miles to the south. He sees only a bulbous clump of gray-green evergreens and the tin-domed silo and the two barns and a patch of leafless woods at the top of the hill and then a big field studded with black-and-white and butter-brown cows. When the truck coughs into life one of the cows looks up from whatever thin strands it is pulling from the ground, looks first at the truck and then at the boy and then drops its head again and roots around for more grass—green grass, the boy can see, even from this distance. It is the middle of January and thin streaks of snow paint zebra stripes on soil hard as a city sidewalk, but the grass that grows from that soil is still green, and by the time the boy turns back to the truck it has backed out of the driveway, narrowly missing what looks like a fencepost with some kind of placard mounted atop it. The truck would have gone into the ditch on the far side of the road had there not been a tree there. Instead something glass breaks, a taillight that is not already broken perhaps, and when the old man shifts into first the boy hears first the transmission's grind and then the glass as it falls onto the road. The truck goes so slowly that had he wanted to the boy could have run after it, could probably have caught it even, even with his numb feet. But he just stands there swaying, watching the truck recede as if one of them, the truck or the boy, is on an ice floe borne away from the shore by a half-frozen current. By the time the truck disappears over the hill the stranger has walked down from the barns and walked on by. There is smoke coming from a chimney on the left wall of the house and the stranger's pitchfork makes a metallic ping each time it strikes the frozen ground.

Feeling floods into the boy's feet then, as if a pot of pasta water had tipped off the stove and spilled over them. He reels, bites back a cry of pain; catches his breath and catches his balance.

Uncle Wallace? he says to the thin brown back retreating down the hill.

The stranger doesn't stop, doesn't turn around.

Get my hat, Dale, he says. At the door he pauses to look the boy up and down, and then he shakes his head one more time. In the failing light his scalp looks white and cold.

Don't forget your shoes, he says, and walks into the house.

2

IT IS AS DARK as it can get now, and cold. It's not like the sun's gone down. It's like the light has frozen in space on its way here, leaving the boy trapped on the frozen plain of this unfamiliar bed.

This was your cousin Edith's bed.

It seemed to him that his uncle's wife, Bessie—Aunt Bessie—had fussed over the sheets. She'd stretched them taut across the mattress, smoothed out the wrinkles with her palm as though he weren't going to pull them back five minutes after she finished. She worked in silence after that one line though, until the boy realized it was his turn to say something.

I have a sister—

His voice cracked and squeaked into the little slope-ceilinged room. There is a slope to the loft's ceiling as well, on Long Island, but nothing like this steep pitch, which comes to within a couple of feet of the floor on one side of the room. He'd had to duck down to cross to the other side of the bed from Aunt Bessie.

The boy cleared his throat, tried again.

A sister named Edith. Louder: Edi.

In the dim room, illuminated by a single dusty lamp beside the bed, the multicolored squares of the quilt Aunt Bessie fluffed over the sheets seemed to spill out in a patternless yet intricate arrangement that hinted at some as-yet-unseen order, like the twilight stars before the constellations become fully visible. Aunt Bessie turned the top of the quilt down over the nearly featherless pillow, gave it a little plump, then straightened up and looked at him. The expression on her face wasn't inscrutable, but so unfamiliar as to seem that way. No one—especially not an adult, and especially not a woman—had ever looked at him with pity before.

You have a cousin named Edi too. A smile seamed her face, thin but genuine. Edith. Goodnight Dale.

And it's not like he's never had a bed to himself, a bedroom, although it takes a series of events as rare and complicated as a planetary alignment to empty the crowded house on Long Island of father, mother, seven brothers and sisters. The old man on a bender somewhere, his mother pulling second shift, Gregory and Lance at daycare. All three of the girls off at friends' houses, Jimmy knocking about the Pine Barrens collecting bird skulls or redeemable bottles or—if he can find him—the old man and what's left of his pay, Duke doing whatever it is Duke does to keep clear of the old man's fists. If on top of all this the boy doesn't have to go in to Slaussen's—and if he can find a way to make it past Robert Sampson and Bruce St. John and Vinnie Grasso without getting dragged into the Barrens himself—then he will round the corner from school and walk into an empty house, and even if he's not tired he will climb the ladder to the loft and stretch his limbs across the pushed-together twin mattresses that make up the boys' bed and stare at the canted underside of the roof as though the silver nailpoints pushing through it were the uncurtained stars in the sky. He knows from listening to his parents that this is what they mean by peace and quiet, but to him the house, empty, just feels odd, unnatural even, uncomfortable. With so much space on the bed he finds himself afraid of rolling over and falling off the edge; and if he imagines the scene from the point of view of the nails then what he pictures reminds him of a piece of driftwood washed ashore, or the last cornflake in a bowl of milk. And so he lies on the empty bed, not to rest but to wait, for his siblings to spill back into the house like a second helping of cereal. But no noisy horde is going to pour into this room. The thin quilt does little to quell the cold, even its illusion of stars extinguished with the bedside light.

Although a solid wall—paper and plaster over a net of lathe and studs—separates the boy from his uncle and Aunt Bessie, it's not much thicker than the curtain that cordons off his parents' bed at home, and he can hear them talking, their headboard pushed up against his. But unlike his parents, his uncle and Aunt Bessie don't shout, and he has to concentrate to hear what they're saying.

It's not right Wallace. Dropping off his own son like that, no warning to you or the boy. It's not right.

The boy can't make out his uncle's reply. It could be a grunt, or just the creak of wooden bed rails.

I mean, the expense. A boy that age costs money, and this farm—Aunt Bessie's voice disappears a moment, then resumes. And we're not young anymore, we both raised children and aren't exactly at an age to start over again. We're not even—

Another grunt, or creak.

I mean, I made him pot roast, fixed up Edith's bed for him. Now what am I supposed to—another fade, longer this time, and then—into town tomorrow? Just drop him off at school?

This time the boy can make out a few of his uncle's words.

Tomorrow's Sunday Bess.

Well Monday then. Aunt Bessie's voice gets louder, clearer. Am I supposed to take the boy to school on Monday? Am I supposed to do that every day until he graduates? How old is he anyway?

Looks about ten, eleven, to me, his uncle says. Though he speaks quietly, there is a clarity to his voice, a fullness to the tone; the boy isn't sure, but he thinks his uncle actually sounds amused. But ten! The boy bridles with indignation. Anyway, his uncle continues, I think it's a week or two before the winter break ends. After that he can catch the bus right here on 38. If he stays I mean.

If he stays. The idea is sinking in. The old man didn't just leave him here: he sent him here. He wants him to stay, with these voices and the people they belong to. This bed, this house, those, those *cows* outside. If he stays they will become his life. His new life.

If he goes back to Long Island there will also be two more weeks of vacation—two more weeks of dodging his mother when he's not pulling twelve-hour days at the market, but two weeks also of blessed freedom from the boys who decided three years ago to make the one-

25

block journey to and from school the most perilous four hundred steps of the boy's life. Just thinking about *that* has his legs twitching under the quilt, his hands balled into fists. Fight or flight. That's what they call it in school. The instinct to save yourself by whatever means necessary, fleeing your assailant, or beating him into the ground. At school they teach you about the animal roots of human behavior but they still can't explain why three bullies have elected him their personal whipping boy, and beaten him up every single school day for the past three years.

I think Ethel was going to send him to military school, his uncle says now. I think that's why Lloyd brung him up.

And what kind of boy *is* it that he's left with us? A boy who would do something so heinous his own mother would send him away? Is that the kind of boy we want living with us? Some hoodlum in the making?

At the mention of his mother, the boy's fists ball even more tightly, until he can feel his pulse in his fingertips. Although he didn't know until this morning that she wanted to send him away, he does know what he's done. Knows, at any rate, why she would want to be rid of him.

Well Bess, he hears his uncle say. You never met Ethel. Don't be so quick to judge the boy on that account.

It comes back in a rush: the knotted sticky bark of the pine limb in his hand, the enveloping stink of his father's coat and hat, the rivulets of sweat running down the back of his neck and spine and into his drawers. Though the room he lies in is cold as an ice cube—a chipped ice cube really, given the ceiling's slope—he suddenly feels hot, and wants to throw the quilt from his fully clothed body.

It had been the first week of school. This past year? Two years ago? Funny, but he's not sure. What he is sure of is that on the morning of the first day of school Bruce St. John had held his hands behind his back while Robert Sampson used his stomach as a punching bag, and on the morning of the second day of school he'd encountered Robert Sampson alone and asked him what he was going to do without his buddy to hold his arms behind his back and Robert

Sampson had said he was going to use his karate to kick the boy in the ear, and then he had kicked the boy in the ear and later that day, in English, the boy had felt warmth on the side of his cheek and discovered a trail of blood as thick as a pencil running down the line of his jawbone and seeping into his shirt collar. On the third day he'd managed to make it to school unmolested, but that afternoon Vinnie Grasso had chased him into the Pine Barrens, and even though Vinnie is three years older than the boy he never would have caught him if the boy's shoes hadn't been too small—which means it was this year, the boy realizes, this past September. The boy's shoes had pinched his feet, slowing him down, and when Vinnie finally caught the boy he made the boy take off his belt and used it to tie him to a tree, and though the boy struggled to free himself all he managed to do was shake his too-large pants down below his drawers. Vinnie had bowled over laughing at that, held his stomach with one hand and pointed at the boy with the other, and the boy had thought maybe that was all Vinnie was going to do when Vinnie stood up and pulled a switchblade from his pocket and held it to the boy's throat and told him he was going to have to kill him now, so there wouldn't be any witnesses. Or maybe he would just cut out his tongue, Vinnie said. Cut out his tongue and cut off his fingers so he couldn't tell anybody what happened. Couldn't speak, or hold a stick to write in the sand. Or maybe . . . and the knife had trailed south past clavicles and ribcage and solar plexus, and the boy started struggling so wildly that his pants fell all the way to his ankles. Vinnie laughed again, laughed for a good five minutes, and in the end all he did was cut open the seams of the boy's pants pockets. Here hold this for me Dale will you? he said, making the boy take the blade of the knife between his teeth while he pulled the boy's pants up and stuffed his cuffs into his socks and proceeded to dump handfuls of dirt into the ripped pockets of the boy's pants, not stopping until both pant legs were about as filled with dirt as the pillow beneath the boy's head is with feathers. It took the boy a half hour to work his hands free after Vinnie left, and then he'd had no choice but to take his pants off in the Barrens and shake and scrape as much dirt from them and his muddy legs as he could and run all the way to Slaussen's, where Mr. Krakowski, the produce manager, had docked his pay for being late. He had not paid him anything at all, and because it was too warm for a jacket the boy hadn't been able to steal any fruit either. He'd tried slipping a handful of walnuts into his pocket, only to have them roll down his pant leg and clatter on the linoleum floor like marbles.

It was the next day that the boy borrowed the old man's coat and hat. He knew it was a desperate plan, something out of the Little Rascals or a Mickey Rooney movie, but it was all he could think of—there was still a dried crust of mud lining his pants, after all, and a shower of dust fell to the floor when he put his foot down the leg. And his house was on Second Street between Fourth and Fifth Avenues, Brentwood Elementary just around the corner on First between Fifth and Sixth: the only choice he had concerning his route was whether to walk on the side of the street where Robert Sampson and Bruce St. John and Vinnie Grasso hung out virtually every morning and afternoon, or walk on the opposite side of the street and hope that a school bus would run them down when they came after him, which hadn't happened yet.

The coat reached to his ankles, the hat sat all the way down on his ears like Ed's on *The Honeymooners*, and both radiated the old man's powerful odor—not just the smell of sour food but the ammoniac aroma of metabolized alcohol. Though they hadn't been worn since the previous winter, both coat and hat reeked of the contents of the old man's brown bottles so strongly that the boy's eyes watered when he put them on, and as soon as he stepped into the morning heat his own sweat added itself to the mix. It was the second week of September, and even though it was a little after eight in the morning the sun beat down on his dark woolen cloak.

He veered by the Barrens to grab a stick and complete his disguise. The pine bough clung to its trunk with taffylike persistence, and the effort of twisting it off left his hands covered in pitch and his skin even more wet with sweat. He could feel the mud inside his pants absorbing his body's secretions; dirty denim adhered to his thighs like a polyester skirt static-clinging to a woman's pantyhose. At

28

first he just carried the stick in his right hand, used it to tap the ground every other step, but then he realized he needed to lean on it if he wanted to fool anybody. He buttoned up the coat, pulled the hat even further down around his ears. His hobble was so convincing that he actually tripped himself and fell on his face. As he drew close to the corner opposite the school grounds he risked a peek under the brim of the hat—there they were, all three of them, Vinnie Grasso flagrantly smoking on school property—and then he returned his gaze to the point of the stick where it struck the dirt of his neighbors' lawns. As he leaned into it he remembered Vinnie's words from the day before about cutting out his tongue so he couldn't speak. What *would* he write, the boy wondered, if that was all he could do? Would he write Vinnie's name, or his own? Kill him, or Save me? If nothing else, he thought, he could always use the stick against them. It wasn't sissy to use a stick. Not if it was three against one it wasn't, and one of them Jimmy's age to boot.

The sleeves of the old man's coat were so long they slipped down over his hands, making it hard for him to keep a firm grip on the stick. He had to continually push up his right sleeve with his left hand, and each time he did so he was aware of his skin in a way he'd never been before: aware that it was smooth, unspotted, the fingers slim and uncalloused, almost feminine in their youthful delicacy. Terrified his hands were going to give him away, he shoved his left into the ripped pocket of his jeans, rubbed it in the film of mud there, then switched his grip on the stick and did the same thing with his right. Not much came out—it felt worse than it looked—but what did come out looked remarkably like the liver spots that covered the backs of Grandma Dundas's hands.

Throughout the procedure the boy didn't risk another peek at his enemies. By now he'd crossed the street, was so close to them he caught snatches of their conversation. He didn't know what he'd've expected them to be talking about—girls maybe, or baseball, or beating him up—but he was surprised by what he heard.

George Armstrong Custer was headstrong, arrogant, and vain, Robert Sampson intoned as if reading straight from the cavalry manual. He marched into enemy territory against orders and without adequate forces. He got what he had coming.

George Armstrong Custer? As in Custer's Last Stand? Little Big Horn, Crazy Horse, every U.S. soldier dead and Custer's blond hair hanging on a peg in a teepee like an abandoned baseball cap—*that* Custer?

For a moment the boy thought Robert must have been speaking for his benefit, especially when Vinnie said, Me scalp white man good! but then Bruce St. John said, Hey, any-a youse guys know who won the Yankees game last night? and he relaxed just a little. By then he'd breasted his enemies, the brim of his father's hat had slipped below his eyebrows but he dared not push it up with one of his pitch-and dirt-flecked hands, sweat stuck his shirt to his back and seemed to flood his drawers, and he would have sworn there was mud leaking out the bottom of his pants. He could see Bruce's battered canvas sneakers out of the corner of his left eye, the frayed cuffs of his black jeans, and when Bruce lifted one of his feet the boy nearly bolted. But all Bruce did was use his left foot to scratch the top of his right, and then he set it down again. And then the boy was past them, two steps, three, the point of his cane gouged chunks of dry dirt and brittle grass out of the schoolyard beneath the boy's weight and there was nothing fake about its tremor. It vibrated like the gearshift in the old man's truck when it idled at a stoplight.

Hey Bruce you live in a cave or something? The boy was so close he could hear Vinnie drag on his cigarette. Yankees slaughtered them, eleven-three. But by now Bruce was on to something else—something feminine, judging by his whistle, and the mocking laugh that responded to it.

When he could no longer hear their voices behind him the boy picked up his pace a little. He hadn't thought about what to do with the old man's reeking hat and coat beforehand. He could put them in his locker, he thought—but both Robert Sampson and Bruce St. John had lockers almost directly opposite his. They might see him. Then up ahead he saw the bulletin board used to announce future events. PARENT-TEACHER CONF 9–27 FALL H'COMING OCT

30. He ducked down behind it, whipped off coat and hat and stuffed them in the straggled prickly bushes clumped around the sign's masonry pedestal. A couple of girls he didn't recognize looked at him funny but didn't say anything, and the boy was halfway up the school steps before he realized he was still carrying the stick. He tossed it in the hedges beneath the open windows of the receptionist's office, narrowly missing a couple of boys in pressed white shirts and dark narrow ties.

Hey watch it there pipsqueak! You could take out somebody's eye!

The boy's dirty hands curled into fists but just then the warning bell rang. He whipped around, saw Vinnie Grasso grinding out a cigarette on the sole of his shoe. Robert Sampson and Bruce St. John were already cutting across the grass toward the door. Trying not to run, he headed off for first period.

He waved at Lois during morning recess where she was jumping rope with a group of second graders before winning six cents pitching pennies, ran into Joanie and Edi at lunchtime. Joanie had an apple she'd saved for him from last night, but Edi looked at him so plaintively he ended up giving it to her—and besides, the cafeteria monitor had taken one look at his hands and announced that lunch was a privilege the boy hadn't earned today. Of his three enemies, he only had class with Bruce St. John—arithmetic, Mr. Humboldt. Mr. Humboldt was also the vice principal and served as assistant coach to the high school football team, and there was a story that he'd once hung a boy by his belt off one of the hooks at the back of the room for talking during class and left him there for the custodial staff to take out with the trash. It was the safest forty-five minutes of the boy's day, marred only by the numbing dullness of fractions, decimals, long division.

When the last bell rang he didn't bother dumping his books in his locker. Just ran straight for the exit in one of those great universal rushes—to the Red Sea, across homesteadable prairie, out of the starting blocks. Or, in the boy's case, the race to beat the barbarians inside the city walls. He knew there was safety in numbers, or at any rate invisibility, and he let himself be swept along by the wave of arms and legs and hairspray and voices until he reached the bulletin board. The coat and hat were where he'd left them, and he'd just kneeled down and dropped his books to the ground and slipped his right arm through the coat's sleeve when he felt a hand around his left. Fingers that felt thick as hot dogs curled all the way around the thin flesh of the boy's upper arm, and even without looking the boy knew the hand was too big to belong to Vinnie Grasso or one of the other boys.

The first thing he saw when he turned was a pair of thick thighs in dark trousers. He had to crane his head all the way back to see the face of Mr. Humboldt towering above him. The collar of his shirt had flipped up on one side, revealing the noose of his dark red tie. From the boy's vantage it looked as if Mr. Humboldt's round head was a soap bubble poised on the end of its blowstick.

Mr. Humboldt lifted the boy to his feet as though he were a toddler that had wobbled to its knees. Now the boy was faced with the buttons of his teacher's blue pinstriped shirt, straining to hold the expanse of his stomach in place; the flap of his wide red tie curled in at the edges like the tongue of a tired dog. Beyond him, the initial flood of students had already thinned to a stream.

I believe it's Mr. Peck, is it not?

The boy swallowed but didn't say anything. He'd never been this close to the math teacher before. Mr. Humboldt was fatter than he'd realized, but that didn't lessen his impression of enormous size and strength. It just made him creepier. Mr. Humboldt looked like a giant baby, the kind who throws temper tantrums and beats its doll's head into the ground as though it were a drumstick. He squinted now, his small eyes disappearing into the folds of his white cheeks.

May I ask what you're doing? Is there a school scavenger hunt I don't know about?

The boy looked down at his father's coat. Even though it hung off one arm, it was obviously too big for him, not to mention too warm for a day like today. In the bright light of day the boy could see it was stained with who knew what—the smears ran the gamut from white to brown to red to black—and the ragged wool itself had gone shiny with age, until the coat had acquired a rubbery sheen. Its time outside seemed to have done it some good though, at least as far as the smell went. It didn't reek nearly as badly as the boy remembered from the morning.

The boy looked back up at Mr. Humboldt.

It's my dad's coat.

Mr. Humboldt opened his mouth, then closed it. He looked at the boy's coat again. It was not the kind of coat you'd say belonged to your father unless it really did.

Well, uh, yes. Mr. Humboldt licked his lips, then wrinkled his nose. You should probably get it back to him, don't you think?

Mr. Humboldt let go of the boy's arm and stepped to one side. His body was so large it seemed like a curtain was being pulled open on a stage, and there, behind him, were Vinnie Grasso and Bruce St. John and Robert Sampson. They were just descending the steps at the far end of the sidewalk, Vinnie and Robert laughing about something, Bruce scanning the schoolyard for—

There he is!

By now the students had trickled down to one and twos, and Bruce's voice carried all the way down the sidewalk. The three boys started to run toward him, then slowed to a walk when they registered that it was Mr. Humboldt who stood between them and their prey. They didn't stop though. Robert Sampson had a smirk on his face and Vinnie Grasso smacked his right fist into the palm of his left hand while Bruce St. John, the most timid of the three, shoved his hands in his pockets and lagged a little behind the other two.

Mr. Humboldt—the boy began, but then something stopped him.

He thought again of the dilemma the stick had brought to mind. It wasn't that he didn't know how to ask for help: he just didn't know whether he wanted that help for himself, or against his enemies. He wanted . . . he *didn't* want to have to ask. He wanted Mr. Humboldt to offer to protect him. Wanted it badly enough to seal his lips shut and stare at his math teacher with wide-open pleading eyes.

33

Yes Dale?

Mr. Humboldt wrinkled his nose again. He looked at the boy impatiently, if not simply with distaste.

Go on now, he said when the boy still didn't speak. Get on home.

By now Vinnie and Robert and Bruce had stationed themselves on the opposite side of the sidewalk. Vinnie had tucked a cigarette behind his ear as though he were Marlon Brando in *On the Waterfront* and Bruce hung even farther back, his glance shifting nervously between his friends' backs and Mr. Humboldt's. As Mr. Humboldt turned toward the door they shuffled to the left Three Stooges style, keeping out of the math teacher's line of vision. The boy knew he had only a few seconds' head start and turned and started running. It was half a block to Fifth Avenue, where the boy had the choice of turning left and trying to lose them in the Barrens or turning right and running for home. It was his shoes that made up his mind. As soon as he'd started running his feet had protested inside the pinching leather, and at Fifth he veered right, running across the street at a wide diagonal.

In a fight he didn't stand a chance—at least not when there were three of them—but in a race he knew from experience the three boys behind him could never catch him. For a moment he even allowed himself to enjoy the chase, too tight shoes or no. He sucked in air through his mouth and shot it out his legs as though they were pistons, and in his mind's eye the old man's ridiculous coat flapped behind him like the cape of Zorro. He even took the time to turn and flip off his pursuers once he'd crossed Fifth, and when he did he saw that the other boys had already given up the chase. But not because they knew they were outgunned. Instead they stood on the corner of the schoolyard, Robert Sampson and Bruce St. John methodically tearing pages out of the schoolbooks he'd dumped by the bulletin board, Vinnie Grasso holding the old man's hat by the brim like a prop in a vaudeville show. As soon as he saw the boy was looking, he lifted his fist with a flourish and punched it through the crown, and then he waved his hand in front of his crinkled nose and threw the hat into the street like a frisbee. It landed ten feet in front of the boy, the top of the ripped crown angling up like the lid on a half-opened can of peas. Across the street the pages of the boy's books fell straight to the ground. There was no breeze, he realized then. The old man's coat had fallen closed around his body, encircling him in a cocoon of hot dead air, and the pages of the boy's books lay on the dirt as still as fallen tombstones—and when he remembers that the boy starts in the bed in his uncle's house, suddenly remembering the broken windowpanes in the garage door from early this morning. It occurs to him that he is even farther away from home than he'd realized.

The threesome's obsession with the boy was inexplicable, coming and going on a schedule he never could predict or parse. There had been no singular incident to start it off, nor did their altercations seem to have any shape or goal. It was simply a pitstop in their daily routine, the way some people walk to the refrigerator and stare into it, letting the sight of food tell them whether they're hungry for a glass of milk or a baloney-and-cheese sandwich. Today was a light snack day. Within a few minutes the boys had turned their backs on him, left his half-shredded books on the ground behind them. Only Bruce St. John looked back every once in a while to see if the boy dared come after his property. But all the boy did was put his hands in the pockets of the old man's coat, where the knuckles of his right hand knocked against something hard. Perhaps the boy was still trying to figure out how victory had so suddenly been turned into defeat, but it wasn't until he'd pulled the object out of the pocket that he saw it was an empty bottle of the old man's medicine. He stared at it for a moment, then lobbed it as hard as he could at the backs of the three boys. By then they were so far away they didn't hear it hit the sidewalk behind them. The bottle exploded when it struck the concrete, seemed almost to disintegrate. As soon as the shards stopped moving they became invisible and, retrieving his father's ruined hat, the boy headed for home.

Perhaps he was still distracted. The boy doesn't remember now, lying in his cousin's bed on his uncle's farm. How could he possibly have forgotten the two most important facts of his parents' lives? His father's medicine, his mother's—

What have you got on?

The boy looked up at her. She stood in the open door of their house, the baby cradled in one arm.

Good lord. You look like Hobo Joe.

Gregory's head lay on their mother's shoulder facing away from him. His hair was long and slack, the ends just starting to curl the way the boy's hair did, and Lance's too, when they went for more than a few weeks without a haircut. The lanky strands were echoed in the shape of Gregory's thin arms hanging limply on either side of his body. The boy realized his brother was sleeping in his mother's arms. His aching feet carried him inexorably toward her.

She screwed up her face, stared at his coat. Is that— She stopped, looking at the hat now. He was close enough that she was able to grab it off his head, and when she did the ripped brim puckered up in a shape that mirrored and mocked her sneer. The boy didn't remember putting the hat back on his head either.

Is this your father's hat?

The boy looked down at her feet. Watched as one rose from the floor in its thick-soled black shoe and kicked him in the shin.

Look at me when I'm talking to you! Is this your father's hat?

The boy looked up at her. Inside the pockets of the old man's coat his hands balled into fists but he kept them there, hidden. He thought of the bottle of the old man's medicine, wished he'd saved it until now.

Why you—

His mother hit him in the face with the hat in her fist. The felt was soft if scratchy, the rancid odor of the old man's scalp almost worse than the abrasive rasp across his skin. The boy shut his eyes against the blows as his mother swung back and forth, smacking one cheek and then the other, and then all at once she stopped. When the boy opened one eye he saw that the ripped crown had separated from the brim and lay on the ground a few feet away. The open ring of the brim was crunched in his mother's clenched fist like a wobbly figure eight and Gregory, awakened by the commotion, looked at him blearily, rubbing his eyes. He stared at the boy blankly and then closed his eyes and turned his head back onto his mother's shoulder.

Go get the hose, his mother said.

She was impatient that day: she beat him while he was still wearing the old man's coat, and the tattered but still thick wool protected his back from the bite of the metal coupling at the end of the hose. But she beat him again when he got home from work that night and couldn't produce any pay for the last two days, refusing to believe him when he said that Mr. Krakowski had docked his wages for coming in late. This time he had on just his undershirt, and he had to sleep on his stomach that night, and when at some point Lance's arm fell across his back his own cry of pain woke him from sleep. She beat him the next morning when he asked her for money to replace the books that had been ruined the day before—undershirt, outer shirt, and his jacket worn in anticipation, but his undershirt was still stuck to his back when he pulled it off that evening after everyone else was asleep. He slept on his stomach again, to keep from staining the sheets with his own blood, and then the weekend came and he was mostly able to avoid her. Monday dawned a little cooler than the week before. There were still wisps of fog on the ground when the boy went to school that morning, and that afternoon Vinnie and Robert and Bruce ambushed him and cut his lip open and ripped a button off his shirt before he was able to wriggle out of their grasp and run away. They were more persistent that day. They chased him all the way home, and they weren't that far behind—those damn shoes!—when the boy dodged round the fallen shade tree and turned up the front walk, only to be stopped by the sight of his mother in the open door. She held the hose in one hand, the shirt he'd worn last week in the other, and like a dart to the bull's-eye his gaze went straight to the bloodstain on the collar. Vinnie and Robert and Bruce literally ran into him as they rounded the fallen shade tree, knocking him to the ground and piling on him before Bruce noticed the boy's mother in the door. The boys stopped what they were doing but didn't get up. Instead they looked at her expectantly, and the boy on his back beneath his assailants looked as well, stared for a full second at the big woman standing in the entrance to the funny little eight-sided house before she threw his shirt on the lawn and turned her back on him and closed the door behind her.

When the memory releases him from its grip the boy finds himself back in the strange house. He has kicked the quilt off at some point and lies in a ball, shivering, and he retrieves the quilt from the foot of the bed and spreads it over him, and then he peels his ears for some sound from his uncle or Aunt Bessie. He doesn't know how long he's been asleep. Perhaps they are sleeping already in the room behind his. Then:

I suppose you're right Bess. I'll call Lloyd in the morning, tell him to come get the boy.

There is another long moment of silence. Though Duke talks of nothing but leaving home the boy has never thought about it before, but now his first clear thought is that he doesn't want to go back, and he even considers running to the next room to ask if he can stay. But he is held in bed by the same conundrum that held in his tongue when he wanted to ask for Mr. Humboldt's help: he's not sure if he wants to stay, or if he just doesn't want to be sent away.

Well let's not be hasty Wallace. I just said it's not right, what your brother done. I didn't say he had to go back. He spoke very polite to me when I made up his bed.

There is a creak from the room behind his.

Anyway, and the boy can hear the yawn in his aunt's voice. We can talk about it more in the morning.

It seems only a moment later that the boy is awakened by a light knock at the door. When he opens his eyes he's completely lost, and he stares blankly at the strange man whose face emerges in the gap between the wall and slowly opening door. The man opens the door all the way and then just stands there, looking at the boy, and then his eyes shift to the dresser beside the bed. Years later the boy, grown up, will wonder if his uncle was actually looking at him or if he was in fact looking for his only daughter, already long gone, but that morning he only watches warily as his uncle approaches the dresser

38

and drawer by drawer empties its contents in a tattered brown gunny-sack. When he has finished he slings the half-empty sack over his shoulder and turns to the boy.

Ladies won't milk themselves, his uncle says. You can put your things away later.

After lunch his uncle burns his daughter's clothes with the rest of the trash. Dumps them out of the sack and into the burn barrel, and folds up the worn burlap to use it again.

3

NOW HE KNOWS the names of things. He knows the directions: not just the words, but the axes of the earth. The north hill that protects his uncle's land from the worst of the winter winds and the Catskill vista twenty miles to the south, the ancient abandoned house buried in the overgrown cedar break just west of his uncle's property and the hundred forty-five acres of pasture to the east. The pasture spans both sides of County Road 38, a hundred ten acres on this, the north side, and thirty-five more on the south, and on this late April morning there are sixty-seven Holstein and Guernsey and Ayshire and Jersey cows in the north field—the ladies, his uncle calls them, but only among dairymen. The queen of the herd is a four-year-old Holstein whom his uncle has named, sheepishly but proudly, Dolly, and whose teats trail the ground when she walks and yield an average of forty quarts of milk each day. At six cents per, those forty quarts will bring $2.40 from his uncle's distributor, Sunnydale Farms, assuming they pass bacterial and cream-ratio inspections. The boy knows also that the sharp knock-knock-knock his uncle raps on his door at four-thirty is called reveille, and is what he would have experienced had his mother gotten her way and sent him to military school. That's all he knows about military school and, his uncle has told him, it's all he'll ever know, as long as he does his chores.

The bacon is done by the time the boy has dressed and washed his hands and face with cold water from the bowl on his bureau and tiptoed his way down the dark narrow stairs; and the boy sets the table while his uncle finishes at the stove. His uncle drains the bacon grease into a coffee can but leaves the meat in the pan, cuts it into pieces with the blackened end of the spatula, and cracks six eggs on top of it. The can with the bacon grease goes back on the counter, next to another can that contains cooking utensils and a third filled with silverware and a fourth that contains coffee and then the fifth can, the newest, the can that contains the boy's shoe fund. His uncle started the shoe fund when he finished the last can of coffee a couple of weeks ago, and the boy knows without looking that it contains $3.10, and he knows also that a new pair of shoes costs $5.50 at Western Supply. His naked toes curl away from the cold floorboards as he sets three places at the table—three plates, three forks, three cups— and he places the third cup face down and lays a napkin on top of that plate to protect it from flies: the third place is for Aunt Bessie, who will sleep for another hour and be gone to her house by the time the boy comes down from the barn for his books. As he lays the paper napkin on Aunt Bessie's plate he sees that his damp hand has left four fingerprints on it, and he is about to replace it when he looks up at his uncle's back. A week after the boy arrived—when he could still hear Aunt Bessie through the wall nearly every night, encouraging his uncle to let him stay on—he had run to the house with a double handful of eggs still warm from the hens' bottoms; he had dropped one as he struggled to open the door and his uncle had smacked him and served him one fewer egg for breakfast. In just over three months it's the only time his uncle has laid a finger on him, and he would sooner brave military school or run ten miles in Jimmy's shoes than give his uncle cause to punish him again.

His uncle divides the food between the two plates while the boy pours them each a cup of coffee. He doesn't fill the cups beyond the halfway mark or there won't be enough left for Aunt Bessie. Aunt Bessie will cook her own breakfast when she gets up but she will only reheat whatever coffee is left on the stove. In fact the boy doesn't really like the taste of coffee. He only drinks it for the cream he can put into it, cream he skims from a galvanized tin pail that has hung during the cool night from a nail just outside the door and, like Aunt Bessie's plate, has a cloth laid over it to keep the flies off. The cream has a sweetness no sugar can improve, a sweetness that has replaced all-butter French loaf in both mouth and mind. He splashes a drop of coffee in his cup and overwhelms it with cream, and he drinks half the dun-colored custardy concoction before he wolfs down his bacon and eggs and half when he is finished, so the thick taste will linger when he heads out to the barn. A few drops dribble down his chin, and even though he catches them with the back of his hand his uncle sees, and as he stands with his plate in one hand he uses the other to pull a napkin from the holder.

Use it if you need it. Put it in your pocket if you don't.

It is the first thing his uncle has said this morning, and the boy stuffs the napkin in his pocket and hurries after him, trying not to feel too disappointed that he has already caused him to speak. His uncle speaks less than any man he has ever met, and the boy has set himself the challenge of seeing how long he can save him from the need to use words. In order to do that he must perform all his chores as quickly and efficiently as he has been taught, wasting neither time nor, more important, the farm's precious resources. He catches the screen door so that its bang doesn't wake Aunt Bessie and then sets off at a run up the hill to the dairy barn. The grass is long and damp, cold and silver in the gray light, but the boy's pants are rolled up almost to his knees and only his feet and ankles get wet. At the barn he grabs two more pails from their own nails. There are two rags in the bottom of one and he takes them out and takes the pails to a spigot and fills them with water. He rinses dried manure and mud out of the rags and drops one in each pail and turns off the tap.

By then his uncle has reached the barn, and he holds the spring-hinged door for the boy so he doesn't spill any water. The boy steps over the foot-high threshold and sets the pails down just inside the door, and by the time the rusty half-sprung coils have pulled the door shut with their vaguely electronic screech— *rrrrrreeeeeeeaaaaaakkkkkkhhhhhh!*—he has run the length of the barn. Faint columns of light dissect the far wall. The dairy barn's siding is called board-and-batten but much of the latter is missing, and sunlight leaks in between the boards, and rain and snow, and, now, the urgent lowing of the ladies. It's been twelve hours since their last milking, and their udders are so swollen that the teats spit milk when they bounce against a rock or log, and the weight of them is a strain on the ladies' backs. It's as if, his uncle has told him, they get pregnant twice a day, and does he remember what Ethel was like when she was carrying any of his younger brothers and sisters? The boy can—Lois, vaguely, and Lance, and more recently Gregory—and it seems to him that the ladies behave much better than his mother. When he slides back the doors to the barnyard they make their way slowly and surprisingly graceful and quiet on the barn's cement floor toward the troughs, their half-ton bodies rubbing against each other with a sound like thunder attempting to slip on a suede jacket. The first few times the boy had to do this he ran out of the way as soon as he'd opened the doors, but now he scratches the ladies' coarse hides as they glide by, nudges this or that one toward one or another trough to make sure they're evenly distributed, slaps the bony haunch of the occasional laggard, Go on, get in there.

The dairy barn contains four feeding troughs: two on either long wall, and two more running next to each other down the barn's center. This is called the milking alley, but the boy prefers to think of the long metal bins as two sets of train rails run side by side, and when the ladies stand haunch to haunch between them they form the ties, and once they're all in place his uncle lowers the electronic boom collars. Each of the four collars is a set of steel tubes curved in a shape that resembles the rounded dentals below the eaves of his uncle's house, an up-and-down notching that descends from the rafters like a pin changer to slip over the ladies' necks just behind the flaring of their skulls. The collars were blue when they were new and they're blue on top still, but their undersides are silver and shiny from years of being abraded by necks as big around as the boy's waist. Their only function is to keep the ladies from walking away while their teats are hooked to the claw of the milking machine: although the four stainless steel nozzles are supposed to slide off with a good tug they don't always, and the boy's uncle has spoken of panicked cows who rip off their own teats in their struggle to free themselves.

While the boy has been herding the ladies in, his uncle has

filled a pile of gunnysacks through a chute that pours down from the silo, and as soon as the collars are in place the boy grabs a fifty-pound sack and pours the shredded corn into a trough. There is a narrow lane beyond each of the outer troughs and another alley between the two center troughs, and the boy walks backward down these alleys to spread the silage evenly and keep it from spilling over the edge of the trough. As he walks, the ladies behind him low in anticipation of his arrival. Their calls make him think that he is a finger running a glissando the length of a giant keyboard, and indeed, it is like music to him, this process—not listening to music, but playing it. The ladies low like a band tuning up, and then, when the troughs are filled, their teeth crunch grain with a regular sound, like a distant marching corps.

Like the collars, the corn's only function is to keep the ladies calmly in place while they're milked; it would be less complicated by far to feed them in the barnyard. Now the boy grabs a stool and one of the pails he filled with water and starts on the nearest lady. There are four teats per lady and four nozzles per claw, but some of the ladies have a shrunken teat and nearly all of them have at least one that is reddened by mastitis, and he lets these hang free, hooking up only those teats that are pale and plump and eager to release their liquid treasure.

The boy pulls the rag from his pail. In the springtime the ladies' teats are covered with mud and manure: they feed and give milk and shit at the same time, and even though most of the latter falls into a six-inch gutter located under their tails some of it inevitably splatters onto the swollen udders. At first this repulsed the boy but now he only notices if some spatters a teat he has already cleaned. He uses his rag to wipe the swollen sacks, squeezing lightly so as not to force out any milk, and when the teat is clean he slips the tip into a nozzle and opens the valve and watches to make sure the suction slurps it in evenly, without pinching the tender skin. As soon as the transparent hose running out the other end of the nozzle turns white he drops his dirty rag into his pail and moves on to the next teat or the next lady. Fifteen ladies per trough, four troughs in the barn. Every station is filled, which is unusual, especially at this time of year. His uncle's herd normally has ten or eleven dries but right now there are only four. There are two bulls as well, meaning there are sixty-one wet cows in the barn: he does thirty and his uncle does thirty, and whichever man finishes first milks the last lady by hand. This is the competition his uncle has set up; this is how the boy earned the money in the coffee can that will buy him a pair of shoes: his uncle gives him the value of whatever milk he gets from the sixty-first cow. The boy knows it is just a game and that his uncle will buy him a pair of shoes as soon as he is able, and he knows also that his uncle could best him without even trying, but, as happened yesterday and the day before, he finishes a half cow ahead of his uncle, and he almost whoops for joy as he runs to find the last of the ladies.

He locates her where she has nosed her way in at the end of a trough. A few of the ladies he recognizes by their spots or scars: Dolly of course, her udder the size of a medicine ball, and the bulls, and the lady with five teats, but despite his best efforts—his uncle knows every one of his herd individually—most of them remain anonymous to him. This is one of the latter. An Ayshire whose face is entirely black except for the insides of her lips, which are as pink as a Negro's, and both her ears, which are white. All of this is distinctive enough, but the boy finds it hard to remember something when it doesn't have a name. He has never dared ask why they don't name the ladies, just as he's never asked why they don't call them ladies in front of people who aren't associated with the farm. Cows, they call them, not cattle—cattle are food—but he puts the matter out of his mind as the black-faced lady turns back to her breakfast. He wipes her udder down as though it were a baby's face, and then, using both hands, lifts up the milksack and tries to gauge from the heft of the warm aqueous bag how much it will yield. This is less game than intermission: the pail holds five gallons, twenty quarts, and only Dolly has ever required a second one. But the boy knows a full pail is worth more than a dollar and he likes to think of the warm weight in his palms as pennies that will buy him a pair of shoes that will cover his feet as softly as warm milk. And, too, he likes the water-balloon shape of the udder, the soft down that covers the pink skin and the slip of the teats through his fingers. Once, just after Lance came home from the hospital, he'd snuck beyond his parents' curtain and lifted his newborn brother from his crib. Lance was neither as plump nor as warm as a cow's udder but it is the closest the boy can find to a twin to this feeling, and it is almost reluctantly that he squeezes off two teats between the thumb and forefinger of each hand and begins to milk.

Good practice, huh?

The boy tries not to jump at the sound of Donnie Badget's voice but he feels his cheeks turn as pink as the udder before him.

Squirt squirt squirt. You been practicing upstairs? Maybe up in the hayloft? Milking it to get ready for the girls?

The boy tries to concentrate on his task but he jerks the tender teat and the black-faced Ayshire looks up from her feed. She stamps one of her hind legs, nearly upsetting his pail.

Careful there, Amos. Don't want to pull too hard. You'll give the lady blisters.

The boy gets up from his stool, heads toward the vat room. His pail is hardly half full and the Ayshire's udder isn't completely drained, but he wants to escape Donnie Badget's insinuating tone.

The holding vat is an enormous stainless steel cylinder that can take five thousand gallons of unpasteurized unhomogenized whole milk—twenty thousand quarts, or twelve hundred dollars—which his uncle's ladies produce every ten or eleven days. The duct is sealed by a valve that has a handle like the handles on submarine doors to emphasize how valuable the farm's sole commodity is—a gallon of milk costs four times a gallon of gas, as his uncle has pointed out—and when he unscrews the valve it opens with a buttery hiss so thick you could cut it with a knife and spread it on toast. After he flips back the hatch the boy lays a rusty screen atop the opening to catch any flies that might have drowned in the milk pail. Of all the implements involved in the milking process, this screen is perhaps the most precious to the boy. Through it pass a thousand quarts of milk every morning and evening, and yet it is tiny, less than a foot across and nearly weightless. Even the grease guard Aunt Bessie lays over the top of the skillet has a handle and a metal rim, but the screen is unbordered, its edges unraveling like an old blanket. And yet it is indispensable, a vital link between the ladies and the vat. His uncle has spoken ominously of the one time his milk was rejected by the pump man for too much matter—flies mostly, and flecks of greenery that might or might not have passed through a lady first— and the entire contents of the vat had to be dumped in the barnyard.

The boy lays the screen carefully over the valve, then pours the pail through and leaves the seal open. By now the milking machine has finished the first ladies, and he and his uncle and Donnie un- hook them from the claws and cart the oversized buckets of steaming milk from the milking alley to the vat room. The milking machine's buckets are rectangular, with soft edges, like a suitcase stood on end. They hold ten gallons apiece and, when full, weigh seventy-five to eighty pounds—the boy himself only weighs a hundred thirty but, like his uncle and Donnie Badget, he carries them two at a time, for ballast. The work is backbreaking but over in just a few minutes, and when they are finished the boy dumps the screen and its dozens of dead flies and seals up the vat again. Immediately he grabs a shovel and wheelbarrel, and he's about to clean the manure gutters when he sees his uncle standing in the open door of the barn looking down at the barnyard. The only time the boy has ever seen his uncle stand still is the day the old man dropped him off, and the sight is so unset- tling that the boy sets his shovel down and goes to see what's wrong. He hopes it is nothing he's done, but his breath is tight in his lungs as he passes the black-faced lady and her half-full udder.

His uncle glances down at him when he comes up, then turns back to the fields. The boy relaxes then, but only a little. He knows his uncle is waiting to see if he can spot what's amiss. But even though he scans the barnyard and the hill to the north and the pas- ture to the east he sees nothing but the sun, which has just cleared the stand of new-growth oak and chestnut and maple trees at the southeastern edge of the pasture. The boy watches its diagonal as- cent for a moment, then turns back to his uncle.

His uncle remains silent another moment. Then:

Fence is down.

He points to a line of fenceposts just beyond the scrubby willows and poplars that clot the muddy crease between the barnyard and the hillside pasture. Several of the posts lean at angles as sharply pitched as the barn's roof and two, defeated, lie flat on the ground. Slack ribbons of wire curl with the wild arcs and loops of some futuristic rollercoaster, catching sparks of morning light.

Been so wet the ground's a swamp. Gonna have to move the posts to drier land, rewire em. Means pasturing the ladies in the south field today. His uncle points again, this time at the rising sun. Best finish them gutters before the bus gets here and get your shoes on. You can help me and Donnie after school.

The boy returns to his wheelbarrel, fills it with manure he scoops from the narrow gutters with a square-bladed shovel. He works faster now, not because of the manure, whose grassy sweet odor he hardly notices, but because the task reminds him of the old man. Wheelbarrels full of shit, he'd said the day he took the boy away from his mother and his seven brothers and sisters. The boy tries not to think about any of them as he pushes the flat edge of the shovel across the concrete, the sound a mechanical rasp he feels in his ears and his fingertips. There is only the boy and his uncle in the house down the hill, and Aunt Bessie in the evenings, and even though he goes to sleep in the center of his empty bed he always wakes up at the edge, and sometimes he lies down in his clothes because not even an entire blanket is as warm as Lance's belly pressed against his back.

He is emptying the tenth load when he hears the bus in the hollow at the bottom of 38 where it curves around his uncle's land. His uncle looks up from the liniment he is rubbing into the neck of a particularly tall brown Guernsey with a face like the sole of an old leather boot. The Guernsey's neck has been chafed by the boom collar, and his uncle pushes the salve into the patches of pink skin with fingers as blunt-tipped as the shovel in the boy's hands.

Go on, get your shoes on.

Just a couple more loads, Uncle Wallace.

Donnie'll get em. Don't keep the bus waiting. Hold up a minute, his uncle says then, and when the boy turns back his uncle is digging in his pocket. His hand emerges with three quarters, two dimes, more pennies than the boy can count at a glance. Who'd you end up with this morning?

That black-faced Ayshire, the boy says. The one with the white ears, he adds, not sure if his description is adequate.

The one with the nigger lips? How much you get from her?

Two gallons maybe. Maybe two and a half.

His uncle hesitates a moment, then plunks two quarters in the boy's hand.

Gotta be more selective when you set the ladies up. Ayshires ain't the best milkers. High milkfat, and they tend to last a year or two longer than the other ladies, but if it's volume you want go for a Holstein every time. The boy is not sure but he thinks his uncle winks at him. Who knows, maybe you'll get Dolly one-a these days.

Aunt Bessie has packed the boy a lunch and left it with his books on the kitchen table. He drops the quarters in the shoe can— $3.60!—and grabs his lunch and his books and his old shoes and runs out the front door just as the bus pulls up to the T-intersection of 38 and Newry Road between his house and the Flacks'. As he dashes under the line of elms in front of his uncle's house he sees that their branches are dotted with leaf pips as pale as lima beans and curled like . . . like orecchiette, he remembers, one of the twenty-seven different pastas he'd stocked at Slaussen's Market. Babies' ears, Mr. Krakowski called them. Smaller than conchiglia but bigger than orzo.

The memory stops the boy in his tracks. He is standing there looking up at the leaves and trying to remember the names of other noodles—linguini, capellini, tortelloni, lasagna, manicotti, ravioli over in frozen foods—when Kenny and Flip Flack come around the front of the bus. Kenny has his younger brother in a headlock and is administering an Indian burn.

49

Hey hillbilly, Kenny says, looking at the shoes the boy is carrying. They go on your feet.

Hey hillbilly! Flip squeezes out of his brother's grip and runs onto the bus.

The boy shakes himself and gooses Flip as he walks past him down the aisle, and it is only when he gets to his seat in the middle of the bus that he realizes he has forgotten socks, and he curses the old man for the thousandth time. He doesn't realize he's sworn aloud until Julia Miller turns around and regards him over the back of her seat. She tucks a loose strand of hair behind her ear, pale brown, not blond like Joanie's—and not half as pretty to the boy's mind.

They might talk that trash down in New York City but we use clean English up here.

I'm not from New York City. I'm from Long Island.

Well you *sound* like Jimmy Cagney and *he* was from New York City.

I'm from *Brent*wood. It's on Long *Is*land.

Well *I'm* from Greene County. My people used to own *your* uncle's house.

The boy pauses. He knows this has something to do with the metal sign that is posted in front of his uncle's house just east of the driveway—the pole he'd taken for a fencepost when the old man had nearly run it over on the day he left him here.

SITE OF
EARLY TANNERY
ERECTED BY DANIEL MILLER
WHO CAME FROM EAST HAMPTON

is what the sign says in butter yellow letters painted on a midnight blue placard, and although the boy's uncle has never commented on the sign the boy senses its importance, else why would his uncle let it remain on his land? Still, the boy has never asked his uncle about it, and he doesn't ask Julia about it now. All he does is stare Julia down until she tucks the same lock of hair behind her ear and turns around. Then he squeezes his feet into Jimmy's shoes and laces them as loosely as he can. Still, by the time he gets home that afternoon the backs of his heels and the tops of his toes are covered with blisters, some of them broken open, and as he limps off the bus it's all he can do to hold back tears of pain and frustration. Ahead of him Flip skips down the stairs and dashes toward his house, but the boy descends so slowly that Kenny comes up hard behind him and steps on the back of his left foot. When the boy whirls around with his fists clenched his neighbor throws up his hands, palms open.

Whoa there hillbilly. It was an accident, honest.

The boy stares at him as the doors of the yellow Bluebird close and the bus heads east down 38. His fists remain drawn for a moment, then all at once he throws his books on the grass, plops down and unlaces his boots, chucks them into the ditch. There is a splash as one of them lands in a puddle and at the noise the boy throws himself on his back and stares up into the pale green five-fingered leaves of the silver maples in the Flacks' front yard. Star pasta, he thinks, but he can't remember its proper name.

Criminy hillbilly, Kenny says. Looks like you been walking on hot coals or something. He is silent for a moment and then he says, Heard about you in gym today.

The boy arches his head back, looks up at Kenny's inverted body. He is not as old as Duke and not as tall, but he has Duke's manner of looking away when he has something to say. He is looking up at the leaves where the boy was just looking.

What'd you hear?

Heard you threw your shoes at Coach Baldwin, then beat Billy Van Dyke in the four hundred.

Billy Van Dyke runs like a girl.

Billy Van Dyke is the fastest kid in eighth grade. Kenny looks down at the boy. Or he was.

The boy rolls over on his stomach, pulls a few blades of grass from the ground and shreds them into pieces one by one.

It wasn't nothing. I was mad.

The screen door of the Flacks' house bangs across the yard.

Kenny! Mom says to get your butt up here and eat your cookies and go help Dad with the cows!

Aw jeez. Flip, you little Nerf ball, you better run!

As Kenny lopes up the yard Flip squeals and disappears around the house. Kenny turns and jogs backward.

Billy Van Dyke does run like a girl, but a really fast girl. Way to go hillbilly.

Kenny sprints around the corner of his house then, and a moment later the boy hears Flip's screams of delight. At the sound he feels a sharp pang of homesickness. Flip's squeals sound so much like Lance's that the boy can feel his little brother's heaving ribs beneath his fingers. He pretends that the girls are holding Lance down and torture-tickling him, that he is heading off to Slaussen's Market and that in six hours his brothers and sisters will be pulling the apples and bananas he has stolen for them from the lining of his jacket. He gathers his books and shoes slowly, but as he crosses the road he notices his uncle's ladies in the south pasture and remembers the downed fence behind the dairy barn. In a moment he's forgotten his siblings. He dumps his shoes on a bluestone flag outside the kitchen door and drops his books on the kitchen table and grabs an apple and heads up to the barn at a trot. He is trying to run and eat his apple and roll up his pants all at the same time—Duke's pants, a good six inches too long for him—and just as he goes through the barnyard gate he falls, his face narrowly missing a cow patty, his half-eaten apple rolling away into the mud.

Nice one.

The boy looks up to see Donnie coming out of the barn. He is shirtless and his stomach and jeans are covered in cakes of mud and he carries a short-handled shovel in each hand. As the boy scrambles to his feet Donnie throws a shovel to him one-handed, and when he catches it he feels the sting of Donnie's strength in both his wrists.

What's the rush Amos? Fence ain't going nowhere.

It's already four. Milking time's in an hour.

Donnie uses his empty hand to scratch at the dried mud on his stomach.

Jesus, Amos. You ain't been here but three months and already you're an expert in dairy farming? The ladies won't curdle, relax.

Donnie has only a fourth-grade education and is ten years older than the boy, and the boy has seen with his own eyes that he is a hard worker. But he has a short temper too, as short as the boy's, and for some reason the boy's presence has riled him since he arrived. It is an antagonism that feels edgier, more personal than that of Vinnie Grasso and Bruce St. John and Robert Sampson, who always beat on the boy as if he were the perennial loser in some game they played. Donnie has never actually hit the boy, but he communicates his antipathy nonetheless, and now, with the shovel in his hands, the boy feels years older. If his uncle wasn't waiting down at the bottom of the barnyard he might. He just might. But his uncle is waiting, and the boy turns away from Donnie still picking mud flecks off his stomach as though they were blackheads and hurries down the hill.

The barnyard slopes steeply down the hill behind the barn until it meets the even bigger hill that stretches up for a quarter mile to the north end of his uncle's property. The crease between the two hills muddies up each spring but has never run water according to his uncle. The moss-covered remains of a collapsed stone fence run down the center of the crease in a tangle of poplars and willows, blackberries and wild rose and fiddlehead ferns he picked a few weeks ago with Aunt Bessie, and just on the other side of it is the wire fence that actually divides the barnyard from the pasture. The boy runs over steppingstones laid in the hoof-churned mud and slips as one of them spins beneath him. He would fall but for the shovel in his hand, which makes a sluicing noise when it stabs the earth.

Watch it there Amos. Wouldn't want you to get your pants all dirty.

When the boy looks up the first thing he sees is that Donnie's fingers have left red marks where he scratched the mud off his stomach. The marks are almost as bright as the skin of the boy's half-eaten apple, which is the next thing the boy sees. The apple is pinched in a pitcher's grip between Donnie's thumb and first two fingers.

Hey Amos, Donnie half coos, half sneers. You forgot to finish your after-school snack.

The boy is still off-balance, more of his weight supported by the shovel than his splayed feet, and he can only watch helplessly as the red ball streaks toward him. It strikes him squarely in the chest, erupts in flecks of mud and apple meat. A hollow ringing fills his ears as though his chest were an empty metal bell, and when it clears he finds himself standing with the shovel held in both hands like a bat. Donnie is walking past him on the steppingstones, moving lightly from one to the next.

Little late on the swing, Amos, he says, pushing the shovel off the boy's shoulder with one hand. Strike two.

The blade of the shovel smacks the wet earth a second time, and mud squirts from beneath the stones Donnie steps on with a squishing sound. The boy jerks around, ready to lunge after him, but the first thing he sees is his uncle standing spraddle-legged by a small pile of fenceposts. He is staring at the boy, a pair of posthole diggers in one hand, and even as they make eye contact an expression flickers over his uncle's face—a frown, it looks like to the boy, but whether he's frowning at the boy or the swampy soil he labors over is hard to tell. He lifts the diggers up and drives them into the hole between his feet, but the ground is so wet that little more than a pinch of mud comes out in the blades, and on the next downward thrust the diggers strike a rock. His uncle sighs then, lets the diggers sit in the hole, which is less than a foot deep. By then the boy has reached him, and he looks up the crease between the barnyard and the hill of the north pasture. He counts eighteen new fenceposts. His uncle and Donnie have been at it since seven this morning, and it's only just past four. There are still six more posts in the pile.

The boy can tell from their bark and from a pile of twigs that have been stripped from them that the fenceposts are fresh-cut cedar, their sawed ends marbled brown and white. Cedar's scarce on this side of the river. The abandoned house just west of his uncle's is surrounded by them, but that land doesn't belong to his uncle, who would have had to range far and wide over his own property in order to find this much cedar. But it's a hardy water-resistant wood, well suited to the wet ground it's going in—worth the effort, his uncle would say. Do it right the first time and you won't have to do it again.

The back of his uncle's shirt is soaked with sweat and his pants all the way up to his thighs are splattered with mud. Useless work, he says now, taking a folded handkerchief from the pocket of his shirt and refolding it in an effort to find a dry patch. He wipes his forehead and eyes and puts the handkerchief back in his pocket. Useless place to put a fence.

Since his uncle has spoken first the boy feels justified in asking a question.

Why don't you move it further up the hill?

Wire won't reach that far.

What about closer to the barn?

Barnyard'd be too small then.

The boy is wondering if he should ask his uncle why he put the fence here in the first place when his uncle says, Wouldn't never have put a fence here myself, but you make do with what you find. He is about to start up with the posthole diggers when he sees the boy still looking at him, and he lets go of the diggers and wipes his face with his handkerchief again. He looks down at Donnie, who is digging up one of the old fenceposts at the other end of the barnyard, and then he looks back at the boy.

What do you know about where you come from?

The boy looks at him, his fingers brushing at his chest.

I'm from Brentwood? he says. Long Island?

But his uncle is shaking his head.

Long Island, he says, scowling, is not a place people come from. It's a place they end up. They come from somewhere else. You, he says, and then he corrects himself. We are from further north. Your grandfather, mine and Lloyd's father, had a farm in Cobleskill.

The boy can't imagine what a farm twenty miles to the north

and west has to do with his uncle's fence, and all at once he stabs his shovel into the ground and reaches for his uncle's posthole diggers.

Here, I'll help.

His uncle puts a hand on his arm.

You should know this, Dale.

The boy lets go of the diggers reluctantly. He looks around, finds his shovel again, holds it with both hands between himself and his uncle.

Me and my father didn't get along so well, his uncle is saying. Which is why your father inherited our farm.

My father is a cook? the boy says, but he isn't even sure of that now. He works at Pilgrim State Mental Hospital?

Your father is a farmer. Just not a good one. He ran our place into the ground. Or didn't run it you could say. Drank it away's more like it, sold off the cows one by one and traded the land acre by acre for a couple of dollars or a bottle until finally the government seized what was left for taxes, while all the while I spent years working for other people until I managed to scrape up the money to put the down payment on this place. Not exactly the best land in the county but it'll buy you a pair of shoes, eventually. That is, he finishes, if we ever get this fence up and get the ladies in the barn.

He lifts the diggers and brings them down hard and the blades strike the rock they struck before and sing like a tuning fork. His uncle shakes his head and almost under his breath he says, Damn Lloyd. Drank away the farm and Nancy and—

He stops when he sees the boy is still standing there, his eyes wide, the shovel gone slack in his hands.

Aw no. You never heard of Nancy neither?

The boy can only shake his head, not trusting himself to speak. He has never heard of their grandfather's farm and he has never heard of Nancy either, but while the former is intriguing and scary and mostly very far away, there is something about the way his uncle had said the word *Nancy*—something about the way he'd said the word *and* right after it—that reminds him of the way the old man had said *not again* that day in the truck.

His uncle's handkerchief is too wet to do any good but he uses it anyway, and after he's swiped at his forehead he holds it in his hands.

Well listen. You know how your dad wasn't the first man your ma was married to? Duke and Jimmy?

Ma wasn't married before she was married to Dad. Dad says that makes Duke and Jimmy bastards.

Right. Well, your dad *was* married before he married your ma. He was married to a girl named Nancy Mitford. He married her right out of high school, was with her a good six, seven years before she left him.

If his uncle had told him to get to work he would have. But he doesn't. He just stands there wringing the handkerchief in his hands. The boy wishes his uncle would tell him to get to work but he doesn't, and so he says, Dad says Duke and Jimmy are double bastards because they don't even have the same old man. Jimmy's last name is Dundas just like Grandma and Grandpa but Duke's last name is Enlow. We don't even know anybody named Enlow.

Mitford, Dale. Your dad's first wife was Nancy Mitford.

Dad says Ma ain't nothing but a whore.

Don't you talk about your ma that way, unless you want me to wash your mouth out with lye.

The shovel is shaking in the boy's hands. He has to drop it to the ground for fear he will strike his uncle with it.

And?

His uncle catches his breath before replying, one hand reaching for the diggers in the hole.

What do you mean, Dale?

You said *and*. You said Dad lost the farm and Nancy *and*. And what?

His uncle shakes his head.

It's not important. Nancy's long gone, your dad's built a life with your ma now.

You said *and*, Uncle Wallace. You *said* it.

His uncle shakes his head. The boy remembers how his uncle had shaken his head at the old man when they first came to the farm.

57

That shake had meant no but this shake means something else. His uncle lets go of the diggers, reaches instead for his handkerchief. He starts to wipe his forehead with the back of his hand, then stops when he sees the boy holding out the napkin that has been in his front pocket all day.

You said and, Uncle Wallace.

His uncle takes the napkin, wipes his forehead, eyes.

They had a son, Dale, he says. Lloyd and Nancy had one son. There is still something incomplete about this information, and the boy waits until his uncle puts the napkin in his pocket and says, Named Dale.

The boy doesn't understand at first.

You mean I'm—

No, no, you're Ethel's son all right. But there was another Dale before you. Another Dale Peck. Nancy took him away with her when she left and when you was born your father give you the same name.

All of a sudden the boy is out of breath. He feels like he has carried two full milk pails the length of the alley, only to discover the vat is missing from the vat room, and the barn missing when he turns around. Shaking with his burden, all he can do is nod at his uncle, and then he takes his shovel and goes to help Donnie dig out the old posts, and the work is so exhausting, the wet earth so heavy and full of stones, that he barely has time to think of this other Dale, the first one. The old man's firstborn son.

Most of the old posts are so rotted that their trunks can be twisted off by hand, but his uncle wants each post's root dug up and the hole filled in so that one of the ladies doesn't break a leg on her way to the barn. The boy goes at it methodically, driving his shovel through the root and grinding the fibrous wood to bits, then shoveling dirt into the holes and tamping it down with his bare feet to make sure the earth is packed solid until at one point Donnie calls out, It ain't a cemetery, Amos. Pick up the pace a little, it's after six.

In the silence after he speaks the boy can hear the lows of the ladies on the other side of the barn and the house and 38. It's another half hour before all the old posts are out of the ground, and even as

the boy lets the shovel fall from hands almost as blistered as his feet
his uncle is putting a pair of pliers into them.

Gotta get the wire off the posts.

The boy and his uncle work at opposite ends of the barnyard
fence, Donnie in the middle; and so it is Donnie who an hour later
says to the boy, Aw Jesus Christ, Amos, I don't believe it.

The boy ignores him. He opens the pliers wide and closes the
sharp metal shears at the back of the pliers' jaws over the wire right
next to the staple. He squeezes and twists and just as the wire snaps
Donnie slaps the pliers out of his hand. They skitter into the mud
and disappear like his apple three hours ago.

What the hell do you think you're doing Amos?

The boy launches himself at Donnie's waist. Donnie grabs him
by his shirt and belt and throws him backward and the boy lands on
his bottom in the mud, feels some of it spill like thick cold water into
his drawers. He is scrambling for a second lunge when his uncle says,

All right, all right, what's going on here?

Will you look at this, Wallace. Amos cut the wire off the posts,
it's in pieces. It's ruined.

The boy bites his tongue because this is indeed what's he done,
and as soon as Donnie says it aloud he senses he's done something
wrong.

That right, Dale?

Wasn't that what I was supposed to do?

Jesus, Amos. Donnie reaches a hand into his breast pocket and
pulls out a handful of rusty bent staples, which he throws into the
mud. You were supposed to pull the staples off the old posts and
leave the wire whole so we could restring it on the new ones. We're
gonna have to buy a whole new roll of wire now.

The logic of Donnie's argument shames the boy—and the
fact that it comes from Donnie's mouth makes it that much worse.
How could he have been so stupid? He watches mute as his uncle
digs into the same pocket that had produced his quarters earlier in
the day. Now he pulls out a few wrinkled bills and hands them to
Donnie and his voice seems to sink into the mud like the pliers.

59

Best see if there's anything in the milk can. I'd just as soon not put this on credit.

The milk can is in the vat room. It contains the change their neighbors leave for a quart or two of fresh milk. It is his uncle's equivalent of the shoe fund: he uses it for incidentals, spare parts for the milking machine, patches for a leaky tire, chicken feed, and occasionally he takes a quarter from it to buy the butterscotch candies he likes to suck on in the afternoons.

Milk can's empty, Donnie says. I used it yesterday to gas up the tractor.

His uncle frowns. He takes the napkin from his pocket but it is nothing more than a wet ball, and he throws it on the ground. The boy stares at the white spot on the dark earth because he finds it hard to look at his uncle. He would like to crawl under the mud himself. But how can he be expected to know about moving fence when he doesn't even know the old man was married before he was married to his mother? That there is an earlier incarnation of him out there somewhere—a first try, perhaps even a better one. Someone who knows how to take down a fence without cutting the wires like they were so many lengths of spaghetti.

He has to clear his throat before the words will come.

You can use my shoe fund, Uncle Wallace.

His uncle looks down at him with a funny expression on his face. He has seen the first Dale, and the boy wonders if he is comparing them in his head. Wonders how he measures up.

That's all right, Dale. I'll charge it, pay it off next time we pump the vat.

No, Uncle Wallace, it's my fault, I want to pay for it.

His uncle shakes his head then, but he is pointing to the house.

Go on then. But hurry it up so Donnie can make it to the supply store before it closes.

It takes Donnie an hour to return with the wire. During that time there is nothing to do but gather up the staples, the ones the boy left on the old fenceposts and the ones Donnie threw on the ground, and try to ignore the confused lowing of the ladies across the road. As the boy works the sun sets behind the same hill the old man had driven over the day he left him here, and the boy lets himself imagine the red spots of the taillights glowing like an animal's eyes even though there had been no taillights left on the truck by then, and from there it is easy to imagine that the old man wasn't driving back to Brentwood but instead to retrieve his other son. His firstborn. The first Dale Peck. The ladies' calls float up the hill, gaining volume and depth until they seem to roll over him like snowballs in reverse, chilling his skin inside his clothes—Duke's clothes, Jimmy's clothes. He roots around in the mud with his bare feet until he finds the pliers and washes them off in the trough. He washes his face too, to soothe the burning in his cheeks and forehead, and when he sees his dim reflection in the rippled water of the trough he has to wonder if this, too, belonged to someone else before it belonged to him.

He hears his uncle's voice behind him.

Don't let him get under your skin, Dale. He's just frustrated because he ain't got nothing of his own.

It takes the boy a moment before he realizes his uncle is referring to Donnie. He takes a last look at his face, then swats at the flecks of mud on his chest and the clots on the seat of his pants, and even though he knows he shouldn't he says,

Neither do I, Uncle Wallace.

His uncle doesn't say anything so the boy keeps going.

I'll pack my things as soon as we're done here. He stares at his uncle's muddy thighs. I guess Ma was right. I guess military school's the only place for me.

His uncle's legs stiffen in their muddy sheaths, and when his knees bend the mud cracks like the crust on a loaf of bread. He brings his green eyes level with the boy's.

You're not going nowhere. Anybody can make a mistake but there's no place for self-pity on this farm. His uncle's voice softens. I'll get you those shoes, Dale. Next time we pump the vat I'll drive you straight to town and buy you a pair of brand-new shoes.

The boy nods his head, unable to meet the watery intensity of his uncle's eyes, so like the old man's. He doesn't understand how defeat has been rendered victory—cannot wrap his head around the mitigating factor that is his uncle's love—and so he mistrusts his reprieve, and when Donnie gets back the boy launches himself into the rewiring of the fence to demonstrate his worth to the farm, prove he can earn his keep. The three of them rewire the fence by lantern light, and then, with Donnie helping, it only takes an hour to get the milking done. Even though the boy hurries it's Donnie who ends up milking the sixty-first cow, and he tells the boy he'll have to find something else to pull on tonight, and aims one of the teats in his hand at the boy and squirts his foot with a jet of warm milk.

It's nearly eleven by the time they head in for dinner. The arc of the Milky Way bands the blue-black sky like a spray of water shot from a hose and the dew on the grass washes the mud off the boy's feet as they walk down the hill. The dew is cold but it stings the blisters on his feet. At the bottom of the hill the little L-shaped house is dark save for the kitchen window, a square of light cut into the wall, a trapezoid where the light angles away on the ground. Dew-wet pebbles glint in the light.

Have to pick up those wire pieces in the morning, his uncle says as he pulls open the door.

Yeah, Amos. Maybe you can make yourself a pair of shoes. Steel toe, Donnie says, and the boy feels Donnie's boot on his wet butt.

The boy doesn't answer, just picks up Jimmy's boots by their laces and lets them thump together to knock the dirt off them. The left one is still wet from being thrown into the ditch, and the boy winces in anticipation of sticking his blistered foot into the stiff leather six hours from now.

Inside, Aunt Bessie is looking at the *Reader's Digest* at the table. There is a big pot of something on the stove and the empty can that had contained his shoe fund is missing from the counter. He looks around until he sees it by the door to the hall, right next to a pair of boots he doesn't recognize. The boots are black and broken in but not worn out, and it looks like someone has run a brush over them to bring up the shine.

Kenny Flack came by while you were out in the fields, Aunt

Bessie says, ladling what looks like beef stew into Uncle Wallace's bowl. Said he thought they might fit you. Said it'd be another couple of years before Flip grew into them and they were just taking up space in his closet.

The boy nods his head, sits down at the table. Kenny Flack, Flip. The names bounce between his ears but his brain is blistered as his hands and feet, too tired to run after them and pin them to their proper faces. And anyway, the boy finds it easier to think of them as empty—easier to think they can be swatted away like flies when they buzz too close to his ears. Kenny Flack. Flip. The words flit through his head, as untenanted as the name Dale Peck has become since his uncle told him he inherited it from another boy.

His old boots are still in his hands and he starts to put them in his lap, then puts them under his chair. He looks at the new boots by the door, the empty can next to them, and then at the empty bowl in front of him, and when Aunt Bessie's ladle interposes itself between his eyes and his bowl and empties its contents into the bowl he picks up his spoon, and as they eat Donnie tells Aunt Bessie how the boy cut up the fence wire and had to spend his shoe fund on a new roll.

Looks like Kenny Flack knew just what was going on out there.

The boy's uncle doesn't say anything during the meal, doesn't mention the other farm, the first farm and the first wife and first child that went with it, the first Dale Peck, but it is all the boy's tired brain can think about, and as soon as he's finished eating he excuses himself and starts toward the stairs.

Don't forget your boots.

The boy turns toward his chair, but Aunt Bessie is pointing to the door. She has an innocent smile on her face, and when the boy doesn't move her smile hardens slightly. She glances down at Kenny Flack's boots, back up at him. They're just shoes to her, a neighborly gesture, brotherly love, and the boy looks at them, sitting next to the empty can with their laces tucked neatly inside their hollow ankles. They're a solid simple thing, but so was his life until a few hours ago. Now the boots seem more substantial than he is, but even so the boy is afraid to claim them, lest they too turn out to be an illusion.

Donnie and his uncle are looking at him now, Aunt Bessie sitting there with her spoon in her right hand and her paper napkin unfolded in her lap, creased into four panes like a curtained window. Under their collective gaze the boy can do nothing but pick up the new boots and turn toward the stairs. They're a hand-me-down just like his other clothes, his name, his face even, but they're also all he has, and he cradles them in his arms like a baby, and carries them up to his empty room.

4

THE DAY AFTER they restring the fence the boy steps off the bus in the shoes Kenny Flack has given him and sees a car parked in the driveway of his uncle's house. Neither boy had said anything about the shoes that day, but when he ran into Kenny at lunch the older boy had introduced him to his friends. This is the boy who beat Billy Van Dyke in the four hundred yesterday, Kenny told his friends. He talks funny but he's all right.

The car is a late-model Buick, its creamy underside separated from its red roof by a wide chrome dart, its polish unflecked by age or mud. It is all angles and lines next to his uncle's bulbous black '48 Ford, but all the boy thinks is, Town car.

The Buick turns out to belong to Mr. Baldwin, the gym teacher, a fussy man who wears brightly colored ties with his short-sleeved white shirts. He sits with his uncle and Donnie Badget at the kitchen table with a cup of coffee in front of him, and as soon as the boy walks in his uncle says, Ernie here says you threw your shoes at him yesterday. Like to knock out his front teeth, Ernie says.

The boy sees Donnie looking between him and Mr. Baldwin, and his gaze seems to link them together, as if the boy is as much a townie as this teacher with the creases ironed into his shirtsleeves.

Says you want to run track and field, the boy's uncle says now, and Donnie shakes his head and looks down into his cup of coffee.

That's not true, Uncle Wallace. He asked me and I said I had chores to do after school. I said I wouldn't have time for his stupid track team.

His uncle nods his head, his lips pursed as if he is considering a

65

business proposition. Donnie's shoulders are shaking and the boy thinks he is laughing into his cup.

It's true you do have your chores, his uncle says thoughtfully. But Ernie here makes the case that a boy should have a sport, especially one he's good at. He looks up at the boy. I told him you could have an hour after school plus time off for meets. How's that sound?

The boy looks back and forth between Mr. Baldwin and his uncle while Donnie stares at him with an inscrutable smirk on his face.

But there's a uniform. Shorts, a tank top. He looks down at his new boots. And sneakers.

Mr. Baldwin covers his mouth with his hand when he coughs.

The school would provide those, of course. If he letters he'll have to buy his own letter jacket, but we'll get him started with the uniform. And shoes, as long as he doesn't throw them at me. He smiles at his uncle. I think he shows a lot of potential.

Again, his uncle nods his head.

Thought that about him myself. I still do.

As he is getting into his car and the boy is about to head up to the dairy barn, Mr. Baldwin says, Nice herd of cattle you have here, and it takes the boy a moment to realize he is talking to him.

They're not cattle. They're cows.

Cattle are food, his uncle explains, already heading to the barn.

Donnie knocks against the boy's shoulder as he walks past him up the hill. Played football myself, he says without stopping. When I was a kid. Always thought track was a bit of a sissy sport myself.

The boy doesn't say anything, just starts to run past Donnie up to the barn, but his uncle's voice stops him.

Donnie and me'll get the ladies. You best go find that wire you clipped up last night. Gather it up before one-a the ladies pokes an eye out.

By then Donnie's caught up with him, and he bumps the boy's shoulder again as he saunters past.

See you in the barn, Amos.

The boy gathers the wire as quickly as he can. He finds twenty-three lengths in all, each about fifteen feet long unrolled but the size of a cereal bowl after he curls it around his fist. The individual wires are nearly weightless but when he strips the leaves from a willow switch and spools the twenty-three coils onto it they weigh as much as a gallon of milk. He stores the coils in the hay barn near a row of glass jars that contain rusty nails and screws and the leftover staples from last night's rewiring, and makes it into the dairy barn just in time to pull a stool and pail up to the sixty-first lady. There's no money in it for him, but he can't resist flashing a smile of triumph at Donnie.

The next day he practices with the track team after school. An hour of drills and weights and time trials, and then he runs the mile and a half home and helps his uncle and Donnie with the ladies. Monday, Wednesday, and Friday evenings he does an additional four-mile loop after the milking's done, setting off and finishing at the sign that reminds everyone who reads it that this land belonged to the Millers before it belonged to the Pecks. That the Pecks lost their place in Cobleskill and had to resettle here, and on Long Island. His loop takes him east and north along 38 until he cuts west on Daniel's Road. Julia Miller lives on Daniel's Road, in a house that has no plaque in front of it but has a full second story and a slate-roofed barn the size of the school auditorium and, as well, the uneclipsed magnificence that is the 1956 Chevy. Sometimes the boy sees her when he runs by, helping her mother in the vegetable garden or playing tetherball with her sister, but even when she waves at him he pretends not to see her, so that the next morning on the bus she can lock her hair behind her ear and say, I waved at you yesterday, and he can blush and say, Sorry I didn't see you. But more often than not he actually doesn't see her, doesn't even look for her, preferring to maintain the solitude of running free of Julia or Donnie or the far-flung members of his family. He follows Daniel's Road west until it dead-ends in Route 32, and then he follows 32 south back to 38. Shepherd's Bush sprawls over the four corners of that intersection, and by the end of May the little resort is hosting its first weekend visitors. On Memorial Day weekend the boy sees a wet-haired girl in a green two-piece bathing suit just as she raises her arms and swan dives off the diving board. He runs backwards until she surfaces at the far end of the pool and climbs up the ladder and presses the water from her hair, and although the boy can't actually see the water from this distance, he imagines its course down the channel of her spine and into the delta where her hips flare out of her bathing suit.

The following Saturday, the first in June, he has to help his uncle irrigate a constipated Holstein. They tether her to one of the new fenceposts and the boy sits atop the post and holds her tail while his uncle coats the nozzle of the hose with bacon grease and slides it up her as she bleats bloody murder, and when, a few minutes later, water spits out around the hose, they run like hell. Murky water spews out for a good five minutes, and then, when it runs clear and they've untied her, the Holstein trots off to join the other ladies under the chestnut trees that shade the top of the hill.

If I didn't know better I'd think she enjoyed that, his uncle says. I'd almost say she had a spring in her step.

The boy cleans the hose and coils it up and then he and his uncle drive to the supply store to pick up a fuse to replace one that had blown in the boom collars that morning. The fuses come in packages of two, and it takes his uncle a couple of minutes to talk the counterman into splitting the package and selling him just the one he needs, and after they've screwed the housing back on the collars' motor his uncle drops the glass fuse in a jar next to his jars of nails and screws and staples, and the coils of wire hanging on the willow switch. He uses the fuses as insulators, he tells the boy, on the electric fence he runs around the hog pen, when there are hogs in it.

Before they leave the barn the boy notices that there are two C's hanging above the shelf of jars—the shelf itself is one of the horizontal joints in the barn's frame, and the nails the C's hang off poke through from the other side, meaning they're part of the barn itself, not nailed into the wall for the sole purpose of holding them up. But he cannot imagine what use the C's once had, or will have again. Perhaps they're remnants of a sign that once spelled WALLACE PECK? The C's are carved from wood in Gothic style and painted gold, most of which has long since flaked off, and the boy is about to ask his uncle about them when he hears the tractor pulling up outside. It turns out to be Donnie, hauling a cube of hay bales piled on the two-wheeled trailer behind his uncle's old John Deere. Donnie waves to the boy's uncle with his cap even as he whirls the tractor around and backs the trailer up to the hay barn. He pilots the tractor smoothly, one hand on the wheel, the other on the gearshift, and the boy watches his performance intently, but it isn't until Donnie shuts off the tractor that the boy remembers the ease with which the old man used to back out of the alley behind the Jew's pharmacy. There is something else that links their activities—something about the finesse that the truly impoverished bring to behavior in lieu of property—but the thought is half formed, finds its only expression in one of the boy's bare feet, which lifts off the ground and scratches the top of the other; and then a backfire makes the air between the barns and the house vibrate like a fly buzzing too close to his ear; and there is Donnie, hopping off the tractor and running his fingers through sweat-wet hair to separate it from his scalp.

The boy's uncle pulls off his own cap and scratches his head as Donnie puts his back on. A thick red line rings the older man's nearly hairless scalp like the orbit of a moon.

Thought I gave you weekends off.

Donnie looks without blinking into the boy's uncle's eyes.

Just happened to be driving by that field on 81 and noticed it was ready to mow. Thought I might as well get on it.

Donnie continues to stare at the boy's uncle for another moment, and then his eyes drop and he traces a circle in the dirt with his boot. The boy's uncle rubs at the red line circling his head and then puts his cap back on.

Guess we best unload it then.

The cube is rectangular actually, its shape a magnification of the bales that compose it—ten bales wide, ten long, ten high. It takes a good hour to loft it into the hay barn, and on three separate occasions Donnie calls out Hey Amos! and throws a bale of hay at him. The first two times the fifty-pound bales knock the hundred-and-thirty-pound boy down, but the third time he manages to catch it and remain on his feet—at which point Donnie throws him another bale and knocks him to the floor. When they've finished the boy's uncle invites Donnie to take the noon meal at Aunt Bessie's house in town, and after they're gone the boy eats a few slices of cheddar and a couple of last year's apples—a tart Granny Smith, a sweet Macoun—and changes into his running shoes and sets off for his first eight-mile run.

The route he's planned will take him up and around the Alcove Reservoir, which he drives past when he goes to church with Aunt Bessie. It's almost ten miles roundtrip in the car, but he figures the back roads he'll take will shave a couple miles off that. Still, eight miles is a big jump up from four and he tells himself before setting out that it's okay if he has to stop and walk part of it. But Coach Baldwin has also said he wants the boy to compete in the half marathon next year—thirteen miles—and the boy looks on this run as a test of his mettle.

He starts out east at an easy trot. Thirty-eight is a broad dirt road with no shoulder, just two shallow ditches that are mowed twice a year to keep the tree growth down, and so he runs on the right side of the road until he reaches the bottom of the hill where 38 curves north and a narrow rutted lane continues on to the east. His path takes him between the two parcels that make up his uncle's land, the grass in the pastures long and fronded with seed and already yellowing as the June heat dries up the last of the spring runoff. At the boggy eastern edge of his uncle's land the pasture has reverted to a strip of forest, and the boy thinks of the twenty-year-old trees as a miniature arboretum. Poplars seem to spring up the fastest, reaching head and shoulders above their neighbors. Their bark is still almost as smooth as a birch's, just beginning to hoar up on the lower part of the trunks, but they're weak trees, and scattered few and far between the hardier slow-growth oaks and maples and chestnuts. A row of black locusts is bunched at the side of the strip like a crowd waiting to get into a movie theater, and the spindle-branched sumacs that grow under the locusts look enough like the larger trees that they could be their children. The sprays of sumac leaves, already tinted red along their seams, make a thin but effective wall that hides the undergrowth deeper in the forest—which is mostly itch ivy anyway, as the boy found out a few weeks ago when he ventured in barefoot to retrieve one of the ladies. Here and there a constellation of white leaves marks a dogwood, and earlier in the year he'd seen a lone redbud, glowing in the shadows like a barber's pole.

It takes him just as much time to tick off these names as it does to run past his uncle's land, and something seems fitting in that, as if a true correspondence existed between the land and language, the living trees and the forest taking root in his head. The damp soil, rich but rocky, the flume of silver and brown trunks erupting from it, the thousands and thousands of leaves as different each from the other as snowflakes. He notes the way a chestnut's teardrop leaflets radiate from a common point like the spokes of a wheel whereas a locust's smaller ovals are lined up along its stem like a string of Black Cats, sees how a maple's leaf is five-fingered like a hand and how an oak's is that same hand gnarled by amputation or arthritis. And he notes also his own limbs, his muscles and breath. It only takes a dozen paces before the soreness has melted out of his hamstrings and calves, a few more before his breathing falls into a rhythm with his feet, two steps per inhale, two per ex, as Coach Baldwin directed him. He listens to the sound his feet make when they strike the hard earth. Coach Baldwin—who despite his horn-rimmed glasses and permanent-press shirts has a mouth like a drill sergeant on the field—has pointed out that his feet are flatter than a whore's back, and he has to take extra care to make sure he lands on the balls and not the heels. It's all in the sound. Coach Baldwin told him that a hammer makes an awful racket when it pounds a half-penny nail into a two-by-four but the nail makes almost no sound at all: the boy wants his feet to be nails, not hammers. What the boy thinks is that running is like giving milk. Something else does all the work and he is just pulled along in its wake, and by the time he leaves the asphalt his mind has separated from his nearly silent feet and follows along like a balloon on a string. When a car honks and swerves past him he jumps a little, because he hasn't heard it coming. By then he has left even his body behind, has given himself over to the land, this land that his uncle knows with a respect that goes beyond love. The boy wants to learn its language fully, wants to read it as his uncle does. Not just road signs and historical markers that hint at the past, but its moods, its temper. There are days when it seems to the boy that his uncle is tied to his farm as surely as he is to his shadow, and the boy hopes that if he surrenders to it as completely as his uncle has then perhaps the land will replace his own unwanted shadows, the old man, his mother, his brothers and sisters and especially the boy who walks around in his name just as he walks around in Kenny Flack's boots. But it is hard to run away from something when all you know is that it has the same name as you.

Once he leaves 38 behind, the landscape darkens. To his left there is an old hemlock forest, to his right a younger stand of white pine. The hemlocks are grizzly but still shapely trees, the pines neater but more variegated in appearance, their soft wood easily molded by wind and weather. The splinter road has no ditches and the two forests crowd its track, dusting its northern edge with feathery hemlock needles and its southern with longer pine pins, and the peaty brown soil stretching out from both sides of the road is nearly devoid of undergrowth, just a little horsetail and gorse and here and there the occasional laurel still in bloom. He doesn't know who owns the hemlock forest but the pines are part of his Great-Uncle Felter's land. He planted them himself, by hand, more than a quarter century ago. Great-Uncle Felter is the old man's mother's brother, and though Mary Felter Peck is long dead Great-Uncle Felter lives on in a white house on Route 32 on the southern side of town. He splits his own firewood with a sledgehammer and iron wedge and sows the seed corn in his garden with a soup of chicken guts, and he considers everyone from the boy's uncle's generation hopelessly lazy and everyone from the boy's generation enslaved to machines, if not simply robots clothed in human flesh. The boy has only met Great-Uncle Felter twice, and on neither of those occasions did he see the man sit or stand still, even to eat, and he imagines that he sleeps on the run, mowing his lawn or reshingling his house or vetting a hog for the next morning's bacon. His uncle only took the boy to see him once, out of duty. The second time they ran into him at the feed store, and they spoke fewer words to each other than they did to the man behind the counter.

His uncle has never volunteered an explanation for his distance from Great-Uncle Felter and the boy hasn't asked, but snippets have come out in the same way that the story of the old man's first wife and son came out. Apparently Mary Felter Peck had continued to live with Lloyd and Nancy and the first Dale Peck after they took over the farm in Cobleskill, and when Lloyd lost it, lost farm and wife and child, she had moved into Great-Uncle Felter's house because the boy's uncle wouldn't take her in. This had something to do with the fact that his uncle's first wife, Ella Mae, was dying of cancer at the time — died right there on that couch, his uncle told him one evening after supper, giving the boy a queasy feeling because he happened to be sitting on the couch — and Mary Felter Peck, who suffered from her own host of ailments, was a burden he wasn't prepared to accept. But still, it seems like ancient history to the boy, and he can't understand why they don't bury the hatchet while there's still time.

Actually Ella Mae wasn't his uncle's first wife: she was his only wife. Aunt Bessie is not actually married to his uncle, which is why she keeps her own house in town and returns to it every morning to feed the two cats that still live there, and tend to the small garden from which she is always bringing radishes and carrots and tomatoes and cucumbers. Aunt Bessie also has a dead spouse, a man named Irving van Clouton, and she has two sons, Joel, who lives out in Rochester, and William, who grows organic vegetables in greenhouse pontoons on a farm in Cherry Hill, New Jersey. On this list of never-seen relatives there is also his uncle's child Edith. In six months all he has learned is that she was widowed at the age of twenty-seven by the Korean War and is now raising a son whose name his uncle has yet to mention. It was Donnie Badget who told the boy that Edith had met her son's father at a dance in Coxsackie just before he shipped out, and there is some doubt as to whether he gave her the wedding band she wears or if she bought it for herself when she found out she was pregnant. At any rate, her son's father's name is on his birth certificate, but his uncle has never said that name aloud either. Donnie said Edith lives in South Westerlo, less than twenty miles away, but for all his uncle has spoken of her she could be as lost as the old man's first wife and child.

This time it's a truck that rumbles past the boy, a flatbed Jimmy like the old man's—a farm truck he understands now, where before he'd always thought the old man drove it because there wasn't a car big enough to carry his entire family. Two boys sit in the back of the truck as different in age as Kenny and Flip Flack but as alike in all other things as ears of corn cut from the same stalk. They stare at the boy and he stares back at them, and when the truck has put a little distance between them the older of the pair raises his hand and waves and turns back to his younger brother. By now the boy has left the pine and hemlock behind, and a pasture stretches out on the south side of the road, the fleur-de-lis shapes of a field of knee-high corn on the north. And why *is* this field pasture—freshly mowed, purple clover swirling low over the soil like heavy smoke—that field planted in corn? Is it because the former has poor drainage and tends to swamp up in the spring, a condition that doesn't bother the ladies but doesn't particularly agree with tractors; or is it because the latter belongs to the Kahalens, who think dairy farming is common and dirty? There is so much to learn.

His breath is still as smooth as when he started, his feet strike the earth with the clean sound of Aunt Bessie's hoe clearing spidergrass from the front walk. They are fifty-four years old, Uncle Wallace and Aunt Bessie both, and have been together for nearly a decade, and sometimes Aunt Bessie jokingly asks his uncle if he's ever going to make an honest woman of her. He will, his uncle jokes, the first day the ladies let him have off he will.

The boy figures he's done about three miles. He's taken his shirt off at some point—doesn't remember doing it, but it flaps from the waistband of his shorts—and although his torso is wet with sweat he feels he could run forever. He does a hundred paces marching band style, snapping his knees so high the tops of his thighs nearly touch his belly, and then he turns around and runs backwards another hundred paces, then runs backwards while doing jumping jacks. The sun is beating straight down on his head but to him its rays are strings holding him up, pulling him along like Apollo in his chariot. He sprints for an imaginary audience. *And Peck comes into the homestretch now, the competition's nowhere in sight but this kid's still giving it all he's got—and there it is, Peck by a mile! Another victory for the Golden Eagles!* He pretends his fingers are a finish-line tape snapping across his chest, and then he leaves them there, feels the swell where his chest muscles rise off his ribs. Swinging hay bales and feed sacks over the past four months has changed his body. Jimmy's football jersey pulls across his shoulders when he puts it on now, and a few nights ago he was so impressed by the sight of his biceps in the bathroom mirror that he kissed them. He is only in eighth grade but he drills with the high school track team, and he has decided he will be captain by his sophomore year. He is polishing a caseful of trophies and listening to the jingle of a dozen gold medals dangling off the bright gold G of his letter jacket when he rounds a bend in the road and comes upon the reservoir. The water is clear and brown and dark all at the same time, and seems to hold the clouds in it as though they were tufts of algae. It is small as reservoirs go, and unusual in that no stream or river runs into it: it collects the water of half a dozen springs as well as the runoff from the foothills hemming it in, and its waterline is all around as jagged as a broken one-by-six save for the single sharp line of the concrete dam on its southeastern edge. An osprey floats in an unraveling spiral high above, but is rewarded by nothing save its own reflection on the flat surface of the water.

Aunt Bessie told him there is an easy footpath that runs around the whole thing—she walks it early in the spring to pick the ramps and morel mushrooms that grow in the pine forests clotting the higher hills on the north and west side of the reservoir, and over the course of the summer she comes back for raspberries, blackberries, wild strawberries, and plums, all of which the boy has tasted in preserved form, and then finally the fruit of one fine old walnut she says not even the squirrels have found. He will have to wait until Christmas to taste the tart she'll make from ground walnut and venison sausage, but as soon as he sees the water he has to have it. He hurdles a low wire fence and high-jumps his way through burdock and tangles of rushes and last year's rusty loosestrife until he comes upon the beaten red earth. Instinctively he veers east, preferring to run in the open air while he's still relatively fresh and cool, saving the shadowy forest stretches for later.

The footpath is slippery with broken flat shale and then uneven with the half-exposed roots of wind-twisted willows and junipers, but in the patches of bare earth he can see the tread of boots and bicycle tires and horseshoes, dogs and deer and raccoons and birds. From the moment he'd seen the water he'd noticed an increase in the insect population too, greenhead flies especially, and now they seem to be winning a game of dodgeball with his hands as he swats head, shoulders, chest. His flailing arms upset his gait until he works them into a tempo with his legs, and when sometimes he actually hits a fly he feels its exoskeleton crunch against his scalp like a blueberry bursting its skin. He can see how Aunt Bessie could call the path an easy walk, but it's hard running. The slap of his rubber soles against the earth, his uneven in- and exhales, now long, now short, completely out of time with his feet. His legs still feel strong but his shoulders ache a little—Donnie's damn hay bales, he thinks. Just happened to be driving by that field on 81 my ass, the boy thinks. Trying to make himself look good is more like it. Trying to prove he's still needed. It's a little cooler by the water but the boy feels a hot flush on his skin as he thinks about Donnie's naked attempt to curry favor with his uncle. His breath is hot in his lungs, and he tells himself he must have done at least five miles. I played football, track is a sissy sport, I played football when I was a kid. The boy'd like to see Donnie Badget try to run *this* distance on those bandy little legs of his. He suddenly remembers running from Vinnie Grasso and Bruce St. John and Robert Sampson. Screw all of you, he thinks, streaking along the water's edge. Screw you all.

First he tells himself he'll stop when he reaches the pine forest and then he tells himself he'll stop when he reaches that wedding-cake rock and then, no, he tells himself, he'll push on to that big smooth slab of granite. He sets his sights on a gigantic poplar next, as thick as he is tall and growing at such a steep angle over the water that it seems to have tipped the world off its axis. The path is more root and rock than earth, and the pine pins covering everything make each footfall a bit of a guess; three times he skids and nearly falls. The reservoir looks small from the road, on the way to church in Aunt Bessie's old Chevrolet, but then the only thing he has to compare it to is the Atlantic Ocean. To make it worse its shore-line sticks out and dips in and seems constantly to be doubling back on itself. Each sharp turn in the trail seems to lead to yet another V-shaped tree-shaded bug-infested inlet, and he's finally decided he has to stop when he sees a bicycle leaning up against a rock. A girl's bicycle, with a dropped center strut and wicker basket mounted in the handlebars and big white-wale tires. He isn't sure but he thinks it's—

Why if it isn't the star of track and field.

When he stops running it seems as if some part of him, his powerplant, his energy, keeps on going. He watches it streak around the reservoir, free of the burden of his body. Six miles, he tells himself. At least. Surely. And then he lets himself fall to his knees.

God*damn* I'm tired.

There he goes, talking that trash again.

Julia Miller is tucked into a little glade of thin birches wearing a white one-piece bathing suit and a pair of flip-flops. The criss-cross straps of her bathing suit meet in a little loop of bunched fabric just above her breasts, forming an open circle the size of a quarter through which the boy can glimpse the merest hint of cleavage. She has a notebook in her lap, and when his eyes linger too long on the circle of flesh and shadow she picks it up and holds it to her chest, just below the loop of fabric. The boy feels himself blushing, and hopes that the general flushed tint of his skin covers it up.

Hi, Julia. What brings you here?

77

His words sound slightly ragged to his ears, his breath still hot in and out of his body. Six and a half, he wonders. Maybe even seven.

I'm doing that paper for Mr. Borden's ecology class.

She speaks as if she expects him to know what she means, and he says, I'm just in general science.

Oh. Julia puts her pen in her mouth. Looks thoughtful. Then: Congratulations.

Huh?

Heard you did good at the Schoharie Invitational. A stunning debut, Mr. Borden said.

We come in second.

But you were in fourth when Jimmy Orstler handed you the baton.

The boy blushes.

Jonny. Jimmy runs second leg.

Well anyway, I heard, Julia says. She looks at the boy for a moment and then she looks at her notebook, then scowls. She rips the page from the notebook but only half of it tears out, on a diagonal, and she wads it up and throws it on the ground. Ooh, she says, this paper's going nowhere.

The piece of paper is wadded into a ball, falls straight to the ground, but even so the boy's mind is suddenly filled with a vision of the handkerchief that had flown off the Jew's head on that last morning, and suddenly everything is different. The glade is no longer as isolated as it once was, or, rather, he becomes conscious of its isolation, aware that this conversation is only taking place because it is so far away from everything else: as soon they are back in the world it will no longer be possible. Julia will tuck her hair behind her ear and blush but that is as far as it will go because Julia's name is on a sign in front of his uncle's house and his name is on another boy. No matter how far she strays from that sign Julia will never forget where she comes from and no matter how far the boy runs he will never find out who he is. But at the same time this realization makes him bold, and it is with sadness—a sadness that accentuates rather than obliterates all those other teenage emotions—that the boy reaches out and uses his hand to do the thing that Julia normally does with her own: he locks her hair behind her ear, lets his hand follow the soft curve of it down until his fingers come to rest on her collarbone and his thumb lands softly on, then under, the strap of her swimsuit.

I was wrong.

Wrong about what?

Julia's voice is curious but not confused, confident but not brazen. Completely unafraid. For one moment the boy loves her more than he has ever loved anything in his life. The emotion hangs in the air between them as clearly as a thread of milk shot from an udder, and then it is gone.

My sister Joanie has hair like yours. A little blonder maybe. When I first saw you I thought hers was prettier but that's just because I miss her so much. Yours is prettier.

It doesn't have to be. Her hair can just be her hair and my hair can just be my hair. You don't have to compare us.

The boy shakes his head. She is sweet but she doesn't understand.

When you come from a family like mine everything goes back to it. Everything I'll ever know I learned in that house first.

Julia's face clouds for a moment and then it brightens and she says, Even this? and just like that she helps his thumb do what it wants to: she slides the strap of her swimsuit off her shoulder. She slides the other one off herself but the top of her swimsuit doesn't fold down just yet. Not until the boy slides his hands inside the loosened fabric and cups her breasts in his hands does the top of her swimsuit roll down below her sternum.

And he's a dairy farmer, he can't help but make the comparison. There's almost none, save the warmth. Each of Julia's breasts is small enough to fit into his cupped hands, and their softness has no milky slackness but is instead almost muscular. And there is a pulsing too, in the crease where they meet her body. It is the beat of her heart.

These are mine, Julia says, not understanding that the boy has never thought of making such a statement about anything, including his body. I want you to kiss them.

He blushes. A sound almost escapes him then—it would have been a giggle. He is thirteen years old and a girl has asked him to kiss her breasts.

He bends his face to them. All he can do is breathe them in at first. They are slightly damp in his hands but in his nose they're dry and an odor of baby powder lingers. With dry lips he kisses the top of each of them—it is no different than kissing a shoulder, a knee—and then he stands up suddenly, blushing so red it colors his vision.

With a laugh Julia steps back from him and dives into the pool and the boy dives in after. And the water is freezing. Fucking freezing. Its coldness makes the boy feel as though he has jumped through a concrete wall. For a moment he is paralyzed and hangs suspended a few inches above the bottom of the pool, a few inches below the surface, and then one foot finds purchase in the loose pebbles and he kicks himself above the water.

Jesus Christ!

Julia is laughing hysterically. She has swum the few feet to the shallow end of the pool and dragged herself onto a mossy rock and slipped the straps of her swimsuit back up her shoulders. She points at him with first one hand and then the other as she adjusts her suit, laughing all the while.

It's fucking freezing!

The boy is so cold he can't think what to do. The water only comes up to his ribs but he hops from one tiptoe to another, and then he runs toward Julia. The water shallows quickly and in a moment he is on the rock beside her, shivering uncontrollably.

Why didn't you warn me? My God, I thought I was having a heart attack!

Julia giggles.

Haught attack.

Through chattering teeth the boy says, Huh? *Hnnh.*

Haught attack. Mutha, fatha, sista, brotha. You talk funny, city boy.

I told you, I'm from—

I know. Long *Guy*-land. What *is* a guy-land?

The boy has to admit he doesn't know.

Just a place where people talk funny I guess. *Tawk.*

Julia smiles.

Say something else.

Say what?

I don't know. She splashes some ice-cold water on his chest and he yelps. Say water.

Wauta.

Julia kisses him, a little peck on his nearly numb lips.

Say . . . say all right you guys.

Awl right youse guys.

Julie kisses him again, longer this time.

Say the porter took the water and threw it on his daughter, even though he ought to have thrown it on her courter, who was . . .

Shauta? Than his daughta?

This time she kisses him for so long that he has to slide off the rock into the water. It is freezing and it only comes up to his thighs but he crouches down so that only his head sticks out. He had jumped in the water not so much because of the sudden tightness in his shorts, but because the tightness reminded him of the one time he'd tried to wear the pair of Lance's drawers the old man had packed in his bag.

Say baseball, Julia says, still in love with her game.

Joe DiMaggio.

She laughs.

Say sports.

The New York Yankees.

Say mother.

Whore.

Julia claps a hand over her mouth. She looks at him with wide eyes and then through her fingers she says, Say father.

No-good dirty drunk.

Sister.

Pretty, the boy says, but only after a pause during which he resists the urge to say *gold*.

Brother.

At first the boy doesn't say anything, and then he says his own name.

Julia has pulled her feet up out of the water and wrapped her arms around her knees.

You're weird, Dale Peck. But I like you.

The boy nods. When he hears his name in Julia Miller's mouth he suddenly understands why his uncle doesn't name his ladies. He understands that you only name something when you don't know what it is. You name it to squeeze out all the parts you don't know so that you can hold on to what you do know—what you need, what you think you can control.

I like you too, Julia Miller.

Later, after she gets back on her bicycle, he sees the wadded ball of paper she'd torn from her notebook. He doesn't unwad it, just puts it in the pocket of his damp shorts and heads home. But his timing's off, his muscles sore. Long before he clears the reservoir a cramp in his left leg has slowed him to a near-walk, and his uncle has already brought the ladies in by the time he gets back to the farm. He can hear the rumble of the boom collars' motor as they lower in place, and he fills a pail with water, grabs a rag, hurries through the door.

Before he can start with the first cow his uncle tells him to change out of his running uniform. By the time he gets back his uncle has hooked all the cows up. There is no sign of Donnie, but his uncle is seated in front of Dolly herself, milking her by hand. The boy hauls the buckets of milk to the vat room, ignoring the ache in his shoulders and legs but unable to tune out the ringing in his ears of his uncle's oppressive silence, and as soon as all the buckets of milk have been dumped in the vat and rinsed out he finds the shovel and wheelbarrel and starts in on the gutters, and he scrapes up every last flake of manure and even hoses the gutters out when he's done.

Come here, his uncle says then, and the boy hurries over, hoping that he'll be able to do something that will ease the hardness from his uncle's face and voice. Lay a mile of fence or build a castle out of hay bales or skim all the cream from the holding vat with a teaspoon.

His uncle is standing in front of a little Jersey girl with long brown whiskers. She is tossing her head agitatedly, banging it against the boom collar.

Looks like someone got a little too curious. Poking around where she don't belong.

The boy blushes and is about to apologize when his brain catches up with his ears and cheeks, and he realizes his uncle has said *she*. He looks at the Jersey more closely, sees interspersed with her whiskers the barbed darts of half a dozen porcupine quills sticking out of the pinkish white skin of her muzzle.

With a quick gesture his uncle slips a coil of rope around the Jersey's neck, pulls it tight.

Hold this. Higher up, keep it tight. And watch it now, she's liable to go for you.

His uncle uses a pair of pliers to pull the first quill out. He has to jerk hard to work against the barbs, and the boy can feel the Jersey's pain in his hands and forearms and the biceps he kissed the other day, which aren't strong enough to prevent her from snapping the back of her head against the boom collar. The collar's hollow piping echoes like plumbing and the Jersey spits a cup of red-spotted cud onto his uncle's overalls. A few of the ladies look up from their feed momentarily, then resume eating.

Hold it tight now. Come on, Dale, she'll hurt herself worse than she already is.

The boy puts all his weight on the rope until the Jersey's triangular head sticks straight out from its thick neck like a bull snake's. The Jersey's ears are laid flat against her skull and her eyes rolled back to display two crescent moons below the dark brown irises and her top lip rolls back to reveal a thick pink wedge of gum. Though neither boy nor cow is moving it feels like he is pulling on a tree trunk vibrating in a storm. He wonders if this is what sailing feels like, tacking into the wind, carving sky and sea to your will, and even as he braces his bare feet against the lady's hooves and watches his uncle work there is a part of him that misses the ocean with the longing that only the island-born can feel.

His uncle works quickly, squeezing, pulling, squeezing, pulling, and each time he pulls out a needle the Jersey makes a sound like a fan belt about to break. Thin streams of blood marble her muzzle as though she has just slopped up a tomato or a raw steak. As the last quill comes out the Jersey lunges forward, and the boy barely has time to feel her teeth on his forearm before his uncle smacks her on her inflamed nose. When the knob of the Jersey's skull strikes the boom collar the whole barn shakes.

The boy looks down at his arm, sees first the single crescent of toothmarks and a smear of the Jersey's blood on his skin, and then a half dozen rubies of his own blood bead up through the thumbnail-sized tears in his forearm. The drops of blood well up, coalesce, drip to the floor, but the wound doesn't hurt, yet.

The boy looks at the single crescent of toothmarks and remembers that cows only have incisors on their bottom jaw.

First his uncle rubs some liniment onto the red nose of the pricked Jersey, deftly dodging her swipes at his fingers, and then he takes the boy outside and puts his arm under the spigot. The water is cold but not as cold as the water in the Alcove Reservoir. It runs pink off his arm and the cuts immediately burn, but the boy can see that none of them is very deep.

I seen them snap bone. You were lucky.

It is only a moment before the water runs clear and then his uncle shuts it off and smears a thick dab of liniment on his arm, the same liniment he'd rubbed on the Jersey. The liniment is clear but unguent, like bacon grease, and even though his uncle rubs it in vigorously the boy resists the urge to flinch. Through the oily sheen coating his arm the boy can see a bit of blood well up, though not enough to push through the liniment.

You'll want Aunt Bessie to wrap that in a clean rag, his uncle says, and then his voice changes and he says, Listen to me, Dale.

The boy looks up from his arm. His uncle is twelve years older than the old man but their faces are the same, soft, slightly babyish, held in place by cold green eyes. He squats in front of the boy, one hand still holding the boy's injured arm, the other the tube of liniment.

You don't go making someone depend on you and then up and let them down. You don't do that. You just don't.

His uncle pauses. Looks down, then looks up again, and when he looks up the boy recognizes the hardness in his uncle's eyes as the same hardness the old man had in his the day he brought him here.

I'll tell you something Dale. I didn't want you here. I told your father to take you back to the island with him. But you earned your place. You work hard and you learn fast and you've got a real feel for the ladies. The boy looks down at the bite on his arm and his uncle says, That ain't nothing. I been bit more times than I can count. But listen to me, Dale, I ain't done yet. I gotta know I can depend on you. That you're not gonna go out for a run and come back six hours later smelling like perfume.

The boy blushes and his eyes fall to his feet, but then he steels himself and looks back into his uncle's face, and he sees that his uncle's green eyes have gone soft like grass after it rains.

Don't let me down, Dale. You went and earned a place here, don't go and let me down.

The boy has thrown his arms around his uncle's neck before he knows he is going to do it. He squeezes his chest against his uncle's and beats back the urge to cry.

I'm sorry, Uncle Wallace. It won't ever happen again.

It's rare for him to touch even one person during the course of a day. Not like Long Island, where there was always a brother or sister all over him, or the back of his mother's hand, and mixing with the still shapeless joy his uncle has filled him with—no, dipped him in—he is disturbed by the fact that there is an ill-defined but inescapable similarity between this embrace and the one he had given Julia Miller.

It's not until he's getting ready to go to bed that he remembers the ball of paper she had thrown on the ground. He's torn then. He

85

doesn't know if he should read it or throw it away. He decides that he will smooth it out without reading it and put the wrinkled white triangle in his top dresser drawer containing his socks and drawers and the old man's medicine. Edith's dresser really. The boy remembers how his uncle had methodically emptied the dresser of its contents, waited until he was burning the rest of the day's trash before burning them. At the time the significance of the gesture was lost on the boy, but as he reaches for the drawer-pull a shiver shakes him up and down as he realizes what he has come so close to losing.

The old man's bottles clink when he slides the drawer open — not against each other, but against the silver medal he won in the Schoharie Invitational, and despite himself, he looks at Julia's words.

Water is
you can't
irrigate our
either. Your
water, in ways
would die of thir
Luckily the
unlimited supply of
which flows into the
New York, is located
should be thankful that
of our most precious nat
deserts do not have all the
as a result they are often ver
who live near polluted water
but it is not clean enough to dri
So when it rains be thankful
you are blessed to live in temperate climes
It makes your life a whole lot easier.

The boy notes that Julia hasn't signed her essay, at least not on his side of the page, and then he closes it up in the drawer.

86

5

ABOUT A MONTH AFTER the boy arrived a man had come around with a petition to improve 38. The petition claimed the dirt road was dangerous, impeded commerce, and impassable in winter, none of which was true, but the boy's uncle, like his neighbors, signed it anyway. That's the last we'll hear-a that, he told the boy, and indeed, they all forget the man had been by until the week before the boy is due to start high school in September, when, out of nowhere, a road crew shows up.

The crew fascinates the boy. The precision, the elegance with which the operators use their machines as extensions of themselves: these flannel-shirted men in thick work gloves wield jackhammers and chainsaws as delicately as Aunt Bessie handles needle and thread. Their treadling bulldozers peel away the old road an inch at a time, the arms of their backhoes lift and swivel and stab as methodically as a heron hunting fish in the shallows of the reservoir. The crew rips the old road apart and leaves a new one in its stead, and where cars and trucks once rattled over washboard ruts they now hum over spongy tar; but by then the crew has moved on to the next stretch of road. Bulldozers widen it, backhoes deepen the ditches on either side. Dump trucks stop the gash with tar that a steamroller, its platen as big as the holding vat, presses flat, and then finally a paint truck bisects it with a double yellow line down its center, as if to say: CUT HERE. When the double line is in place the road suddenly reminds the boy of the frozen river he had to cross to get here, the great sheet of ice and the single channel in its center. The line is like the seam in his life, he thinks, the chasm he doesn't like to remember because he no longer knows which side he'd rather be on, or if he wants the tear open or closed.

The crew works in stages, destroying a stretch of road and replacing it and then moving on, and from the end of October through the middle of November the length of 38 in front of his uncle's house is in fact impassable, and he and Kenny and Flip Flack have to catch the bus on Newry Road. The pump truck uses Newry Road as well. It's able to reach the Flacks' dairy barn via the two-track they drive their tractors on, but even though the muddy wash of 38 is less than twenty feet wide—less river than muddy creek—the pump truck cannot ford it to reach his uncle's land. When the boy's uncle protests that it is costing him two weeks' income the driver says, I'm sorry, Wallace, I get this baby stuck it'll be my ass, I'm truly sorry. And he does sound sorry, but not sorry enough to risk his job.

Meanwhile there are the ladies, whose udders care nothing about infrastructure or broken axles or two cents a quart, and in the end there is nothing for it but to dump the contents of the vat. The boy's uncle doesn't say anything as he hooks a rubber hose as big around as a sewer pipe to the vat and runs it out to the barnyard, but Donnie curses and stamps his feet and seems on the verge of picking a fight with the road crew, until finally his uncle says,

No use getting riled up, Donnie. It's just the government's way of helping out poor folks. Raising their taxes and then depriving them of their income in return for the favor.

Donnie kicks at the hose spewing forth a solid column of milk like an endless tube of toothpaste. The column squiggles, straightens out again.

It ain't right, Wallace. It just ain't right.

The boy's uncle continues to stare without expression into the torrent of milk spewing from the hose. Then he looks up, not at Donnie but at the boy.

No use crying over spilt milk. Ain't that what they say?

His uncle laughs then, but two weeks later, when the vat has to be dumped a second time, he makes Donnie and the boy do it alone, and sets off down Newry Road, where he has parked his car for the meanwhile.

As the boy watches him pick his way across the mess of 38, he realizes the season has changed. Fall is over, winter setting in. The leaves on his uncle's elms were golden two weeks ago. Now they're as faded as old newspaper, and fall off the branches like drops of water off a cow's whiskers. The maple leaves in the Flacks' yard have gone from red to rust and they too fall to the earth, a brown drizzle that clacks on the frozen soil with a hard mournful sound. It hasn't snowed yet, but a week's frosts have left the ground hard as concrete, and when his uncle clears the churned-up road his heels clink on Newry Road as if on metal. The boy listens to them fade away until they stop, and a moment later the slam of a car door shakes him from his reverie, and he hurries off to the barn to help Donnie.

The boy doesn't like working alone with Donnie, who is always on his back. Grabbing tools from his hand, correcting errors visible only to him with a look on his face like, Jesus, Amos, ain't you learned nothing yet? But this morning Donnie seems too genuinely angry to affect it, and in a few minutes they've hooked the hose to the vat and run it outside, and when the boy opens the valve the milk rushes from the hose as from an open hydrant.

It ain't right, Donnie says, staring at the milk as it runs down the frozen slope of the barnyard. A man's honest labor, wasted. I tell you, it ain't right.

Where the milk spews from the hose it seems so solid you could pick it up like a rope, but five feet on it suddenly disintegrates, rippling and spreading out like a wet bedsheet fallen from the line. It isn't right, the boy thinks, but it *is* beautiful. The milk is thick as paint—whitewash, he thinks, Huck Finn, something like that. Its widening ripples are as gentle as ocean waves on a windless day. Whitened stalks of grass stick out of it like upright icicles, stalagmicicles, and here and there a cow patty makes a chocolate-colored island in the alabaster sea. Frost crystals glitter in the cow patties but the forty-degree milk steams as if it were boiling.

Just look at that. It's no wonder an honest man can't get ahead.

The boy tears his eyes from the steaming milk. Donnie is standing with his foot on the end of the hose behind the metal coupling, as if it were the head of a poisonous snake.

I heard there's farmers get paid by the government not to raise crops. They let their fields sit empty and get paid anyway. You think Uncle Wallace could get some of that money?

Donnie looks at the boy as if he is speaking a foreign language.

Shut up, Dale, he says finally. He kicks the hose and the boy has to jump to avoid getting sprayed. When he looks up Donnie is stalking toward the dairy barn. I'm gonna clean the gutters, he calls over his shoulder. Keep an eye on the hose, Amos.

Keep an eye on the hose Amos, the boy says under his breath. As if gravity needs his help emptying the vat. As if he's just a kid, useless to do anything but watch his uncle's hard work flow toward the crease between the barnyard and the north hill, wetting the cedar fenceposts they'd labored so hard to set in the spring. Why don't *you* keep an eye on the hose, the boy says out loud. Don, Don—Donald Duck.

The insult is hardly satisfying, but it doesn't matter: a new sting has replaced it. Although it's the second time they have pumped the vat, it's not until the boy hears the word coming out of his own mouth that he associates this hose with the one his mother used to beat him with, and now the memory takes him over completely. The fear, the pain, the rage. The two hoses are the same, the boy sees now. Black rubber with metal couplings at either end—only this one is larger. The one at home is attached to the washing machine. Foamy gray water drains through it into the backyard at the end of every cycle, and when his mother swings it through the air it releases a clean bleachy smell, as if she is beating the dirt out of him, the impurities, the stain of the old man's blood.

A cold breeze chills the boy's neck, and when he pulls his jacket around him he feels the remembered pain in his shoulders and back at first, but then he feels the constriction of the material itself. It's getting too small for him, just like everything else. The boy buries his hands in the torn lining and wiggles his toes in Kenny Flack's boots and feels the tips of his toes rub against the worn leather. He kicks the spewing hose, and this time it reminds him of something else. It reminds him of Julia Miller. For two weeks after their meeting at the Alcove Reservoir the boy had avoided her on the bus and at school, and then summer had come to his rescue. All through June and July and August he had kept his gaze focused on the ground whenever he ran past her house so he could tell himself he hadn't seen her wave; mostly, though, he'd stuck to his new route along the reservoir. He remembers his impression that his love for her was like a thread of milk shot from an udder, and he finds himself measuring that thread against this river, against all the sacrifices entailed by life on the farm. He has been here less than a year, already lost his family and first love to memories that wash over him in waves of heat and coolness. But now he wonders: how much has his uncle given up? And what could he possibly have left?

The boy feels trapped by all these thoughts and he wills the milk to hurry and drain from the vat. It took a good twenty minutes the first time around, and he's only been out here for about ten. But then an Ayshire calf trots into the barnyard, her nose high in the air, the smell of milk reining her in visibly, like a lasso. The Ayshire bleats like a sheep as she runs up to the flood of milk, and even though the boy knows he should chase her away he wants to watch her—wants to devote his whole attention to something that's no more comprehensible to him than his memories, but at least doesn't hurt. And besides, he thinks, it would be a shame if no one profited from the farm's loss.

The Ayshire wades ankle deep into the pool. She twirls about in a circle, kicking white drops every which way, paws at the milk with one hoof as if trying to get to the ground beneath it. Finally she stands still, panting slightly, head lowered, and then, with the delicacy of a cat, touches her lips to the milk. She weaned more than a month ago, but the boy wonders if she retains some memory, some regressive urge toward suckling, helplessness. But the Ayshire reacts as if shocked, jerking her head up and running across the barnyard like a colt. The boy can hear her bleating her discovery to the rest of the herd, but if any of the other ladies understand what she is trying to say they don't respond, and when the last of the milk has finally drained from the hose he flushes it with water to keep it from curdling and molding, and then he shakes the water from the hose to keep the rubber from freezing and splitting, and then he rolls up the hose and puts it back in the vat room and heads off to school.

That afternoon as he runs home from cross country practice the boy heads down Newry Road so he can avoid the mess of 38, and as he passes the spot where Uncle Wallace and Aunt Bessie have been parking their cars he notices that Uncle Wallace's car isn't there. Aunt Bessie's is exactly where it was when he caught the bus that morning, and Donnie Badget's battered Ford pickup is still there as well, but there's no sign of any of them at the farm. The cows have wandered in close to the barnyard in anticipation of the evening milking but other than a few calves running through the pasture the fields are silent. In the kitchen both his and his uncle's breakfast dishes are still in the sink and Aunt Bessie's plate is still on the table, its napkin still laid atop it. Normally they would be gone, as would the dishes from the noon meal, and the beginnings of supper would be on the counter or the stove. But the house is quiet and the fire in the kitchen stove long extinguished, and so the boy changes out of his sweats, exchanges his school-bought sneakers for Kenny Flack's boots, and then, not sure what else to do, he cleans the ashes from the stove and builds a new fire, and then he sits at the kitchen table and eats a slice of apple pie and a wedge of yellow cheddar cheese, which is to say New York cheddar, made from New York cows, rather than Vermont cheddar, which is white and mealy. The boy eats his snack off Aunt Bessie's breakfast plate, but before he starts he fits her unused napkin back in the holder carefully. The fire and his fork scraping his plate clean are the only sounds in the little house. Outside, the light dims perceptibly. Within a half hour of his return it's nearly dark, and he can hear the first impatient calls of the ladies, eager to be relieved of their burden of milk. It is nearly five.

The boy puts his plate and fork in the sink, and then, instead of heading up to the barn, he turns back into the house, going not into the living room or up to his bedroom, but instead into the west half of the house. The main part of his uncle's house is divided by a central hallway. The eastern half, which connects to the kitchen wing, contains the living room downstairs and two bedrooms upstairs, but the western half remains shut up all winter to save on fuel costs. The big room downstairs and two small rooms upstairs mirror those on the eastern side of the house, but the beds and couches and chairs they contain are disassembled or broken or piled over with unmarked boxes and crates and layer upon layer of dust. The boy pokes randomly through a couple of boxes as he has done three or four times before, thinking he might find something that belonged to his deceased Aunt Ella Mae or absent cousin Edith, maybe even a relic of the farm in Cobleskill, but everything he touches is anonymous and empty, Mason jars, brownware crocks, frayed extension cords, and he is about to leave the room when a flicker of light in one of the west windows catches his eye. The light is tiny and winks in and out of the overgrown cedars surrounding the abandoned house that abuts his uncle's property. The cedars are so thick it takes the boy a moment to realize the light is in fact inside that house. A hundred feet away there is someone standing in a window as he is—smoking.

It turns out to be Donnie Badget.

Well if it isn't Amos, he says as the swollen front door squeaks out of its frame on crooked hinges. He takes a long drag on his cigarette and the lit end glows brightly. Come to tell me I shouldn't be smoking here, I'll bet. That I could burn the place down. Or maybe you just wanted to remind me it's time to get the ladies in?

Donnie's words have a force to them, as if he has been waiting a long time to speak them, or some version of them. The boy is glad it's nearly dark and Donnie can't see him flush. He had thought of saying both things.

I don't care what you do. Burn the place down, I don't care. It ain't Uncle Wallace's, it don't concern me.

What's your uncle's is yours. That how it goes, Amos?

The boy is about to leave without replying when he notices an ashtray on the narrow mantel above the fireplace, and then, when Donnie crushes his cigarette on a worn pine floorboard, the boy sees a few other butts scattered around his feet. He glances around the tiny room then, but all he can make out in the dim light is that time has stripped it of everything, not just paint and plaster and straight lines but size, space. Although the room was probably the house's main parlor, the boy cannot imagine it ever being large enough to contain anything besides himself and Donnie and that ashtray. A real ashtray, not a recycled can of tuna fish or green beans but cut glass, gleaming dully in the thin light, and cradling a dozen white butts like eggs in a nest of ash.

Who owns this place?

Donnie's eyes follow the boy's, see him looking at the ashtray.

Not your uncle, that's for sure. Not you. He taps the soft curve of the plaster wall with his foot. Used to think I might buy it someday but it looks like that ain't gonna happen either, thanks to you Amos. He kicks the wall again, harder, and the boy hears grains of plaster trickling through the lathe. This house was built in seventeen hundred and sixty-one, Donnie says with something like awe in his voice. It is older than our nation.

With a glance the boy takes in the four corners of the room. It seems hardly larger than one of the stalls in the hay barn. He is five feet two inches tall, but he's pretty sure that if he wanted he could touch the ceiling with his fingertips. Were people shorter then, he wonders, before the Declaration of Independence?

Donnie is lighting another cigarette.

Thought I had my future all mapped out. I did. Work with Wallace until I'd put back enough money to buy this piece, then pick up Wallace's too, when he was ready to retire. Who knows, maybe he'd've even left it to me. It don't look like he and Edith are gonna bury the hatchet any time soon. But all that was before you come along and decided you wanted to be a dairy farmer. I gotta hand it to you, Amos, you played your cards right. You work hard, keep outta trouble. You're a regular Tom Sawyer, Amos, a true credit to the family line.

The boy has to stand on tiptoe to run his fingers along the ceiling, but when he does a puff of plaster dust falls on his face, and just before he closes his eyes against the dust he suddenly sees that the little room is not empty, but as full of Donnie's empty future as the west wing of his uncle's house is filled by an equally untenable past. When he rubs his eyes it is less an effort to wipe the dust from them than to clear those shadow lives away, and when he speaks his voice surprises him almost as much as it seems to surprise Donnie.

What were you gonna do with two houses?

His voice surprises him because even as he asks the question it occurs to him: *he* has two houses. Here, and on Long Island.

What?

I don't understand, the boy says slowly, why you would need two houses. Uncle Wallace don't even use all of his.

Ten people sleep under one roof in the house on Long Island—nine, with him gone—and although that house has many inconveniences he never once thought it too small. He swipes at his eyes again, clears his throat.

A man can't live in two houses, he says as forcefully as he can. He's got to choose.

Donnie drops his half-smoked cigarette to the floor, but when he speaks there is a fire in his voice where the cigarette had been.

I don't know, Amos. Maybe I wouldn't choose. Maybe I'd sleep in one house one night and the other house the next. I'd have options. Two beds instead of one. Breakfast here, dinner over to Wallace's, flip a coin for supper. Maybe I'd tear one down and live in the other, maybe I'd pitch a tent on the front lawn and leave em both empty. Two houses is options, Amos. But thanks to you I don't have no options no more. Once your uncle finishes teaching you everything he taught me I probably won't even have a job.

He pauses then, uses his heel to grind out the smoldering cigarette on the floor. In the dim light his face is nearly invisible, his expression inscrutable, his voice as cold as the butt beneath his boot.

But I guess you didn't figure on Wallace getting married, did you, Amos? That throws a wrench in the works, don't it?

95

The boy blinks.

What?

Wallace and Bessie, Donnie says. You might have noticed they ain't around? They're getting married, Amos. They're down at the courthouse this very minute.

As always the boy finds it hard to pull his head from Long Island once it goes back there, and he has to shake it back and forth to empty it.

I don't understand.

What's not to understand, Amos? Wallace is making Bessie his wife and heir and this farm you thought was yours is gonna go to her and hers.

Uncle Wallace and Aunt Bessie . . .

Who knows, Amos, maybe they'll even have a kid themselves. Their own boy, instead of a hand-me-down. I guess we'll find out soon enough. Wallace said he'd be back by suppertime. When the boy doesn't say anything Donnie stamps on his cigarette butt one last time. Guess we'd best get in the ladies, huh Amos?

Donnie pulls the door closed behind them, locks it with a padlock the boy hadn't noticed when he went in, puts the key in his pocket. As they are pushing through the tangled cedar break—the boy thinks Donnie deliberately lets a branch snap back and smack him in the face—the boy says, How'd you know how old it was? The house?

Donnie doesn't say anything until they have made their way out of the cedars, then just jerks a thumb back at the house's roof. The point of the eave sticks above the cedars. Nestled beneath it the boy can just make out four rusted numbers: 1 7 6 1.

Don't take a high school diploma to figure that one out, Amos, Donnie says when the boy trots after him. Any more questions?

Technically, Donnie's prediction comes true. It is after eight when the boy's uncle and aunt return, but he doesn't eat until they come in. Instead he goes to his bedroom and does his homework after he and Donnie finish with the ladies, and he stays up there until he hears voices on the front lawn. Just one voice actually, Aunt

Bessie's, punctuated by the shapely silence with which his uncle asks and answers questions.

As if commemorating their new status, his aunt and uncle enter through the front door instead of the kitchen. His uncle is dressed in his work clothes but Aunt Bessie sports the dress she wears to church. A shiny smile cuts her chin as if stamped there by a cookie cutter, but in his uncle's eyes the boy sees the same defiant cast he'd seen in the old man's the day they drove up here. For a moment he imagines his uncle is drunk but then he realizes his uncle is afraid. Of himself. Of what he's done.

They wear mismatched rings—the rings each wore for their first marriages—but Aunt Bessie shows hers off like it is brand new.

Your uncle is a crazy man Dale, she says, holding out her hand. There is a flush to her cheeks, a wild dazzle to her eye. You would think she'd just married a soldier the night before he ships out. She lets the boy examine her ring then heads for the kitchen. Pots and pans rattle out of cabinets behind him, something thumps and wobbles on the warped cutting board.

His uncle is still standing in front of the door, looking at him. His right hand twists the ring on his left for a moment, and then he puts his left hand in his pocket. From where the boy is standing he can see the two doors that open off the hallway: the closed door to his uncle's left that leads to the unused part of the house, the open one to his right, leading to the empty living room.

Wild, Aunt Bessie says in the kitchen, as if the men have followed her in. Impulsive. Devil may care. Happiness bubbles out of her voice like water from a tap even as her knife clunks through whatever's on the cutting board.

The boy can see his uncle's left hand outlined against the thin fabric of his pants, his thumb still playing with the ring on his finger. He stares at the boy with eyes filled with fear and defiance, guilt and pride, and even as he returns his uncle's stare with his own silent question the boy has a glimmer of understanding about how a man can fail to fill up even the one house he has chosen to live in. How he can empty it, in fact, rather than fill it. Lives pour into houses, pour out again, but in the end only the houses remain: names on signs and dates on walls only remind you of what's gone before; cardboard boxes don't hoard the past, they hide it. But all the boy wants to know is, has *he* outlived his usefulness? Is it his turn to be sent away, just like the first Dale Peck? The boy's eyes bore into his uncle's but all his uncle does is twist the ring on his finger inside his pocket, and then he shrugs, as if responding to something someone has said.

You and Donnie get the ladies in okay?

The boy looks at his uncle blankly. It is a question without an answer. His uncle might as well ask him if he lit the hay barn on fire. As if acknowledging this, his uncle strides past him to the kitchen and pulls open the door to the woodstove.

Freezing in here, he says, and puts another log on the fire. He leaves the door open until the log crackles, and then he shuts it and sits down at the table. At the counter, Aunt Bessie's voice sings through slices of her knife and the sharp aroma of onions.

Just let me get this on, I'm sure you're both starved.

When the boy sits down in the chair opposite him, his uncle looks up as if surprised he's there. His eyes dart back and forth. Then:

You and Donnie get the ladies in?

Again, the boy only stares at him, and his uncle's eyes fall to the table. But almost immediately they lift up, and he breaks into a sheepish grin.

I married her, Dale. I said if the ladies gave me a day off I'd marry her, and I did.

It isn't just the memory of Donnie's words that makes his uncle's unpleasant, alien. They're an adult confidence, speaking of a freedom the boy doesn't have. To make choices, whether wrong or right. To take a wife, have children, leave either or both behind.

The boy realizes Aunt Bessie's knife hasn't made a sound for a while, and he looks up to see her regarding him and his uncle with a soft, almost glazed focus. When she catches the boy's eye her smile stamps itself on her face again.

Wasn't really the ladies gave you the day off, she says. More like the county. Or Dale for that matter. Donnie couldn't-a got the milk in himself.

His uncle looks up at her, then looks back at the boy. A smile flickers over the corners of his mouth.

Guess you got a point there, Bess. He nods at the boy. Guess I owe you a thank you, Dale.

Behind him the log cracks in the fire, and the boy feels the room has suddenly heated up ten degrees.

Look at the two of you, Aunt Bessie says. Like enough to be father and son. My boys. My two boys. And she touches the corner of her eye with the sleeve of her dress. Must be the onions, she says, and turns suddenly. It's gonna have to be stew again, she says loudly. If we want to eat before midnight.

The boy turns back to his uncle. What Aunt Bessie says is true: he can see the old man's shape wiggling inside his uncle's in an effort to get out, but what does his uncle see when he looks at him? It's been weeks since he's thought of the other Dale Peck but he keeps coming up tonight, and the boy suddenly realizes he's swallowed his predecessor whole. That he lives his namesake's life as much as his uncle lives the old man's. For a moment everything disappears then, Aunt Bessie, the house, the table and chairs, and there is just the two of them, his uncle and himself, mirror images folded along a seam like an inkblot, both the original and its paler echo devoid of any identity save what is projected onto them.

It's the regular thumps of Aunt Bessie's knife that cut the fantasy away piece by piece: gradually the table resumes its shape beneath his forearms, becomes the same rectangle it has always been. His uncle's forearms rest on the same rectangle and the thin gold crescent on the fourth finger of his left hand, the only thing new to the room, seems as inconsequential as the dirt under his fingernails. They are who they have always been, two dairymen waiting for dinner: dinner, sleep, morning reveille and sixty swollen udders eager to be drained, world without end, amen. Donnie was lying, the boy suddenly realizes, or he was just wrong: his uncle's marriage doesn't have anything to do with him. It doesn't change *his* life. With a sigh, he lets out the breath he's been holding since five o'clock that afternoon, and the air seems to push at the four corners of the little room until everything is back the way it was.

Dolly came in today. Fifteen quarts. That means she's gonna drop soon, right?

His uncle nods his head.

Before Thanksgiving probably. She's had two boys in a row, she's due to give us a little lady. Let's keep our fingers crossed.

The boy's head nods, an unconscious echo of his uncle's. But then something occurs to him.

What happens to the boys, Uncle Wallace?

His voice sounds tight to his ears, but his uncle doesn't seem to hear it. He's gone back to fiddling with his ring.

Not much use for boys in a dairy herd, Dale.

The boy's head nods. So what happens to them? The ones you don't want? What do you do with them?

His uncle looks up then, eyes narrowed, lips pursed. He pauses, then says,

Well, we do keep one or two around, for stud.

The boy realizes his head is still nodding, and he stops with a twitch. But he continues staring at his uncle until the latter's eyes fall to the table.

Veal, he says, shrugging, just as Aunt Bessie turns with a pot in her hands.

Soup's on, she says, and, in a gesture whose benevolence will haunt the boy until the end of his days, she serves him first.

The next morning he wakes to find that it's snowed. Not even an inch, but that first snowfall seems to turn a key in the sky, and for the next several months it snows at least once a week. Shovelfuls of it, from fluffy weightless powder that blows back in his face as fast as he scoops it away to frozen chunks as solid and heavy as broken pieces of granite. Soon enough everything is covered: the front walk, the driveway, the paths to the hay and dairy barns. What had been a thirty-second run up the hill takes thirty minutes or an hour the day after a snowfall, when, for the tenth time that winter, he must shovel the path clear. By the turn of the year the snow has made igloos of everything regardless of its original shape. Donnie's dream house domes over like a funerary mound and even the spindly sign by the driveway supports a translucent white arc as thin as a section of rollercoaster, as though a sheet has been laid over it.

His uncle and aunt's marriage seems to disappear too, as though a sheet had been laid over that as well. The morning after the wedding his uncle put his ring in a box on his dresser—the same box he took it out of to get married—and a couple mornings after that Dolly calved. A boy. Her third in a row. The calf got a week on the farm before the road crew finally finished 38 and the panel truck from Carol's Meats could get in to take him away. The thin asphalt road bisected the newly white fields like a magic marker stripe on a blank sheet of paper, so smooth and quiet that the boy could hear the calf's confused cries long after the truck disappeared over the hill.

But this morning in the middle of February there has been no new snow. It is too cold for snow, too cold even for fog. The dew is one more frozen sheen of white over the farm, and his and his uncle's boots ring with a metallic echo as they make their way up to the dairy barn. Even the teats of the ladies feel cold as he hooks them to the milking machines—at least at first they do. After a half dozen plunges into the pail of cleaning water his fingers are so numb it's all he can do to handle the claw without dropping it. His uncle finishes well ahead of him, and the boy hears him walking the alleys as he struggles to hook up the last of the cows. There are only fifty-seven wet ladies, and the boy is wondering what his uncle is looking for when he hears,

We're missing someone.

The boy looks up to see his uncle standing with his hands on his hips. Beneath the brim of his hat his brow is wrinkled.

A Guernsey.

The boy doesn't question his uncle because he cannot conceive of his uncle erring when it comes to the farm. But he also cannot grasp what it means to be missing a cow, and he says nothing.

His uncle pulls his hat down around his ears.

Have to go and find her.

It takes little more than a glance out the barn door to ascertain there is no black-spotted mass amid the sparkling sea of white. There are only two patches of trees on the land where the missing Guernsey could be concealed—the new growth at the southeast edge by 38, and the older stand at the top of the hill. When his uncle sets off toward the road, the boy makes his way uphill.

He uses a cow path to help him navigate through two feet of snow. The depth of the trail testifies to the ladies' weight, but it is its narrowness that impresses him—though the ladies weigh five or ten times what he does, he must walk Indian style to keep his feet between the snow embankments carved out by their hooves. Their trail parallels the line of honey locusts up the hill, and as the boy walks he peers into their jagged shadows. But though a hundred smooth mounds of snow could conceal a hundred cows underneath, the only things that poke from the wrinkled white blanket are the dark trunks of the trees, creaking in a breeze that picks up as he ascends the hill. The cold wind cuts through his layers, slivers of blown snow sting his cheeks as he looks around. His cheeks throb, as do his hands and feet, and heart, for he dreads both the idea of coming upon a frozen carcass and also the impact a lost cow will have on the farm's fortunes, especially after the disaster with 38 and the pump truck last November.

He finds her near the top of the hill. She lies on her side in a thicket crowding the base of a slanting tree, and even as he takes in the way her thin legs stick out from her torso like toothpicks from balled melon, he notes that he cannot name either the tree or the bushes of the thicket. Without their leaves they are as anonymous as an Angus without its eartag. He sees how the cow's breath had carved a box canyon in the snow in front of her muzzle, sees that the fine black hairs at the end of her tail have gotten tangled in the twigs above it so that it looks as if she is hanging by a frayed rope, and he sees also that his observations are useless to both him and the prostrate animal, two facts at either end of its body and somehow divorced from what lies between. The thicket could be hackberry or deerberry, wild privet or mountain laurel, the tree chestnut or ash. Even if he knew, it wouldn't wake the animal fallen in their thin shelter, her white body blending in with the snow and only the black patches on her coat showing up like splotches of tar.

But his feet do. The Guernsey's ear twitches, and then she lifts her face and looks at him. Ice has made two walrus tusks of her whiskers, but other than that she seems remarkably fresh, and for a moment the boy thinks everything will be all right. She has merely wandered off the track, overslept; needs only to be prodded. Indeed, she heaves herself to her feet at the sight of the boy, seesawing up her front end and then ratcheting her haunches up to meet it. Her tail switches free of the twigs. But after she is upright she just stands there, holding her right rear leg at an angle, a patient look on her face. If her expression had been pleading, if her eyes had asked for succor or empathy, the boy feels he might have been able to do something, but the look she gives him is transcendently inhuman. She is merely waiting for him to right the world. To make it worse, her crooked leg is wrapped round and round by a knotted helix of shiny wire.

He falls twice in his flight down the hill. It is a good half mile to the road, a half mile that takes more out of him than any half marathon he ran in the fall, and by the time he finds his uncle he can barely pant out what he has to say.

The lady. The hill. Her leg. A wire. I'm sorry, Uncle Wallace, I'm sorry, I'm sorry.

The slowness of his uncle's steps maddens him, and it is with relief that he takes off to the barn when he is told to fetch a halter and lead, a pair of snips. By the time he makes it back up the hill his uncle has reached the injured Guernsey, and he takes the halter from the boy and slips it over her face. The Guernsey stretches her head out eagerly for the halter, her faith in their ability to fix things absolute. She lets his uncle lead her two limping steps to a tree trunk, lets him tie her frozen nose against the rough brown bark. It's not a birch, the boy thinks. Not a beech either, or a poplar. At least he knows that much. At least he knows what it's not.

The Guernsey's not young, the boy sees now. Six, maybe even seven. You can tell by the udder: at this time of the morning it should be plump as a fully inflated basketball, but instead it's stretched out, its milk pooling at the bottom like a horde of loose change in the toe of a sock. One of her teats is wrinkled too. Wilted really, shrunken like a desiccated radish.

Talk to her. Pet her, try to keep her calm. But watch out for her feet.

The boy doesn't know what comes out of his mouth. Something: the Guernsey's ears flick toward him, as do her eyes. He scratches the frost from her hide, attempts to massage her massive shoulders. But mostly he watches his uncle, who squats on his haunches in the snow and deftly snips off the crooked wire bit by bit. He unzips his jacket halfway and folds each little length of wire into the bib pocket of his overalls as if building a heart out of his lady's suffering, and he works swiftly, silently, until nearly all the wire is gone. And then a sigh escapes his mouth, and he says,

Aw no.

It takes the boy a moment to see what has happened. What's left of the wire is so thin and flimsy there doesn't seem to be any substance to it. But somehow it has managed to puncture the Guernsey's leg, pierced it right through like an arrow through a Valentine heart.

After his outburst his uncle sets his jaw, and then he says, Steady now, and grips the wire in both hands, and then he jerks it free.

The Guernsey screams. There is no other word for it. She screams like a child stung by a wasp even as her leg buckles and she falls into the boy, who feels the seismic impact of her shoulder then finds himself lying face up in the snow several feet away. A leafless branch is displayed against the low gray clouds like a filament from a torn spiderweb—or like a jab of brown lightning, the boy thinks, and it is as if he is waking up all over again in the old man's truck on the day he arrived. The branch he'd seen through the windshield that morning had grown from a honey locust, but this one, well, it could be. But it could also be something else. He just can't tell.

When he stands up he sees that the cow *is* hanging now, by the rope that holds her to the tree. Her front legs shred the snow while her back lies as if trapped within the birth canal, and then it seems as if she remembers how to use them and all at once she is up, her front legs spread wide, her head hanging as low as the rope will allow. Her right rear leg doesn't touch the ground though, but twitches slightly up and down, as though an invisible length of wire still secured it to her hip. A few drops of blood fall from the wound and blot the snow.

The boy's uncle heaves himself out of the snow where he too has fallen. He shakes his head, folds the last length of wire into the pocket of his overalls and zips his coat up over the lump of shredded metal.

Untie her.

When the boy loosens the rope from the trunk he sees that the lady's weight has scored a ring in the papery bark, but he still can't tell what kind of tree it is. He pulls on the lead but his uncle puts out a hand.

She'll come if she can.

They stand about twenty feet from her, downhill, in the direction of the barns, and after a few minutes of heavy breathing the Guernsey lifts her head, looks at them.

Come on girl, the boy's uncle says. Come on.

The boy holds his breath as she takes the first step. Please don't fall, he thinks. Please, *please* don't fall.

She doesn't. Her right hip drops as if her leg is sinking in quicksand, but then it rises again, and she walks slowly toward them. Twice she stops, seems to be contemplating lying down, but she doesn't. A half hour later, just as they make their way through the eight-month-old fence to the barnyard, the boy hears his bus coming round the bend. He turns and sees it sailing up the smooth black river of 38 like a yellow barge, then turns back to the cow.

Isn't that your bus, Dale?

The boy ignores his uncle, turns back to the Guernsey.

Come on girl. Come on now, you're all right, come on.

He stares at the cow as if his sight alone is keeping her upright, and his uncle doesn't mention the bus again. The Guernsey flounders as they veer into untracked snow. Her head droops from side to side as she walks, her muzzle practically dragging in the snow, and the boy begs her, Come on girl, that's it, come on, but even as he speaks he remembers the Ayshire who had tasted the milk from the vat on the day his uncle and aunt got married. Both elements—the injured Guernsey, the endless expanse of snow—seem like the inevitable amplification of that earlier scene; only his uncle's marriage seems to have disappeared. For the first time in his life the boy has the sense that something, the land, history, time itself, absorbs all the things people forgo and forget. That their lives are running out like milk from the vat, no pump truck coming to redeem it for cash, no valve to close it up again. Nothing but an expanse of wet earth to mark its passing, memories as damp and smelly as a bath towel at the bottom of the hamper.

They stall the injured Guernsey in the hay barn to keep her away from the jostles of the other ladies, and when the boy runs to the dairy barn for some food he passes the wire he snipped from the fence last April. The wire is still spooled around the willow switch where he left it. Aunt Bessie has ropes of garlic and onions in the fruit cellar that look just like this string of wire coils, but to the boy's eyes it looks more like an ammunition belt, a string of grenades waiting to go off. The two C's hang above them, carbon-copying some unknown recipient with news of the boy's crime.

The injured Guernsey all but knocks the pail of food from his hand when he returns.

She's got her appetite, his uncle says. That's a good sign. He looks down at the boy. You'd best be getting on to school.

The boy watches her eat for a moment.

Are you going to call the vet?

His uncle shakes his head.

She's too old, Dale. Probably would have had to cull her the next time she calves no matter what happens.

The lady lies down to digest her meal. There is the half-full udder, the wilted teat.

The boy grabs the pail that had held her food.

I'd better milk her.

Donnie'll get it.

His uncle doesn't look at the boy, and the boy has to resist the urge to grab his hand.

I picked up all the wire, Uncle Wallace. I know I did.

The lump of evidence to the contrary bulges in his uncle's bib pocket like a goiter. It is only a little bit bigger than a fist or an apple. Bigger than a baseball, but not as big as a softball. His uncle doesn't say anything, and after a moment the boy tries a different tack.

What're those C's Uncle Wallace?

His uncle's expression doesn't change for a moment, and then he surprises the boy. He smiles.

Game we played when we was teenagers. Used to be a resort down by Cairo called the . . . the something. The C something. It had a big sign out in front. The Cairo? His uncle shakes his head. Funny, I don't remember. All's I remember is that boys used to dare each other to steal the C, when you took it off the sign said something else. Cairo, airo? I don't remember Dale. But it seemed pretty funny at the time. Guess it was, at the time.

The Guernsey rustles in the straw beside him, and the smile fades from his uncle's face.

Go on. Get Aunt Bessie to drive you to school.

The first thing the boy sees when he goes into the hay barn that afternoon is that his uncle has put the ball of wire shards into a jar. They sit on the shelf next to the dead fuses and salvaged nails and string of wire coils, as if to suggest that their potential usefulness cannot be overlooked, despite whatever damage they might have caused, and as the boy looks from them to the stolen C's hanging above them, he wonders which category the latter belong to.

When he enters the Guernsey's stall she does not get up, neither to eat or give milk. She will eat, she will give milk: she just won't get up. She lies on her left side, her injured leg sticking straight out from her body and swollen to three times the size of its healthy twin. The boy's uncle has applied his liniment to the leg, but that is all he can do for her. It all depends on what the wire hit, he says. Muscle, bone, ligament, tendon. But she walked all the way downhill. She's eating. Those are good signs. Now all we can do is hope it don't get infected.

The boy brings the Guernsey breakfast and dinner in a pail, milks her by hand. Because she is lying down he has to milk her into a frying pan, stopping frequently to empty the milk into a pail. He finds the volume of milk heartening; it is nearly normal, for a cow her age. He cleans the manure from her matted tail, changes the urine-soaked straw twice daily. But even though she seems calm and free of pain she makes no move to get up, and the swelling in her leg doesn't go down. By the fifth morning the boy notices that the pursed lips of the original wound have begun to ooze a thread of green mucus. The leg is hot to the touch, and soft, like an overripe tomato.

When the boy reports this to his uncle he nods his head. He looks at the boy with his mouth set in a line as if he is trying to decide whether to say something. Throughout the ordeal he hasn't mentioned the wire that he pulled from the injured Guernsey's leg or how it might have gotten there, and he doesn't mention it now. Instead he says,

If the fever hasn't broken in the morning you'll have to put her down, and then he goes into the house to wash up for dinner.

The boy cannot taste his food that night. His homework is incomprehensible to him. And yet he manages to clean his plate and fill in the blank pages of his notebook, and after he takes a bath he goes straight to bed. He thinks he is like a cow: his body does what it has been bred to do, leaving his mind free to focus elsewhere. He can hear his uncle and Aunt Bessie talking in the room below his, hears the tinkle of metal and glass echoing up the stairwell when Aunt Bessie washes the dishes from the pie she and his uncle have eaten, and when they go to bed the boy can hear that too: the opening and closing of drawers as pajamas are pulled out, the creak of bedsprings, his uncle's quick steady snores.

When he opens his eyes the curtains of his windows are two pale white squares. The moon is nearly full, and the snow-covered world glints and glows darkly. There's still a light on in an upstairs bedroom of the Flacks' house so it can't be that late, and although the boy knows he should go back to sleep he gets dressed instead. The top drawer of his dresser tinkles when he opens it for a second pair of socks: four medals—two silver, a bronze, a gold—and the old man's bottles. In the moonlit room he can almost see the old man's ghost opening and closing drawers, hear his admonitions against waking his brothers and sisters, his mother. But this bed is empty, the upstairs hallway completely silent. He walks downstairs in his stocking feet and retrieves the new boots he got for Christmas from beside the banked embers of the kitchen stove and takes scant comfort in the fact that they are warm and soft, and fit comfortably, even over two pairs of socks.

He eases out the back door. Outside, the darkness is dazzling, the earth a series of sharp shiny curves like the pieces of a broken glass bowl. But the wide-open silence seems like the hush that follows a great noise, and the boy jogs up to the hay barn with a premonition that he is already too late. Inside, the air has a sharper bite than outside, the refrigerator chill of a car first thing in the morning, but it is the darkness that takes the boy by surprise. He is three or four steps into the barn before he realizes he can't see a thing. He freezes in his tracks, afraid to go forward or back lest a pit open up in the frozen dirt of the barn floor. The vertiginous feeling is not just uncomfortable. It is familiar, and the boy remains poised on the invisible precipice until he remembers the day his uncle told him about the first Dale Peck. He jumps as if someone has touched him on the shoulder in the dark barn, but then he pushes his namesake away rudely, goes back to the door and retrieves the flashlight hanging there on a nail, uses its beam to guide him to the injured Guernsey's stall. She is holding her head up as he pushes open the door, but the flashlight's glow isn't powerful enough to capture any expression in her eyes. When she lays her head back down it lands on the straw with a thud, like something dropped.

109

In this light her leg is soft, featureless, as swollen as a wineskin, the hoof shoved into it like a split cork. The boy need only train his beam on it for a moment to see that the situation is hopeless. His anger surprises him. How could she have betrayed his ministrations like this? He has washed the manure and urine from her coat with his own hands, dried her even, to prevent her from catching a chill. He has proffered handfuls of grain unadulterated by augured silage, held them on a piece of cloth to her mouth so that she could lick them up from her prone position. Doesn't she understand the significance of his efforts? How can she repay him by dying?

The Guernsey sighs, an almost human wheeze reflecting the pain and boredom of illness, even mortal illness, as if she were eager for it to be over. The sigh blows out the boy's anger as if it were a candle, and in a moment he is on his knees beside her head, stroking it, sshhing her, willing her to be strong. The Guernsey's ears twitch but other than that she doesn't respond to his presence, his caresses. The ladies aren't like dogs or cats; their neediness isn't the neediness of pets. She neither tolerates nor welcomes his fingers, but simply lies there, as insensible as the weather. The boy notices he is shivering then. In the dark silent barn with the Guernsey unmoving before him there is nothing to do but feel the cold. Within minutes it is unbearable. A fit of shaking rattles his limbs with the fury of a pot boiling over and he has to clamp his lips between his teeth to silence their chatter. The boy feels guilty for even noticing the temperature. The lady at his feet is dying and all he can think of is returning to his bed. But when he thinks about it he realizes it isn't the empty bed in Uncle Wallace's house he is pining for, but the body-stuffed bed of his parents' house, and before he can think himself out of it he has scooted between the lady's legs and curled up against the swell of her belly.

Its warmth surprises him. It is like pressing against a furry breathing boiler. The boy feels himself rocked by the power of the lady's lungs. It is a gentle movement, slow but full. Sometimes the bed on Long Island would sway like that, when all four boys breathed in and out in time. But her belly is so warm! He curls into a ball, scrunches as much of his body as he can against her. How can this furnace be sick, injured, let alone near death? She is like a campfire you can hold in your arms or put on like a jacket. He wants to hold her in his arms but settles for holding his own belly. His arms snake inside the torn lining of his jacket and encircle his torso. It's warm too, but not as warm as the lady's. He senses her legs on either side of him, holding his curled body like hospital rails. He wants to be held inside like that. He wants to be held inside her belly, be re-born as a calf. He wants to place the soft teeth of his bottom jaw and the gummed bone of his upper around an udder and drink from the well of her body. But he's a boy. What happens to boys? He feels the pink skin of the udder beneath his right cheek. Warm. Milk should be drunk warm. Not cold. He never wants anything cold again. Warm and pink from the blood that made it. Pale pink, like a flashlight shining through your fingers. When he was a child he sucked his fingers until his mother put Tabasco sauce on them and they burned his tongue. Lois sucked her fingers but she didn't put Tabasco on Lois's fingers because Lois wasn't a boy. What happens to boys? His fingers don't burn his tongue now. They don't taste like veal. His fingers fill his mouth with a warmth that trickles down his throat. He misses his mother but the farm has replaced her. He thinks it would have been better if he had never seen her but at least he has the farm now, the warm farm he has crawled inside, that's crawled inside him.

Dale.

For a moment he is able to hold on to the whole of the experi-ence: the dying cow, her warm belly, the frozen barn, the memory of the bed he shared with his brothers, the simple sad fact that he loves his mother and wished she loved him too, and then, when he real-izes the pink glow behind his eyes isn't an udder but the glow of the morning sun, the sense of loss he feels is almost overwhelming.

Come on, Dale. Get up from there.

The boy squeezes his eyes tighter. *No*, he tells himself, *it's not fair*.

Straw rustles. When the voice comes again it is closer, quieter—

and, he suddenly realizes, Donnie's. In a tender voice that marks him apart from the boy's family Donnie says,

She's dead, Dale.

All at once the boy is screaming. You can't make me go! Not again!

He is not sure at what point he opens his eyes, but the first sight he registers fully is the white hill between the barn and the house, and then he sees the bus coming down 38. He runs around the house and throws himself on the bus without a word to Kenny or Flip and when he gets to school he goes to the bathroom and combs the straw from his hair and wipes the dried milk from his chin.

As he gets off the bus that afternoon his eyes fall on the sign next to the driveway. He stares at it as the bus rumbles past in a cloud of exhaust. The letters are obscured by hoar frost, the thin sheet of snow hangs off in an east-southeast line sculpted by the prevailing winds. Kenny and Flip Flack walk up their yard but the boy stands beneath the frozen elms, staring at the sheet of snow hanging off the sign. What he sees now is that the delicate white arc looks for all the world like the polar image of the fence that had gone down in the barnyard last spring, impossibly delicate but resistant—insistent—as well. The sheet of snow is only slightly thicker than a piece of paper, and yet it has endured three months of wind and snow, daytime melts and nighttime freezes. The loops of wire the boy had clipped off the barnyard fence had looked equally delicate, harmless, but now, thinking of that fence and looking at this pole, the boy sees it as a link in a different kind of fence. The sign is a historical marker after all, a pole supporting an invisible wire that stretches from his time to a past that seems not very far away. For a moment the entire fence hangs in the air beside 38, reaching back to a past the boy cannot begin to imagine but which he can feel nonetheless, a past as inevitably a part of his life as the future that awaits him. He whips around then, as if he'll be able to get a glimpse of what's in store for him, but all he sees is the glare of the setting sun glinting off the snow-capped hill behind him.

He turns then, shucks his schoolbooks in the kitchen, heads up to the dairy barn. He and his uncle milk the ladies in silence and he shovels out the gutters after they're done, uses a push broom to sweep a few blown flakes of snow from the front walk, and then he goes inside to do his homework. He comes down for dinner and then he takes his bath and goes back to his room. He hears his uncle and aunt get ready for bed, and then he hears his uncle in the hall outside his door. The floorboards' creak makes knocking unnecessary, but his uncle knocks anyway.

The boy looks up at his uncle. He is a small man in a small door, but somehow scale doesn't correct for proportion. They both seem small, a doll in a doll's doorway, a doll's hand hanging on to a doll's doorknob. But beneath his gaze the boy feels as tiny as an ant.

I'm sorry I killed her, Uncle Wallace.

His uncle's mouth remains level, firm, as does his voice.

I come to tell you something, Dale.

The boy looks at his uncle and knows before he speaks that he is not going to send him away. A feeling of dread fills him then. He has worked so hard to forget all his uncle's revelations. The image of the sign flashes in his mind: what part of his past is his uncle going to drag up now?

But he is surprised by what comes out of his uncle's mouth.

Your father was a good boy, Dale. Just like you. Hard working, honest, a bit of a temper maybe, but a good boy.

He stops again. His hand turns the doorknob but the door is already open.

Then one day—

His uncle stops. The latch clicks when he releases the handle but the boy's uncle stands there as if frozen, but softly frozen—as if cast in soft white wax. He is staring at the floor and the boy studies him. His uncle is looking at the floor and there is a half smile on his face. Later on—in just a few minutes, as soon as his uncle finishes saying what he has to say—the boy will understand what his uncle is looking at, but for the moment he is struck by the awe there, the sense of comprehension. Belated comprehension—belated compassion too—and the boy understands that his uncle is not just speaking to him.

His uncle nods his head. Then:

Lloyd found our father, Dale. In a field, just like you found your lady. I tell you, when I saw the look that was on your face it brought me back. Lloyd was thirteen, Dale, same age as you are.

The boy turned fourteen two weeks ago, but he doesn't say anything.

Our father was shot dead, Dale. Lloyd found the gun. Nobody knew if it was suicide or murder. Some folks even wondered if Lloyd—

He stops again. It is a long time before he continues.

It ruined him, Dale. Just ruined him. He couldn't go on—go back to how it was, go forward to something new. So instead he drank. And of course our old man was a drunk and that was the one thing Lloyd said he'd never be. But he just couldn't face life after he found Daddy like that.

No, the boy thinks. Stop. This isn't right, this grandfather story. It is as though his uncle has laid the corpse in bed beside him, said, See? Your troubles ain't so bad. He wants to say to his uncle, This is your story, not mine. It means something to you, not me. But even as the boy thinks Stop it's already over. His uncle has told his story and the boy has heard it and neither of them can erase his past.

His uncle turns to the boy and addresses him directly.

You got to put things aside Dale, he says, and the boy has never heard him sound so plaintive before, so unsure of himself. Sometimes all you can do is what's right. Do what you have to without thinking about it. Put the mistakes behind you, the bad times, because nothing can fix the past or bring it back.

The historical marker beside the driveway flashes in the boy's mind. No, he thinks again, that's not true, and his uncle must know it too. He leaves the sign there after all.

It's a hard life, his uncle is saying, and there is still that plaintive edge to his voice, as if he is not just willing the boy to believe but asking him to confirm his own beliefs. There's only the future to look forward to, his uncle says insistently. Nothing else. Nothing but. And—His uncle's voice catches, then resumes. And I just couldn't take it if you got stuck like Lloyd did.

His uncle stops then, finally, and this time doesn't start again. He is finished, waits only for some sign that the boy has heard him, understood.

The boy says, I'm fourteen Uncle Wallace, and his uncle nods once, then closes the door.

As soon as he leaves the boy shuts the light off. He lies on the edge of the mattress as he always does, but tonight he's not making room for his brothers but instead for his grandfather's body. The boy doesn't doubt his uncle's story, but he can find no way to attach any meaning to it either. He tries to imagine the old man standing over his grandfather's dead body, and the inevitable happens: he sees himself, standing over Lloyd, the warm barrel of a gun clutched in his hand. He sees the dead Guernsey too, sprawled across the stall. Even after he falls asleep he feels her cold carcass beneath him instead of the mattress, each of her ribs pushing into him like a root pushing out of the ground. Her head is stretched out as if in birthing, her legs stick straight out of her body, two flush with the straw, two poking into the air, and when his uncle raps on his door in the morning he shudders awake, realizing—remembering—that he never actually saw the Guernsey's body. He had run from Donnie's alien sympathy without looking back, just as he had forgotten to look back at his house when the old man had taken him away last year. All at once images from his dreams and his life and his uncle's mouth tumble on him in a rush. The pillowcase beneath his head is stuffed with his brothers' clothes and the old man's bottles and the dead cow's torso, and the pillowcase itself is a net of snow-white wire. The cow becomes his invisible grandfather and he himself becomes the old man, and then Dolly's calf, sold off for veal. The Guernsey, he knows, is already gone, sold off for dog food. Is *this* what makes history so terrible? the boy wonders. This constant effacement of one real thing by another, yet yielding neither? It is worse than death. It is as if the Guernsey had never lived at all, nor his grandfather—as if someone had made the whole thing up.

His uncle knocks on the door again, something he has never had to do in the boy's thirteen months here.

Come on Dale, he says through the closed door. Ladies won't milk themselves.

6

COVERED WAGONS must have gone this slow, the boy thinks. Third gear, hauling a full load—a half ton of tarp-covered manure capped by the fifty-pound bundle of Flip Flack—and his uncle's 1934 John Deere can do no better than three, maybe five miles an hour; certainly no faster than a man walking. He tries to imagine crossing the continent at this pace, the mountains and rivers, endless plains yielding to relentless deserts. Gold Rush? Gold Crawl is more like it. He'll take a brand-new Chevy any day of the week.

The four-cylinder engine protests its heavy load with a sound like a match dropped in a bottomless bag of firecrackers, an endless series of tiny explosions that vibrate their way into the boy's body through his numb bottom and out his tingling ears and fingers. If he concentrates on the noise itself it seems deafening, but long hours mowing fields and hauling loads of hay and manure have taught him to tune it out. Now he inches his way west on 38 in a bubble of sound, peaceful, protected. Though the soundless world is visible all around him, it seems to exist at a conceptual remove, like a three-dimensional silent movie. Inside the bubble there is nothing but the boy and the pedals and knobs and wheel of the tractor, and Flip Flack. Or Flip's voice at any rate, which, though muffled, is still perfectly audible.

I wish Kenny wasn't working road crew this summer. That means I'm gonna have to do all his chores *and* mine too. I practically do as much as he does anyway, so that means I'm gonna have to do *twice* as much as I do now. *Two* times. I don't know why Kenny wants to work road crew anyway. All that stinky old smelly old tar. I'd rather clean up after the ladies any old day, wouldn't you, Dale?

A pair of passing crows seems almost to leave contrails in the sky, a honeybee bounces along like a poorly flicked yo-yo bobbing at the end of its string. The muggy air is bright blue, so thick with moisture that the tractor could be a boat on the river. Chicory blossoms seem almost to be floating at the end of their stems like water lilies. The fluid sunlight pulses through the trees like liquid amber, outlining everything, separating objects one from another. Each tuft and wisp of vapor, each twig and leaf takes on a gilded edge. The film of sweat that covers the boy's body seems part and parcel of the same effect, as if the boy is coated in a residue of sunlight. As if he has been dipped in it. Though it is only the second week of June, the thermometer read 94 degrees at the noon meal, and the radio said the humidity was about the same.

Kenny says he don't want to be a dairyman at all, Flip goes on. Says it ain't no kind of life for a man in this day and age, being chained to a udder. Our dad says real freedom comes from knowing your place but Kenny still says he's gonna do something else with his life, be a carpenter or maybe even join the armed services. Something that won't tie him to one place. Dad said dairy farming was good enough for three generations of Flack men, it should be good enough for Kenny, but Kenny said carpentry was good enough for Jesus Christ, it ought to be good enough for him. I thought Dad was gonna pop him sure. Your butt's sweating.

The boy nods his head; then, when his brain catches up with Flip's words, squinches a little on his perch. The tractor's seat is bare metal, its cushion—leather, vinyl, cloth, whatever it might have been—long since worn away. Sitting on it in the summer is like simmering on a hot stove, and he himself has seen the sweat drip off Donnie or his uncle through the tiny holes drilled in the seat. The holes, as fine as those on a spaghetti strainer, are arrayed like a Jewish star. He doesn't know if they were drilled there to let the sweat out or not.

Kenny says he's taking off after the letter ceremony next week. You lettered, right? Are you going to the ceremony?

The boy nods his head. The letter ceremony. It is why he is driving this load of manure to Shepherd's Bush. He is trying to earn enough money to buy a letter jacket. He finished the year with eight medals to his credit, and by the time his sophomore year begins in the fall he wants them all on his chest, spangled and loud.

Ew, gross. Looks like you peed your pants.

I wouldn't talk, the boy calls back. You're sitting on a pile of shit.

The last half mile of 38 to Shepherd's Bush is one long if not particularly steep incline, and when the tractor reaches the top it's nearly crawling. It takes the two boys almost three hours to unload the half ton of manure by the resort's kitchen garden, and Flip continues to talk the whole time. For the most part the boy lets him prattle without answering, occasionally identifying tender shoots of basil or onion or kale in response to the younger boy's inquiries, asters, vinca, yes, Flip, those *are* morning glories, but they bloom all day. The boy finds Flip's garrulousness soothing, comforting even, the absolute lack of anxiety the ten-year-old has about his family, his future, everything else he doesn't know. When I grow up I'm gonna do exactly what my dad does, Flip says, I'm gonna milk cows and live in our same house, and the boy has no doubt that he will.

When they're finished the boy collects three dollars from the gardener. A letter jacket is fifty dollars, the boy thinks, pocketing two of the dollars and giving one to Flip, who sweeps out the trailer with a push broom. Three months of vacation, four loads of manure each month at three dollars per, a dollar to Flip, say, every other time, and . . . the math gets lost in his head. He spreads the tarp over the ripe-smelling planks and Flip tosses his broom and the shovels on top and climbs in. The trailer, almost as old and infirm as the tractor, bounces from one wheel to the other as they rattle back down 38's smooth tarred surface, and once he's got the tractor going the boy drops it into neutral and, freed of the gears' restraint, the wheels pick up speed down the long hill. Flip lies down and lets himself be tossed from side to side, his laughter constant, punctuated only by cries of Faster, faster! The freshly hayed fields on either side of the road are studded with crows and seagulls massacring the field mice whose homes have been mown into bales. The crows and gulls straggle over the fields like two chess teams too busy to notice each other.

At first the boy doesn't recognize the straw-haired girl with the baton walking between the road and the line of elms in his uncle's front yard. She is walking away from him marching band style, the baton resting on her shoulders like a soldier's rifle. From the back she reminds him of Julia Miller. Sunlight streams through the leaves on the elms, which are still small and pale, none bigger than a silver dollar. In a few months they will be as big and dark as dollar bills, the shade beneath them as thick as pea soup, but right now the sun can still sneak through the half-grown, half-green leaves and glint off his sister Joanie's hair, and the first thing the boy thinks when he realizes who it is is that Joanie's hair isn't blond at all, but brown, hardly lighter than his. Then Joanie turns around, and almost immediately jumps up and down and points at him with her baton.

It's Dale! It's Dale!

The boy can't hear her inside the tractor's noise. He still hears nothing besides Flip's giggles and screams as he rolls from side to side in the rattling trailer, but he knows that's what Joanie is saying. He is thinking that the truck must have driven right past Shepherd's Bush on 38 when he and Flip were unloading the manure and he didn't hear that either. He would have thought he'd have heard it— would have thought he'd have sensed his mother's approach like a cold wind on his neck. But he had no idea.

He's so caught up in his thoughts that he nearly rolls past the driveway, and he makes the hard left without braking, nearly tossing Flip from the trailer. Then he has to slam right to avoid running into the back of the old man's truck, and even over the roar of the tractor's engine he can hear Flip's body slam into the other side of the trailer. When he pulls up short he finds himself staring right at the truck's broken taillight, and he turns and looks at the big sugar maple that stands across the road in the northwest corner of his uncle's south pasture. Flip is lying in the trailer, his limbs askew, his belly still shaking with laughter, and when the boy cuts the motor a backfire makes Flip jump and scream and then giggle again, but to the boy the sound is nothing so much as the sound of his bubble bursting. Flecks of grass and manure cling to Flip's sweat-wet cheeks and his eyes are closed. Seventeen months ago the boy had gazed at the broken panes of the garage door on Long Island without knowing why the sight filled him with a sense of loss, but as he looks down at Flip's dreamy smile and quivering stomach he knows full well that he will never see him again, and his only consolation is that Flip is himself unaware of the impending separation.

That was *fun*.

Without the sound of the tractor's engine Flip's voice is more distinct but thinner, and quickly dissipates in the hot afternoon air. Giggles still bubble out of him like bubbles from frogs hidden underwater.

I think I'm *broken*.

A shriek rends the air.

Dale! Dale!

Joanie jumps up on the trailer even as Flip sits up and they miss butting heads by inches. Joanie falls backwards but by then the boy is behind her and he catches her. The rubber tip of her baton hits him in the eye as she whirls around but he binds her to him in a bear hug anyway.

Dale!

It's Dale! It's Dale! he hears behind him then, and he turns and sees Edi and Lois running down the hill, each holding the arm of a little boy he thinks is Lance at first, until Lance pushes open the door of the dairy barn behind them, and he realizes that Edi and Lois are carrying Gregory. When the boy left, Gregory wasn't a year old, still more infant than child, but now, nearly three, he seems like a real person, his tiny legs leaping down the hill, one step for every three or four his sisters take.

Dale's back! Lance calls into the dairy barn before sprinting after his older sisters and little brother. Dale! Dale! He runs awkwardly in a pair of shoes much too large for him, trips once, nearly falls, then keeps on running. Dale! You're back!

Oh gosh, my baton left a mark! I'm sorry!

Joanie is rubbing at his cheek and eye even as Edi and Lois come close, panting. They let go of Gregory and throw their arms around the boy. They're still screaming Dale! Dale! in his ear, but Lois manages to squeeze in a conspiratorial whisper:

Joanie's always carrying that thing around!

Dale, look! Lance is calling beyond their shoulders. Look, Dale, I got your shoes! They're almost too small for me, look!

When he reaches the boy Lance squirms in between his sisters and wraps his arms around the boy's stomach and jumps up and down so vigorously that one of the boy's old shoes flies off his feet.

Dale, look! Joanie says then. She has stepped back a few feet, and now she releases her baton into the air, pirouettes once, and catches it.

Look, Dale! Lance says. Your shoes are almost too small for me now! I'm almost as big as you!

Lois has a boyfriend, Lois has a boyfriend! Edi says. She is holding Gregory in one arm now, and when the boy looks at his littlest brother Gregory turns his face and hides it in Edi's wavy brown hair. Beyond them, Lois is dragging a startled-looking Flip Flack up the hill toward the dairy barn.

Don't be shy, honey, Edi says to Gregory. It's just your bother, honey. It's your big brother Dale.

You took my drawers! Lance says, pulling at the boy's cut-offs as if he might be wearing them now. You can't wear my drawers, Dale, they'd be too small for you!

Flip is looking back at the boy with an expression of mock terror on his face as Lois drags him like a sled up the hill.

Dale, look! Joanie says. He turns, and she tosses her baton in the air.

Joanie was spinning her thing in the truck! Lance says. She hit me on the arm, look!

Lance holds out his arm and the boy pretends he can see a

bruise. He licks his thumb and rubs the spot and Lance giggles and says, Gross!

Just say hi, Edi is coaxing Gregory. Come on, say hi to your big brother Dale. A muffled Uh-uh comes from her hair and Edi smiles helplessly at the boy. He don't remember you, she says. You been gone practically as long as he's been alive.

You took Jimmy's football jersey too! Lance says now. You took *everything!*

Up until now the boy has felt like a spoon in a sugarbowl in the midst of his brothers and sisters, but now he speaks for the first time since he shut off the tractor.

What are you, the family record keeper?

No! Lance says, dodging the punch the boy throws at him.

You think you're almost as big as me? the boy says. Come on, pipsqueak, let's see what you can do. Put em up.

The five-year-old giggles and throws his arms around the boy's bare stomach again, then steps back and looks up at the boy.

Jimmy said he was gonna kick your butt for taking his football jersey but I don't know. You look different. Bigger. Thicker.

The boy is looking at Edi over Lance's head.

Is Jimmy here?

Edi is rocking Gregory in her arms.

Oh, he's with Ma and that uncle person.

Uncle Wallace.

Jimmy's with them in the barn. Look at Joanie. She fixed her feet walking with that baton.

The boy turns and sees that Joanie is walking in the dappled light of the elms again. She walks in a straight line and stares fixedly at her formerly pigeon-toed feet, which now run as parallel to each other as the double yellow line on 38.

When the boy turns back to Edi, Gregory is staring at him with curious eyes.

Hey there, little fella. He reaches a hand toward Gregory's cheek but before he can touch him his little brother blushes and buries his face in Edi's hair again.

It's okay, Edi says, and the boy isn't sure to whom she is speaking. You two don't hardly know each other, do you? She smiles at the boy, strokes the back of Gregory's head.

What about Duke?

Edi nods toward the truck behind him. The slatted panels are up in back, encasing the bed like a giant egg crate.

Says he's gonna join the marines. Says he ain't even gonna finish high school, just join the marines and this family will never see him again.

By then the boy has scaled the panel at the back of the truck. The first thing he sees is Duke's shorn head, gold fuzz glinting in the sunlight. Duke is sitting with his back against the cab, busily pulling slivers of wood from the bed of the truck, and his shaved head looks as bright as the rising sun to the boy. He glances over at Joanie. Never mind Julia Miller—how could he have remembered Joanie's hair as blond, compared to Duke's?

He steps over the back railing and Duke says, Nice pants. Or should I say shorts?

The boy looks down at his legs. Although he never managed to outgrow them—Duke's four years older than he is, after all—he did manage to wear them out, and Aunt Bessie cut them into shorts for him after the last day of school this year.

It was Dad—

Your Dad. Duke throws a sliver over the wall of the truck.

Anyway. Sorry.

No skin off my ass.

In the silence the boy can hear his siblings scatter like a flock of startled pigeons. He looks at Duke until Duke gets up and walks past him, throwing a mock punch as he goes. His fist touches the boy's jaw and pushes it lightly to the side, like a revolving door.

Your Dad, Duke says again, and then he jumps over the back rail of the truck and disappears.

The boy scrambles after him. They walk around the side of the truck and up the line of honey locusts until they reach the woodshed.

Edi says you're gonna join the marines. The boy points to Duke's head. Looks like you did already.

Duke runs his hand over the top of his head.

Just letting everybody know. Letting everybody know that I'm out of here. Any minute now.

Just then Lois runs around the near corner of the hay barn, screaming, Daddy's sleeping in the barn, Daddy's sleeping in the barn! A moment later Flip rounds the barn's far corner and speeds toward his house.

You talk funny! Flip calls behind him. Your daddy's a drunk and you talk funny!

Duke watches the little blond boy until he has run all the way across 38 and inside his house, and then he runs his hand over his crewcut again and looks up at the hay barn.

Wish I had a match.

The boy looks up at the barn as well. It is easy to imagine it on fire, easy to imagine the old man rolling in his sleep, pushing the flames away as though they were an unwanted blanket. He can almost hear him mumbling, Goddammit, open a window, it's burning up in here, and he has to fight back a laugh.

Just one match, Duke says, and spits on the ground. Poof. For the first time he turns and looks at the boy. They said I could sign up as soon as I turned eighteen. I fudged the application, figure by the time they find out I'll be old enough anyway. I'm gone, Dale. O-U-T out of that fucking house, just like you. Out.

The boy doesn't say anything for a moment. Then:

Edith's husband died.

Edi's —?

Edith. She's our cousin. Uncle Wallace's daughter. Her husband died in Korea.

That war's over. Duke shrugs. And I'd rather die than live in that house another day. You lucked out, getting away when you did.

Dale! Dale! Lance is running down the hill. I touched a cow! I touched it right on the stomach. He holds out his hand for inspection. Look, I touched it!

Moo! Duke says, like boo!, and Lance jumps back, putting the boy between him and his half brother. He pokes a finger into the boy's stomach, chest, shoulder.

You *do* look different.

They're called muscles, Duke says. You'd have some too, if you stopped playing with Lois and Edi all the time. You should have some discipline like Dale here, or Joanie and her baton.

Lance blushes and starts back up the hill.

I want to milk a cow! Come on, Dale, show me how you milk a cow!

Duke is still looking at the hay barn as if wondering where to put the match.

I'm sorry about the pants, Duke. I tried to tell him.

Duke nods.

I heard you.

You were awake?

Duke doesn't say anything for a moment. Just stares at the hay barn and runs his hand over his crewcut. Then:

I'm outta there a week from Monday. Ma don't even know yet. As he starts back toward the truck he delivers another mock jab, this time to the boy's stomach. Good luck with all that.

As the boy follows Lance up the hill he sees Lois and Edi swinging Gregory between them. The little boy is shrieking with delight. Then he sees Jimmy come around the corner of the hay barn, his hands thrust in his pockets. When he sees the boy he pivots on his heel, skirting the edge of the barn and staring at the ground as if he has lost something, or is watching out for snakes.

Hey Jimmy.

Jimmy waves at the boy but doesn't speak, or stop. Lance runs back down the hill and grabs the boy's hand, pulling.

Come *on*, Dale!

There are only a half dozen ladies in the dairy barn at this hour, all of them lying down and chewing their cud. There is no sign of the boy's uncle or mother, however. They must be out looking at the fields.

Lance runs to the nearest lady, a Holstein with a white star emblazoned on her black brow. She stares at him without interest as he leans his full weight on her stomach and pushes at her.

Get up, get up!

The Holstein doesn't stop chewing.

Get up, you lazy cow, get up!

She's digesting her breakfast, the boy says to Lance. She don't want to get up right now.

Breakfast! It's almost dinnertime!

A cow spends half the day lying down, Lance. They have four stomachs, they digest their food very slowly. Come on, maybe one of the other ladies will get up.

Lance giggles. Ladies!

Another Holstein obliges them for a couple handfuls of grain. She stands docilely at the trough while Lance tugs at her udders, and only her ears twitch when the little boy screams victoriously at the spoonful of milk he finally manages to squirt into a pail. The boy goes ahead and drains the Holstein's udder, thinking he will serve all his siblings a glass of thick warm milk the way he once served them apples and bananas from Slaussen's Market, and he is helping Lance carry the pail down the hill to the house when he looks up and sees his mother standing right in front of him on the driveway. She stands there in her brown dress, as thick and squat as a tree trunk shorn of its canopy by a bolt of lightning. She stands immobile, and for some reason the boy cannot imagine her walking to or leaving this spot. It is as if she had sprung up there from seed.

Ma, look! I milked a cow!

Lance runs toward their mother and she puts a hand on his head, but she is looking at the boy.

What're you fooling around in that barn for? Those are your uncle's cows, you don't need to be messing with them.

I been milking them every day for a year and a half, Ma.

Don't talk back to me. Get on inside and get your stuff. We have to leave soon.

Lance looks up at his mother's face, then at the boy.

Look at my milk, Ma! I milked it right out of the cow. Dale didn't hardly help me at all! Show her my milk, Dale!

I see it, honey, you did a real nice job. Dale was never one for helping his family out. Hurry it up, she says to the boy. It's a long drive back.

Edi and Lois come around the side of the house, trapezing Gregory between them.

Higher! he screams. Higher, higher!

Lois, Edi! Lance says. Dale's coming home!

Lois and Edi jump up and down, inadvertently shaking Gregory out of his shirt like a pillow from a pillowcase.

Yay! Dale's coming home!

The boy looks down when he feels his mother pull the pail of milk from his hands. She would have walked three steps to get to him, but he didn't see her or hear her. But now she has his pail in her hands and his hands are empty.

It's now or never. I'm not driving all this way again. You want to be a part of this family you go pack your things. If not. . . .

She lets the milk finish her sentence. It hangs in the air in a white bubbly arc, then falls to the ground, its wet shadow hardly darker than the earth it sinks into.

The boy looks at his four siblings jumping up and down, cheering. Even Gregory is jumping up and down, caught up in their enthusiasm. He looks back at his mother. Up until now it had seemed like him and her. Him versus her. But then he looks at his sisters and brothers again. Edi and Lois are trying to swing Lance now, but he is nearly as big as Lois, and Edi is calling for the boy to come and help. God, how he hates the fact that his mother comes with them. She is like the prickly rind on a pineapple. Why can't his brothers and sisters come already peeled?

All the while she stands there holding the empty pail in front of her stomach with both hands. If only she would hit him, the boy thinks. If she would just hit him he would wrest the pail from her hands with the muscles he has built up from slinging hay bails and pails of milk and beat her into the ground, not like a fencepost but like a stake. He would drive his mother into the milky heart of this land he has come to love in lieu of himself, and that does not, he suddenly understands, love him back. If it loved him it would fold up around him and hide him until this woman was gone, but instead he feels its flat indifference all around him. The stillness of the earth reproaches him. You are not of this soil. You are not good enough. You never were. You never will be.

But she does not hit him. She sucks in lungfuls of the same air he is breathing and sprays them back in his face. She defies him to hit her. To hit his own mother. His hands curl into fists but even as they do, even as he imagines striking her down, he feels himself in violation of some fundamental law of the universe. It's as if his image in the mirror had reached out and struck him. His hands unball, his fingers stick straight out from his palms like candles stuck into a cake.

His mother smiles.

Go get your things. Lance, go find Joanie and tell her we're leaving. Edi, Lois, she says, louder, stop swinging that boy around before you pull his arms off. Come on, we're going. Jimmy! she yells now. Jimmy, come on, we're going!

She walks away from him, stepping in the milk-wet gravel and taking as little heed of the sliding pebbles as she does of him. She is reeling in her children like fish.

Tuck your shirt in, she calls when Jimmy appears from behind the hay barn. I didn't raise you to be no ragamuffin.

She lets the milk pail fall to the earth like an empty candy wrapper, and continues heading toward the truck. It seems very important that the boy pick up the dropped pail, but once he has it in his hands he doesn't know what to do with it. He would scoop up the milk if he could, but there is nothing left besides a few nearly translucent bubbles and a fast-fading crooked smear. He twitches back and forth between the barn and the truck, thinking again that his mother is reeling him in but that now he's hooked on a second line. He feels the two hooks pull him in either direction, then all at once he jerks free and runs toward the house.

In the kitchen Aunt Bessie is going through the cabinets.

We'll feed them eggs, his uncle says from the table. All kids like eggs, they'll be fine, Bess, don't worry.

There's a whole *brood* of em, Aunt Bessie says. There's another one every time I turn around.

Uncle Wallace! the boy says. Ma says I have to go home!

Aunt Bessie turns off the water she is running over a sinkful of potatoes and turns around. She has a small wet brown potato in each hand, and she holds them up as if they were as useless as the dirt she pulled them from.

How does she do it Dale? she says, shaking the potatoes. Eight children! I'm exhausted just thinking about it.

She stops then, blinks. All at once her eyes are as swollen with moisture as the humid summer air.

What did you say Dale?

The boy looks at Aunt Bessie for a moment. Sees black shoes, a snood of graying brown curls, a plain blue dress filling the space between, belted loosely at her plump waist. Sees that she is cast from the same die as his mother and yet she is holding a potato up to him—holding two potatoes, and offering to cook them for him. He can feel them in his throat like stones. Swallowing them down is almost more than he can manage. Answering her is out of the question.

I want to stay Uncle Wallace, he says, turning from the sympathy in Aunt Bessie's eyes. I want to stay with you and Aunt Bessie and help you run the farm but Ma says I have to go home and oh, Uncle Wallace! I miss my brothers and sisters. I miss them like crazy. Duke said he's gonna join the marines but everyone else will still be there. Gregory don't even know me. He don't even know I'm his brother. I don't know what to do, Uncle Wallace.

He stops then, and then he thrusts the empty pail toward his uncle.

She poured it out on the ground, Uncle Wallace. Just threw it out like it didn't matter at all.

Throughout the boy's speech his uncle has not looked up from the table where he is sitting. Then he stands so suddenly he knocks his chair over. His hand is shaking as he sets it upright and then he says,

Come on in here.

He walks out of the kitchen into the hallway. He starts to go into the living room but then he stops, whirls toward the storage room, then stops again, wavering between the east and west parlors as the boy had wavered on the hill between the old man's truck and his uncle's barn. The boy stares at him, afraid to follow until his uncle has made his choice. He doesn't understand his uncle's indecision, can't imagine what hooks pull at his uncle nor why the context for the ensuing conversation is so important. All he knows is that the room on his uncle's left belongs to the present, to the lived life of the house, and the room on his right belongs to the past, and when his uncle suddenly pushes into the right parlor the boy's heart sinks, and he thinks he might as well go ahead and crawl into the back of the truck now.

But he manages to tiptoe in behind him, and his uncle shuts the door. The dust in the storage room is thick and warm in the light slanting through the unshuttered windows and reflecting off jars of pickles and jellies stacked on the sagging mantel. The jars were filled by his uncle's first wife, Ella Mae, and they have sat there so long their labels are unreadable under a film of grime—Aunt Bessie will not open them, even when her preserves run out and she must buy some from the store. The boy sits on a pile of newspaper, still holding the empty pail in his lap, and his uncle lets his own hand cling to the doorknob a moment, then releases it and walks over to the window and stands framed by the light pushing through the remains of an ancient curtain. The sunlight is strong, slightly red, obscuring his uncle's face in shadow. It occurs to the boy that it is late in the afternoon. In his lap, the empty bucket still exudes a milky odor. It is almost time to bring the ladies in.

All at once his uncle speaks.

Listen to me, Dale. I know you love your family, and you're right to. They're your family. But listen to me. There ain't nothing for you back there, Dale. No future. You go back there and you'll end up like . . . you'll end up where you started from before you came up here.

For a moment the boy had been sure his uncle had meant to say he would end up like Lloyd. Like his father. It is something his mother has said to him many times.

But I can come back, Uncle Wallace. As soon as I finish high school. Three years and I'll come back and we'll run the farm together. It could be my last chance to see them, Uncle Wallace. My last chance to be with them.

But his uncle is shaking his head.

Didn't you learn anything in your time here?

But Ma said it's now or never, Uncle Wallace. She said she won't drive up here again.

Light pushes through the closed dirty windows, as do Lance's squeals, and the boy knows without looking that Joanie and Edi are holding his arms down while Lois torture-tickles him.

Dale! Lance is laughing and screaming. Dale, help!

When the boy hears his name his mind flashes on the other Dale. He is just a shadow now, something the boy can neither hold nor shake off, and he wonders how long it would take before he became just a shadow to his brothers and sisters if he stayed with his uncle. He realizes he is shaking his own head now. His uncle is still looking at him.

Didn't I teach you anything, Dale? Anything at all?

Uncle Wallace, please. It's not fair. You know I want to stay.

But his uncle just shakes his head.

You're breaking my heart, Dale. You're breaking my heart.

Suddenly the boy's uncle is in front of him. He has the look on his face he gets when he is about to say something about the boy's past but his words, when they come, reveal an equally unreal future. The smell of milk from the pail is strong between them, slightly sweet, slightly rank.

Listen to me, Dale. You're like the son I never had. You're like

. . . you're . . . It's yours, Dale. Everything I have will be yours if you stay here. Stay here, Dale. Don't break an old man's heart. There ain't nothing for you back there, just stay. Say you'll stay and I'll give it all to you. Ah Dale. You're the son I always wanted.

And all of a sudden it occurs to the boy. He *can* stay. He doesn't have to go back. He does have a choice. But as he looks at his uncle before him and listens to his brothers and sisters outside, he realizes he doesn't want to make that choice himself. He wants someone else to make it for him. He wants it not to be his fault. Whatever it is, he doesn't want to be responsible for it.

He didn't even know me, Uncle Wallace. He didn't even know I was his own brother.

His uncle looks at the boy for a moment and then he shakes his head.

Goddamn that Lloyd. First he took the farm and lost it and now he's taking you too. I wish he'd never brought you up.

Uncle Wallace, please.

Come on then. You want to go, come on.

Uncle Wallace, no, I want to stay.

But his uncle is at the door. It slams open and then there is the sound of his boots on the stairs. The boy runs after him, still clutching the empty pail of milk.

Uncle Wallace, no, I'll stay, I'll stay.

His uncle has the pillowcase off the bed by the time the boy runs into his room. He grabs the boy's running shoes from the floor, his shorts and team jersey from the back of a chair. He is reaching for the top drawer of the dresser when the boy remembers what's in there.

Uncle Wallace, don't—

His uncle pulls the drawer open so violently it nearly comes out of its slot, and the bottles of the old man's medicine bounce off each other and off his cross-country medals so loudly that the boy thinks they will break, but they don't. The shallow drawer hangs from the dresser like the cupped tongue of a cow reaching for a lick of salt or tuft of grass, and one of the bottles slides to the lower edge, Lance's drawers half covering it like a sheet pulled back to identify a corpse. For a moment neither of them says anything, then:

They're not mine, the boy says quietly, and his words sound like a lie even to his ears. They're Dad's, not mine.

His uncle is still staring at the bottles.

Yeah, but you kept em, didn't you.

They're Dad's, Uncle Wallace.

His uncle drops the pillowcase to the floor.

I guess they are Lloyd's. And I guess you're Lloyd's son after all. He doesn't look at the boy as he walks out of the room. Go on. Get your stuff and get out of here.

The boy waits until his uncle's feet have made it all the way to the first floor and the front door has opened and closed behind him. Then he packs. When he gets downstairs the first thing he sees is that Donnie has shown up. A string of a dozen shad lie on the kitchen table.

Well if it isn't Amos, Donnie says, looking over his shoulder. Practically jumped into the boat, he says to Aunt Bessie then. He is standing at the counter on the other side of Aunt Bessie, and the boy can hear the sound of a knife squelching through fish flesh. Couldn't hardly keep em out.

Well, thank goodness, Aunt Bessie says. I didn't know *how* I was going to feed all those children. Dale! she says then, looking up and smiling brightly, as if the confrontation of ten minutes ago had never occurred. Come see what Donnie brought for you.

The boy thinks she means the fish, but Aunt Bessie is pulling a jacket from the back of a chair. She turns it around, shows it to him. It is gold felt with white leather sleeves, and on the left breast pocket is a dark outline where the letter G had once been stitched to it.

It's his old letter jacket.

Saw it at the back of the closet the other day, Donnie says, his knife slicing through flesh and bone and clunking solidly against the cutting board. The smell of fish permeates the kitchen. Thought you might as well have it, Amos, since I don't wear it no more. He whirls

134

suddenly, his hands filled with bloody gore. Here you go, Amos, how bout a little caviar to go with your new—

He stops when he sees the expression on the boy's face, the stuffed pillowcase slung over his shoulder. He looks at the boy, his hands filled with pinkish-white sacs linked together by spidery bits of tissue. With as much clarity as he has perceived anything else on this day, the boy realizes the sacs in Donnie's hands are the fish's ovaries, filled with roe.

Aw, Amos, you got to be kidding me.

Now Aunt Bessie is clutching the jacket to her chest.

Dale, don't. Don't. You'll break his heart.

The boy thinks it should be a struggle to keep his voice level, but it comes out as flat and smooth as the frozen river.

Tell Uncle Wallace I'm sorry.

As he is about to climb into the back of the truck Aunt Bessie runs out the back door and presses the jacket into his hands. Donnie says you should take it anyway. She kisses him on the cheek, then runs back into the house.

When he mounts the back of the truck he sees first the back of his mother's head in the cab and then, beyond her, through the front and rear windows of the cab, Jimmy leading the old man down from the hay barn. The old man is batting at Jimmy's hands but lets himself be led like a half-trained puppy.

Duke sits at the head of the truck, his half siblings arrayed on either side of him like a family sitting down to dinner absent table or food: Edi with Gregory in her lap on his right, Lois beside her; Joanie with baton on his left, Lance next to her. The boy sits down next to Lois and she rests her head on his shoulder.

I'm glad you're coming home Dale, she whispers in his ear. Joanie and Edi didn't miss you as much as I did. I'm your littlest sister, I missed you the most.

The boy puts his arm around her back and squeezes.

I missed you too.

The door cracks open and the old man climbs into the cab. As the door slams closed Jimmy climbs over the back wall of the truck.

Your father, is the first thing he says to the boy in a year and a half, is a drunk.

Muffled yelling comes from the cab of the truck.

Jimmy takes his place opposite the boy but doesn't sit down. Instead he leans over the railing and looks out at the pasture, where the cows are making their way toward the barn for the evening milking.

Moo, Jimmy calls to the cows in the fields. Moo-oo.

Lance giggles, stands up and joins his half brother at the railing. Moo! Moo-moo!

They don't moo, the boy says then. They low.

Jimmy turns around.

They what?

Low. It's called lowing. He makes the sound as best he can, and one of the cows rewards him with an answer even as the truck's engine turns over.

Lance giggles. Me-aw! he says, sounding more like a donkey than a cow. Me-aw!

The truck lurches into reverse, nearly knocking Jimmy over. He catches himself, then sits down heavily.

Stupid cattle.

They're not cattle, the boy says. They're cows. Cattle are food.

You still eat them, Jimmy says. After they're done giving milk you eat them. Your uncle told me.

Uncle Wallace never ate one of his own cows. He has special instructions with the butcher.

Jimmy makes a move as if to get up but Duke stretches out his boot and puts it on Jimmy's ankle.

I'd think it over, Jimbo. Looks like Dale's put on twenty pounds of muscle in the last two years and you're the same momma's boy you always been.

Jimmy looks at Duke and then he looks at the boy and then he settles back against the side of the truck.

Me-aw! Me-aw, me-aw!

Lance crawls across the truck as it starts up the hill away from the farm. Me-aw! He crawls away from Jimmy until he is next to the boy, and then he lies down with his head on the boy's lap.

I'm glad you're coming home, Dale.

The boy tousles Lance's hair.

Will you go to work at Slaussen's again? If you do go back to Slaussen's I like bananas the most, followed by oranges and then grapes and then apples. If you go away again will you take me with you?

The boy looks down at his little brother. For the life of him he can't imagine what expression must be on his own face. He tries to smile but all he can manage is a nod.

Lance smiles up at him for a moment, and then his face clouds.

Guh, he says. Guh, guh. The boy doesn't understand until Lance reaches up and traces the outline on his chest.

G, the boy says then. It's a G, Lance. He pulls the right half of the jacket over the left, covering up the shadow of the letter.

Lance nods thoughtfully. Then all at once a smile splits his face. G! G stands for Gregory, Dale? Is that what it stands for?

The boy looks down at Lance, who stares up at him guilelessly.

Did you get it because you missed him? Why didn't you get an L? I really missed you and my name starts with L. L for Lance.

L for Lois too, Lois says sleepily.

The boy thinks of the letter ceremony he won't be attending, the medals he left upstairs on his cousin's dresser, in his cousin's bedroom. He places his hand against the worn patch of felt on his chest, and thinks it is like a missing puzzle piece where his heart should go.

Over Lance's head the boy can see Jimmy staring at him. When he sees the boy looking he looks down at his chest, and the boy turns and looks at Gregory, who has fallen asleep in Edi's arms.

They were all out of L's, the boys says, turning back to Lance. He pulls him all the way onto his lap. But I missed you too.

7

No, MEOW. Like a cat. She thought she was a cat.

Don't they usually think they're a king?

I said *cat*, didn't I? She thought she was a cat.

In my experience they usually think they're a king. Or something like that. Delusions of grandeur, ain't that what they call it?

The boy's parents' voices scale the ladder as though a pair of cats themselves. They settle heavily on his chest next to the lighter weight of Gregory's hand. Downstairs the pipes cough when his mother turns the faucet on, and then, when he hears the water run smooth, the boy presses his thighs together. Friday morning, eight A.M.: he has been awake for two hours—desperate to pee for a good forty-five minutes.

A *cat*, Ethel. She crawled out on the ledge like a *cat*. Stark naked of course. Meow, meow, kitty cats don't wear no clothes, meow. Why it is the crazies have to get naked I'll never know.

The water stops, a pan settles heavily on the stove.

Well, his mother says, and the boy can hear the self-lighting stove click for several seconds. Like she said. Cats don't usually wear no clothes. The burner ignites in a quiet *whoosh!* and a whiff of gas floats up to the loft.

They don't usually talk back either. Which is more than I can say for some people.

Since Duke left at the beginning of the week, Gregory has been sharing the bed with his older brothers, but this is the first time he didn't sleep wedged in the crease between Lance and Jimmy. He was there on the edge of the outer mattress when the boy came in from

Slaussen's last night, and when he woke at milking time his brother's arm had been slung over the boy's torso, his elbow on the boy's stomach and the slightly cupped fingers of his left hand on top of the boy's chest. His mouth had hung open and his breath on the boy's cheek had been wet and sweet—stale, but sweet too—and the boy had decided to stay in bed a while longer. No cows to milk after all. But he'd waited too long: the old man had stumbled in from the hospital just before seven, waking his mother, and now the boy is stuck in the loft until his mother goes to work and the old man passes out. Unless, of course, he's willing to risk a confrontation this early. Which he's not. Instead he tries to concentrate on the tiny weight of Gregory's fingers, cupped over his heart like a stethoscope. Tries to ignore the heavier pressure in his bladder and ears. Down by his hips his fingers are curled into loose fists as if squeezing an imaginary pair of teats, and he tries to ignore that as well.

Born naked, his mother is saying now, as if that answers the old man's question. An egg cracks against the side of a pan, sizzling as soon as the albumen strikes the hot metal, then a second joins it. They usually get naked when they think they're a king too. Emperor's new clothes, right?

A *cat*, Ethel. Jesus Christ, how many times do I have to say it? And besides, it was a girl. Girls can't be kings.

Can't be cats either.

A third egg cracks into the pan, and the sound of the percolator joins the cacophony. The boy doesn't understand how his brothers and sisters can sleep through it. Doesn't understand how he used to, before.

Anyway, the old man's rasp cuts through all the other sounds. The orderlies can't get her to come back in. They're all like, Come on, Jeanie, come back where it's safe, and this girl Jeanie's all like Meow, meow, kitty cats *like* to crawl on ledges, *meow*. The old man screeches the last meow with particular relish.

I know what a cat sounds like, Lloyd.

Meow!

Lloyd—

Gregory turns in his sleep and the bed creaks beneath him. He turns away from the boy, his face searching for a cool spot on the pillow, then turns back toward him again. In the process his hand slides off the boy's chest and wedges between his own skinny thighs, his cheek presses against the boy's bare shoulder. If the boy looks down the tip of his nose he can just make out Gregory's mouth, puckered open like the rim of a fishbowl between his plump cheeks. At two and a half, Gregory's face is still baby fat, but his arms and legs are as skinny as an old man's.

Don't go waking them kids, Ethel. You'll be cooking eggs for the next hour.

His mother's spatula scrapes loudly over the surface of the pan.

Joanie and Edi can cook em breakfast if it comes to that, they're old enough to take some responsibility around here. His mother snorts. Besides, it's probably just *your son*, pretending to be asleep.

The boy can smell it now, her breakfast. Eggs and coffee. He hates the fact that the odor makes his mouth water, his stomach rumble. Hates it almost as much as the fact that when he gets downstairs he knows he'll find nothing but a pan with a residue of dried egg on it.

What's that? the old man says now. What'd Dale do?

He didn't do nothing, his mother says. As per usual. Boy's as useless as his father.

My boy, the old man says dreamily. My own boy.

His mother's spatula scratches viciously at the pan.

Useless as tits on a bull.

My only boy.

That's it Lloyd, his mother says, talk yourself to sleep.

I'll go to sleep when I'm good and ready, the old man says, louder. I'm trying to tell a story here.

And I'm trying to enjoy a few minutes of peace and quiet before I have to head off to the loony bin, so hurry it up already.

The old man doesn't say anything for a moment. Then:

What were you saying about Dale?

I didn't say nothing about Dale, finish your story.

Whatever's on the table jumps and rattles under the old man's fist.

He's not going to no military school, I'll tell you that much. My son is *not* going to military school.

Nobody said nothing about military school, Lloyd, finish your goddamned story already.

Boy belongs with his family.

Lloyd.

All right, all right. Where was I? Right. So I says to them, I says, Is that any way to call a cat? And they says back to me, Mr. Peck, Mrs. Bonnaducio is very obviously *not* a cat. And so I says, Yeah, but *she* don't know that. And they're all like, Mr. Peck, don't you work in the kitchen? And I was like, Yes sir, I do work in the kitchen. I been working in the kitchen for fifteen years and I was a farmer before that, which is why I happen to know that if you want a cat to come you have to give it a saucer of *milk*. The old man chuckles. Yes sir, I said. If you want a cat to come, you have to give it a saucer of—

Finally! his mother's voice cuts through the old man's. I thought these eggs were never gonna cook. A plate settles on the table, and the boy hears her spatula scrape the contents of her pan onto it. A chair slides across the floor.

Pass me the salt, will you, Lloyd.

The salt shaker comes down heavily on the table. For a moment the only sound is his mother's fork clinking rapidly against her plate. Then the old man's voice:

She jumped.

The boy's mother's fork continues moving rhythmically over her plate.

Okay she didn't jump. She fell.

Pass me the milk, Lloyd, the boy's mother says, but only after taking several more bites.

The old man's chair scrapes across the floor. The refrigerator opens, and when the milk bottle clunks on the table the boy has a sudden vision of them in his head, the milk bottle and the salt shaker, two clear glass containers filled with white and standing beside his mother's white plate like a father and son at the racetrack, and then, when the old man speaks again, he has retreated to his bed. His voice comes from directly beneath the boy.

Okay she didn't fall but she nearly did. She would have, if I hadn't set out that saucer of milk.

Just happened to have a bottle with you? his mother calls across the house. That it, Lloyd? You just happened to be bringing a bottle of milk home to your *family*?

The boy hears the bed creak beneath the old man's weight.

Well she wasn't a real cat, Ethel. Why should I waste real milk? He speaks quietly, but both the boy and his mother hear him.

I know what kind of bottles you had on you, Lloyd. His mother's plate lands in the sink so loudly the boy thinks she must have tossed it. And don't think I won't find em. I swear, sometimes I think *I* should be the patient at that hospital. I must be crazy, to stay married to a no-good drunk like you.

The bed creaks again.

That's it, Lloyd. Go to bed now, now that I'm leaving. That's it, stick your head under the pillow. Run and hide, Lloyd, just like you tried to hide *your son*. One of these days, Lloyd. One of these days you're gonna drive *me* out on that ledge, and no *saucer of milk* is gonna get me back in. You hear that Lloyd? No saucer of milk is gonna fool *me*.

The boy waits until his mother leaves and the old man's muffled snores fill the house before he gets out of bed. He tucks the sheet around Gregory even though it's hot and stuffy in the loft, and then he fixes the hanging sheet between the boys' bed and the girls'. Now that Duke's gone and Jimmy's taken his place on the far side of the bed, it's continually bunched up in the center of the rope, Edi's head visible at one end, her feet at the other, like a magician's assistant about to be sawed in half.

The old man managed to take off his shoes, the boy sees as he descends the ladder. He lies on his bed spread-eagled, his soiled kitchen whites only slightly lighter than his dark socks and only slightly darker than the pillow over his face. The quilts hang on their ropes on either side of the bed like the curtain at a puppet theater, and the boy draws them around the old man's crooked limbs before heading first to the bathroom and then to the kitchen, where the coffeepot's still on the table, still warm, an oaken cutting board beneath it as a trivet. A pair of flies mate on the lip of the open bottle of milk—the salt shaker's right next to it, just as he'd imagined—and the chairs around the maple table have almost as many names as the family that sits in them: a one-armed Windsor at the far end, an armless at the near, in between a mixture of rickety ladderbacks with unraveling rush seats, uncomfortable straight-backed school chairs, and one kitchen stool, ostensibly Gregory's, though all the children like to sit in its high seat and use their feet to open and close the hinged steps via which the stool is converted to a stepladder—a convenience the low-ceilinged house has no use for at all.

The boy adds some water to the coffeepot and puts it back on the stove, then sits on Gregory's stool, holding a bowl of corn flakes in his hands and eating it while the coffee comes back to a boil. He's halfway through his second cup when he hears tiptoeing in the loft above him. A giggle trickles out from behind pressed-together fingers. The boy keeps his head cocked as though looking down into his cup but peers up through his bangs at the loft. Lance and Gregory and Lois are lying on the floor in a row, only their eyes visible between the edge of the loft floor and the lowest rung of the guard rail. He stares at the guard rail a moment, a pale pine two-by-four, nearly white save for one whorled knot which glows out of it like the eye of a peacock feather. Since he's come back from the farm he's noticed things like that, the fact that the cutting board is made of oak, the kitchen table of maple, the guard rail pine. The names of all those chairs. It bothers him a little bit, the fact that his uncle's and his parents' houses are built from the same materials. But things seemed to fit together naturally Upstate, whereas here they are merely cobbled together, fastened roughly with half-hammered bent-over nails and waiting to break beneath your weight.

Gregory giggles, and Lois sshhes him loudly. The boy sips the last of his coffee, pretending to ignore the steady stream of giggles and whispers above him, then stands and takes his cup to the sink. Up above him his siblings press their faces to the floor like ostriches, the sleep-tangled tops of all three heads plainly visible. His mother's plate is in the sink, a white disk eclipsing the black cast iron skillet in which she'd cooked her eggs, and the boy stares at them a moment, then suddenly grabs the wet rag and whirls. His shot catches Gregory on the top of his head, and his scream ignites Lois and Lance. Within a minute they're running screaming around the loft, and then he's up there with him, Gregory under one arm, Lois and Lance curled around his ankles like a pair of ball-and-chains, all three of them screaming and laughing at the top of their lungs.

Got me a sack-a feed here, the boy says out loud. Guess I'd better go feed the cows.

No, no! Lois screams. He's not food, he's a boy!

The boy drags his feet one after the other toward the edge of the loft. Them cows is pretty hungry, I bet. Liable to eat up a whole sack of feed.

No, I'm a boy! Gregory screams.

Yes sir, I'm gonna pour this sack-a feed into the trough, feed me some cows.

A boy! Gregory screams, I'm a boy, a boy!

The boy holds Gregory by his ankles over the edge of the loft and shakes him like he is dumping out a sack of food. Gregory's arms flop over his head and then his undershirt rolls down as well, so that only his hands are visible beneath the hem, like a two-handled umbrella.

Daddy, help! Gregory screams through his laughter. Wake up, Daddy, Dale's feeding me to the cows! Wake up! Help!

Jesus Christ, Dale, give it a rest already.

The boy looks over to see Jimmy propped on one elbow in bed.

It's nine o'clock in the fucking morning, some of us are trying to sleep.

In his hands, Gregory is still twitching, even though the boy has stopped shaking him.

Jimmy, help! Dale's feeding me to the cows, help!

Don't you have to go to work? Jimmy says, then turns over and pulls the pillow over his face.

When the boy looks back at Gregory he realizes his little brother is wearing the pair of Lance's drawers he took Upstate with him last year. Lance, all of whose clothes do time with one or two or three older brothers before coming to him, made a big show of reclaiming the drawers and then presenting them to Gregory, the first thing he's handed down, the first thing Gregory has received. The youngest Peck has worn them every chance he's gotten since then, even though they're too big for his tiny waist and thin, thin legs. His ankles are no bigger than a cow's teats, the boy thinks as he lifts him back over the top railing—a warped pine one-by-six riddled with knots and furzed here and there with strips of bark.

When the boy sets Gregory upright his brother continues to hold his shirt over his face like a lampshade. The boy can see the top of Gregory's head over the inverted hem, but Gregory stares right into the white field in front of his eyes.

Play! Gregory says in a baby voice. No work! Yes play!

No, Jimmy's right, the boy says. I gotta get ready to go.

Play! Lance says. He and Lois are still clinging to the boy's ankles, and they shake him as though he were a coconut tree. Play!

Play! Lois echoes.

The boy tries to step free of them but they refuse to let go.

C'mon, guys, I gotta take a bath.

No bath, play! Lance says. Bath bad, play good!

In front of the boy, something is happening to Gregory's undershirt: it seems to be spiraling down a drain like bath water. The boy realizes Gregory is chewing on his shirt.

Gregory, what are you doing?

Behind the shirt, Gregory makes a sucking noise.

I'm a baby cow, Dale, he says, his voice muffled by a mouthful of white cotton. He giggles. I'm sucking on my mother's tit.

All at once the boy grabs the shirt and rips it off Gregory's head and throws it to the floor.

Enough with the goddamned *milk* already. The word is *calf,*

145

Gregory, and boy calves end up in the veal pens. And you'd better not let Dad hear you using language like that or you'll be sucking on more than an undershirt.

Gregory stares at his brother with a stunned look on his face, not sure if they're still playing. His naked arms are still standing straight up from his shoulders.

The boy rips his ankles from Lance's grip, Lois's.

Let go, I gotta take a bath. You guys can entertain each other for once.

His three siblings stare after him mutely as he heads out of the loft. He is halfway down the ladder when he sees Joanie lying on her stomach on her bed, looking at him.

You okay, Dale?

He pauses on the ladder, his head just above floor level. A miniature mountain range of dust swirls underneath the bed closest to him, his and his brothers'. Jimmy's shoes are there as well—a brand-new pair, bought just before the boy's return—and a single white sock.

Yeah, I'm fine. I gotta go to work, I'll see you later.

The boy runs a few inches of cold water in the bath, telling himself it's too hot to build a fire in the stove in the basement. But it's too cold to sit in the water for more than a couple of minutes and he scrubs himself quickly and then tries to rub some warmth back into his limbs with a towel. By the time he's finished he's wet all over again, with sweat, and Joanie is in the kitchen pouring bowls of cereal for Lance and Lois and Gregory. Jimmy and Edi are still asleep upstairs, the old man snoring in his quilted-off bedroom.

The boy gives Joanie a little kiss on the forehead before he heads off to the market.

You're prettier, he whispers.

Gregory, don't you dare throw that cereal at Lance! Lance, what did I just tell Gregory! She looks up at the boy. What'd you say?

Nothing. I'll see you later, sis.

Joanie squeezes his hand.

I'm glad you're back, Dale.

146

The boy squeezes back, but doesn't say anything.

At the market nothing is heavy enough. Nothing tires him out. Crates of Florida oranges and Long Island cabbages, jumbo cans of pineapples and peaches and peas. They're so light he could juggle them. They don't seem worth the trouble of moving from the truck to the storeroom, the storeroom to the floor. He can hardly believe people are willing to pay for them. There is nothing in the market with the real weight of a pair of milk pails, one in each hand, or a bale of hay as big as he is. Nothing that could possibly exhaust him, so that when he goes home he will be able to sleep through another night of his mother and the old man. Even though he pulls nine hours—he was only scheduled for four—he still feels he could run a half marathon. Not that that would do him any good. His mother has already told him he won't be taking up that foolishness when school starts in the fall. The family needs his earnings from his job at the market and he won't be taking time off for practice. His earnings to-day consist of a bag of oranges. Seven of them. Mr. Krakowski, the produce manager, knows that there are eight children in the Peck household, but he doesn't know Duke has joined the marines. Sorry Dale, he says with a smirk when he pays him. Guess someone's gonna have to share.

And now he cannot walk home slowly enough. For a year and a half he ran from one task to another on the farm, never enough time to get everything done in a day. Now he doesn't know how to stretch out the minutes, the blocks. Before he knows it he is standing in front of his ridiculous house. In a street of identical single-story rectangles sided in asphalt shingles, the one-and-a-half story wooden octagon his family lives in juts out like a guard tower on the edge of a prison wall. The house had been Brentwood's first school, years and years ago, before they built the modern brick building around the corner on First Street. It had been falling apart even before his family moved in, suffered from its middle-of-the-last-century construction: no electricity, no plumbing or gas, no interior walls. Just one room with eight sides, each a little bit shorter than a regular-sized couch. Over the years, in brief fits of sobriety, the old man had built the kitchen and bathroom wing, turned the attic into a loft for the kids, plumbed and wired it, even built the garage, and it occurs to the boy as he turns up the driveway that the old man must have some natural ability besides drunkenness. The materials he worked with were cheap and not particularly sturdy, but they're still standing after more than a decade of hard use. The appliances work, and the fixtures. At some point the old man must have showed a lot of promise, the boy thinks, even as he gets ready to climb up the soft incline of the shade tree that has lain in front of the garage door ever since the old man cut it down five years ago. Five good-sized saplings have sprung up from the base of the tree. They ring the stump like candles stuck into the edge of a birthday cake, and even as the boy pushes them out of his way he remembers how one of the cedar fenceposts he'd planted with his uncle last year had sprouted up the same way. As soon as he saw them his uncle sheared off the saplings with a hatchet. Let it keep growing, he said, and it'd pull your whole fence down. The fencepost had put out seedlings all through summer and fall that his uncle had diligently excised until the frost set in, and the following spring—this spring, the boy reminds himself, just a couple months ago—it had admitted defeat. That's what you want, his uncle had said. You don't want it to grow. You just want it to *be* there.

The boy is climbing onto the slanted trunk when he sees a red plastic ribbon tied around one of the saplings, and even as he is fingering it he realizes he saw several such ribbons on his walk home. He looks over at the big tree in the Slovak's yard next door, notes first that there is a ribbon tied around its water heater–sized trunk and then that it is an elm, and then he looks further up the block. Almost every yard has an elm in it, and every elm is belted by a bright red ribbon. The boy doesn't know what they're there for but he knows it can't be good news.

The boy pushes the saplings aside, mounts the slanted trunk and works his way up the rough bark from branch to branch. About halfway up the trunk one of its branches lies alongside the window to the loft, and the boy, following Duke's example, has often used it to sneak out at night, and sometimes, as now, to sneak in. But today he needn't have bothered. Gregory and Lance are upstairs playing with a set of Lincoln Logs, and they scream when the boy crawls through the window, abandoning their tiny unroofed cabin to jump up and tackle him, almost tumbling him back out the window. The boy barely has time to set down his bag of oranges before they knock him to the floor, and he is lying beneath them pretending to be pinned when his mother's voice cuts through the warped plywood the three boys are piled on.

All right, enough-a that nonsense. Get on down here.

She doesn't say his name but she doesn't have to.

We got him Ma! Gregory calls. We got him pinned!

I can hear that honey, but let him up now. He's got work to do.

The boy kicks off his shoes before heading downstairs. He takes the bag of oranges with him, so he won't have to come back up for it. The first person he sees is Jimmy, sitting at the kitchen table in Gregory's stool. His mother is sprawled on the couch with a *True Confessions* in one hand, which she rolls up and points at the bag.

What do you got there?

The boy gives her the bag and she sits up and dumps it out on the floor, using her magazine like a shepherd's staff to keep the oranges from straying too far, then counting them. She counts them twice, touching each orange with the tubed magazine as if she were conferring benediction or playing duck-duck-goose, then looks up at the boy.

What, you couldn't wait until you got home, eat with your family?

The boy doesn't say anything.

Well then. Since you already had yours. She picks up an orange. We'll say this one was Duke's. The sharp nail on her thumb punches through the rind and peels off a section.

Jimmy, come get you an orange.

Jimmy doesn't get up from the table.

Thanks Ma. Not hungry right now.

His mother pops a fragrant segment of fruit into her mouth.

Suit yourself. Now then, she says, pausing to spit a couple of seeds into her palm. Listen up. There's gonna be some changes around here. With Duke gone. You're gonna have to pull your own weight around here. No more sneaking in and out the upstairs window thinking I don't hear you, thinking you can hand out your little oranges and bananas to your brothers and sisters to get them to do your chores and such. That stops right now.

The boy still doesn't say anything. Just stands there and watches his mother rip his orange into pieces and devour it. He *had* been going to give them to his brothers and sisters, but not in exchange for doing his chores. But now the first orange is gone, just a few fragments of peel on the floor and a handful of seeds in his mother's left hand, and the rest are piled up between her feet where she sits on the couch.

Additionally, she says, you're gonna start going with Jimmy when he collects your father's pay.

The boy turns and looks at Jimmy, who refuses to meet his gaze. He turns back to his mother.

But Ma—

The magazine catches him full on the side of the cheek. It's not that he doesn't see it coming—his mother is heavy and slow, and sitting down to boot—but he knows dodging will just lead to worse.

Don't you sass me unless you want the real thing. She smacks the other cheek for good measure. Now. It don't do no good for just one of you to go tramping through the Barrens trying to find that drunk. Maybe you'd like it if I sent one-a your sisters?

She points at him with the rolled-up tube. It is only inches from his face. So close he can smell the ink. And you might think he'd have to fight back the urge to hit her, or flee. But it's the opposite. He is so rigid he thinks he will fall over—fall into the tunnel of her magazine and disappear into its well of words.

Good boy. Now get on out there and find him. Six oranges ain't gonna feed seven kids no matter how you slice em.

Isn't Dad working right now?

I called Billy, he said he never made it in. Now stop wasting time and get out there before he drinks up his whole paycheck. The boy continues to stand there, and his mother waves the magazine in front of his face. What, you want me to get the hose? What're you waiting for?

The elm — the shade tree.

His mother half raises the magazine.

I swear to Christ Dale, don't make me get off this couch.

The shade tree. It's got a ribbon tied on it. There's one on all the elms in the neighborhood. Do you know what they mean?

I don't know nothing about no ribbons. Now get out of here, unless you want me to get the hose. Get!

As they leave Jimmy grabs an orange from the pile on the floor and eats it as they walk toward the Pine Barrens. He peels the rind back like a candy wrapper, exposing the globed top of the orange and biting into it, spraying juice on his cheeks and hands. The boy isn't sure if the sucking noises he makes are meant to be lewd, or are simply greed, or hunger. The boy knows his parents think he dislikes his half brother, but they're wrong. He dislikes only the fact that Jimmy wears his mother's maiden name like a suit of armor, that he has never been strong enough to shirk off her favoritism nor smart enough to see that his beknighted status is an oppression, not just to the boy but to himself. On his own he is a happy-go-lucky sixteen-year-old in brand-new boots, and within a few blocks the two boys have settled into a silence that, if not exactly easy, is not strained either, punctuated only by Jimmy sucking on the orange and boisterously spitting his seeds into the street. Then:

You want half?

Jimmy is holding out the mangled remains of the orange, which is noticeably less than half.

No, thanks. I'll eat later.

Suit yourself.

They pass another elm. In the falling light the ribbon tied around its trunk looks like a mourning band.

They got some kind of disease, Jimmy says then.

A disease?

Yeah. Dutcher's disease, dutchie's disease. Something like that. City's gotta cut em all down to keep it from spreading.

For some reason the boy suddenly thinks of the cow that had died beneath his head from a piece of wire he'd failed to pick up from the field, and then he thinks of Dolly's last calf, marked at birth for the veal pens. And then he thinks of Gregory.

Can't they save em. Give em some kind of medicine?

Jimmy spits the last of his seeds into the street, drops the rind into the gutter. He wipes his cheeks with his hands and his hands on his pants and sticks his hands in his pockets.

Guess not. All they can do is cut em down to save the other trees. What was it like on that farm?

Jimmy's voice changes when he changes the subject. There's an edge there, but the boy can't tell if it's aggression or just nervousness. He looks over at his half brother, but Jimmy is looking down at his feet like he always does.

Why you wanna know?

Jimmy shrugs.

Just asking.

In answer the boy sticks his arm out and flexes his biceps.

It's hard work day and night. The kind of work that makes a man of you.

He brings his bicep close to Jimmy's face, as if forcing him to acknowledge the truth of what he says, or daring him to defy it. But all Jimmy does is shrug again.

Ma says farm life beats the man out of you. Says farming makes you a slave to the elements, and dairy farming makes you a slave to a cow to boot. A dairy farmer ain't no more free than one of his cows, Ma says. That's why she made your dad give up his farm and move down here.

The boy has a sudden vision of Flip Flack in the trailer behind the tractor, saying almost exactly the same thing—saying *his* mother had said almost exactly the same thing as the boy's mother had. The image of Flip orating from his perch atop a pile of tarp-covered manure fills the boy's brain in crystalline detail, almost at the same time as the realization that it is an invented image, as false as his mental picture of the dead cow he never looked at before he ran out of the hay barn that morning: Flip was behind him. He never turned around. He never saw him, just as he never saw the cow—an Ayshire? a Holstein?—after it was dead. Then he says,

What're you talking about? Ma didn't even know Dad when he had his farm. It was gone by then.

Hey, I'm just repeating what she told me. She said she only married your dad because of you, but only on condition he give up farming. Jimmy shrugs yet again, his lack of interest in the boy's father's biography apparent. Anyway, it's ancient history, right? Nothing to do with us. We weren't there, right? Or not really anyway.

The boy muddles this as they walk on. He knows the first part of what Jimmy has said is true. His mother tells him as much every chance she gets—don't you go thinking you're any better than *my* sons, you're a bastard just like they are—but the second part contradicts what his uncle told him. His uncle had said nothing about his mother's demands, had said only that the old man drank their ancestral farm away, cow by cow, acre by acre. Renunciation not for love but for drink. If Jimmy had said this to him two weeks ago the boy would have dismissed it out of hand. But in his banishment he is less inclined to accept his uncle's words as gospel. Still, what is he to do with the discrepancy?

And even as he thinks back to his time on the farm, all he remembers is hardship, struggle, a series of small failures. A life whose rhythms were indeed tailored to the ladies' needs rather than their keepers', as witnessed by the fact that the boy still wakes up at five in the morning, still gets antsy at the same time every evening. But no, he realizes, that's not true. He wakes up a little later every day—today it was nearly six before he opened his eyes, as if proof that any habit, no matter how deeply ingrained, can be eroded by the same process of repetition that produced it. But he still feels that the problems he faced on the farm were smaller than the ones down here, simpler. Surmountable. The questions Upstate had answers—all of them except the last, that is, the choice put to him by his uncle and his mother—whereas the questions down here are not even questions, but conundrums, enigmas. For example, why did his mother marry the boy's father, rather than Jimmy's, or Duke's? And why does she hold this fact against the boy, and not Joanie or Edi or Lois or Lance or Gregory? Of all my children, she has told him point-blank, you are the only one I regret. You are the only mistake. You are the cause of my lost freedom. He can understand why his uncle was hurt that the boy wanted to see his family again, but if his mother really does regret having him then why did she insist he come back? Certainly not for the occasional bag of oranges or apples.

By now they have reached the edge of the Pine Barrens, and the boy drops back to follow Jimmy into the scrub. All that grows here is the dwarf white pine that gives the Barrens its name, a tree stunted by thin sandy soil and twisted by the Atlantic winds. The occasional chokecherry is equally gnarled, and splotched with lichen and mold besides, and close to the ground is a tough sharp grass that will cut your ankles if you're not careful. That's all there is, besides the litter of brown and white paper, cellophane, empty beer and soda bottles. In the falling light the contorted shadows of the trees make the place even more inhospitable, and the fact that it is a state park seems like a bureaucratic irony. The pines are too short and sticky with pitch to climb, their needles too thin to provide substantial shade during the summer; the chokecherries won't kill you if you eat them, but they will make you sick if you manage to keep them down. The only games the neighborhood children ever play here involve hiding, or violence, or death. The boy has been in it thousands of times before—taking the roundabout way to school, to work—but never on this errand. He knows about it, of course, not so much from Jimmy as from Duke, who never lost an opportunity to deride the boy's drunken father. The Barrens abuts the back of the hospital grounds as well as two or three bars, and for the past few years it has been his older brothers' summer task to find the old man where he has passed out on his way to or from one or another of these establishments, and lift whatever's left of his paycheck from his pockets.

Don't know why she sent us out so early.

Huh?

He don't usually leave the bars till after dark. Says he feels safer looking for a foxhole when he knows nobody can see him.

You talk to him?

Sometimes. He's woken up once or twice. Sometimes we have to follow him around too, until he finally passes out. Usually we keep outta sight, but if he sees us then we gotta go into the bars with him.

I hate going in them bars.

Jimmy shrugs.

You get used to it. Sometimes Duke even gets him to buy us drinks without him realizing.

You drink?

Don't sound so shocked. I'm sixteen years—sshh!

Someone is crashing through the brush a ways ahead of them. As the boy peers through the shadows he sees they are closer to the hospital than he'd realized. Through the feathery curlicues of twisted pine limbs he can see the back of the dark building against the umber sky like a stage flat blocking out the light behind it.

Roll me over, in the *clover*—

It's Dad all right, Jimmy whispers. Your dad, I mean. Damn.

What?

He's just leaving now. Unless he took something from the supply cabinet at work it'll be a couple hours before he's down.

Lay me down, roll me over and do it again!

The boy laughs quietly.

Does that sound like a sober man to you?

Jimmy shrugs.

I'm starving.

The boy nods. He's hungry too.

Can't we just ask him or something?

Jimmy makes a face at him.

We talking about the same Lloyd Peck? He'd sell you for a bottle, Dale, and don't you forget it.

The boy's stomach rumbles audibly. He wishes he'd thought to slip an orange into his pocket before surrendering the bag to his mother. To top it off the wind's coming up as the sun goes down, and he is suddenly cold in his undershirt and bare feet. He is thinking he should have worn Donnie's letter jacket when Jimmy hisses another sshh! The old man's path has suddenly veered in their direction, and the boys duck behind a clump of chokecherries.

He's going to Jack's first, Jimmy whispers. C'mon, let's go.

The boy follows Jimmy. The sandy soil, strewn with pine needles, muffles their footsteps, but they have to watch out for fallen branches. The old man takes no such precautions. You would think he was hacking his way through the jungle with a machete.

Roll me o-o-o-ver, in the clo-o-o-ver—

He sings in a loud voice, exuberantly off-key. A voice full of self-mockery but also self-love. At some point the old man embraced his role as a drunk, and he plays the part with relish if not flair or originality, even when there's no audience around. He can stumble in at three A.M. with the best of them, the boy thinks, miss chairs when he sits down, wet his pants in his sleep and point out the stain to his own children and laugh at the pathetic spectacle of himself. He starts singing Auld Lang Syne in the first week of December and doesn't relinquish it until Valentine's Day. You'd almost think he was *Irish*.

Jimmy stops suddenly, and the boy comes up hard on his heels.

Damn it Dale! Jimmy whispers. Watch out!

Why'd you stop?

The old man answers for him. In the quiet evening the boy hears the faint sound of urine striking the trunk of a tree.

Glass clinks against glass as the old man fishes in his pocket. The urine stream wavers as the old man fumbles with the top of his bottle—Oops, a little on the shoe, Lloyd, hee hee—and then he drinks and pees steadily.

There we go, my pretty pine tree. A little drink for you, and a little drink for me.

Jesus Christ, Jimmy says. Je-sus Christ.

When he has finished the old man stows himself and stumbles

on and the boys follow him. The wet tree steams slightly in the falling temperature, and they give it wide berth.

When they reach the bar the old man stops at the edge of the forest to compose himself. It's as if he knows they are watching: he pantomimes straightening a tie, slicking his hair back in a mirror, then sets off across the back parking lot with a casual but unsteady stride, as if he is just out for an evening stroll through a slalom course. There are a dozen cars in the bar's back lot, the battered vehicles of men hiding from wives or creditors, and the old man pats the flecked chrome on the grille of an ancient enormous Packard with a coffin-shaped snout as though it were some shy Labrador come up to lick his hand. There is a clink when his hand strikes the grille, and it takes the boy a moment to realize it is the old man's wedding ring.

Jimmy walks to a fallen pine and settles down on it. His actions have the air of familiarity, as if he has sat on this tree many times before. The tree is close to the bar's dumpster which exudes a stale odor of rust and beer.

What do we do now? the boy says.

We wait. You're lucky. It looks like he got some syrup from work. They don't usually let him stay more than an hour when he's been hitting the syrup.

An hour!

Maybe an hour. Maybe two.

Two hours! I don't believe it!

Jimmy shrugs.

He's your dad.

The boy looks over at his half brother. He is sitting with his feet up on the trunk, his knees bent, untying and tying the laces of his new boots.

Do you ever—

Jimmy looks up at him sharply.

What?

The boy shakes his head.

Nothing.

Say it.

Do you ever . . . I mean, have you . . . asked Ma . . .

What? Jimmy is squinting in the dim light. His nose is thinner than ours, the boy thinks. It's not a Peck nose. Not a Dundas nose either, for that matter. Come on, Dale, spit it out.

The boy shoves his hands in his pockets.

I was just wondering, you know, if you'd ever asked Ma. Who your dad was.

Jimmy squints into the boy's face as if looking for a sign that he is making fun, one of his hands already balled into a fist. The two boys stare at each other for a long moment, and then Jimmy's face drops and his hand relaxes. He peels a strip of gummy bark off the trunk he is sitting on, wads it up and throws it into the forest.

I don't suppose it matters.

No, I guess not.

What's that supposed to mean?

Nothing. I mean, what's it matter, right?

Jimmy is rubbing his hands together to ball up the pitch that has stuck to them so he can pick it off. He rubs, and picks, and rubs, and picks.

She's a fertile woman, our ma.

The boy laughs.

That's for sure.

Thought she was done after Edi, but then she started up again with Lois.

And Lance. And Gregory.

Who knows how many more she's got in her.

A car pulls into the parking lot then, and the boys sit in silence until its driver has gone into the bar. When the boy looks back at Jimmy, he is still picking at the pitch on his hands like a zoo monkey picking at flies.

You're better off not knowing anyway. At least this way you can pretend he's not a drunk.

Jimmy pinches at his hand.

Yeah, that's probably true.

Hey, the boy says then. Hey, you wanna know something?

Jimmy continues to pick at his hands for a moment, then flings them away in disgust. He looks up at the boy.

What?

Did you know Dad, my dad was married before? Before he was married to Ma?

Jimmy peers at him, not quite disbelieving but definitely suspicious.

Think about it, the boy says. He was twenty-nine when I was born. Who waits till they're twenty-nine to get married, have their first kid?

Or the other way around.

The two boys laugh. If nothing else, they'll always have this in common.

Ma was nineteen when she had Duke, Jimmy says then. He looks up at the boy. But who cares, right? It's not our, our . . . He struggles for a word. Not our responsibility, right? Not our problem. It don't have nothing to do with us.

The boy looks at his half brother. He had been about to mention his namesake, but suddenly he can't face the thought of Jimmy saying that that has nothing to do with him either. That it doesn't affect him, doesn't matter. Because even though weeks might pass between thoughts of the first Dale Peck, the boy still knows Jimmy's wrong. He just doesn't know why.

Yeah, right, he says to Jimmy. It's just, you know, weird. To think that if things had worked out between Dad and his first wife, you know, we wouldn't be here.

You wouldn't, Jimmy says, his attention already drawn back to the pitch on his hands. What isn't weird in this family?

It's almost fully dark now. The boy can't believe Jimmy can see anything on his hand. He is just picking at them for something to do. He picks at his hands and at his shoes and then again at his hands, and neither boy owns a watch, so they don't know how much time has gone by when the old man emerges from the bar's back door. A trickle of music announces his exit, and then a faint but cheerful See

159

ya later Lloyd! and then the old man stumbles out into the parking lot. When the door slams closed behind him he stops suddenly, standing up straight and putting his hand to his chest as though he's been shot, and then he relaxes and shuffles into the Barrens.

Close one, he says, and laughs quietly and pats himself on the shoulder.

The boys hide behind the dumpster until the old man has disappeared into the trees, then set out after him. Darkness and the need for silence slow them, and the boy can hear the old man's crashing shambling progress grow farther away.

C'mon, hurry, he says to Jimmy. We're losing him.

Relax, Dale. We'll just wait and see which way he's going and then head him off.

A branch snaps under the boy's foot then. He feels it before he hears it, its springy resistance beneath his bare sole, and then the crack erupts into the dark forest like a little bomb, and when the sound fades the boy realizes the old man has stopped up ahead of them.

The boy peers through the darkness. The trees are all black spirals, like crazy straws sucking up tar, and visible only against the faint haze of emerging stars.

Who's there?

The boy looks toward the voice. That stooped shadow, wavering slightly? Is that the old man, or just a squat pine shivering in the breeze? The boy can't tell.

Vernon, the old man calls. That you?

The boy wants to ask who Vernon is but doesn't risk speaking. But Jimmy seems to understand, and shrugs an I-don't-know.

Vernon? the old man calls again. Come on, Vernon, don't be sore. I was only joking back there.

A gust blows a few blades of grass over the boy's foot like a spider's delicate stalking, and the boy nearly jumps out of his skin. He suddenly realizes he is terrified and elated at the same time, though he has no idea why. He wants to scream and giggle both, but Jimmy has his finger over his lips.

Sshh.

Hello? the old man calls, and then: Jimmy? Is that you Jimmy? He laughs, Come on out, son, you don't have to hide from your old man.

Something happens to Jimmy when the old man calls to him. Longing and rage seem to compete in his body. His hands curl into tight fists, but his bottom lip trembles and sticks out as if he is going to cry. For the second time that day the boy thinks of his namesake, the first Dale Peck. Does he too long to hear the word *son* from a father's mouth? Does he long to hear it, and kill the man who says it?

Jimmy's breath is so loud through his nose that the boy thinks the old man must hear him for sure.

Hello? the old man calls one more time, and then a moment later he resumes walking. All righty then, he calls as he stumbles and crashes his way through the underbrush. Come and get me if you want me.

The stooped shadow was a pine after all. The old man was several feet to the left.

It takes a long moment for Jimmy to relax and then they follow the old man for a few minutes more and then Jimmy hisses, Damn!

What?

He's heading toward Carl's. He must be on a real bender. We're gonna be out here all night. Be lucky if we get anything off him at all. He pauses, looking over at the boy. It's hard to tell with just the stars and low moon for illumination, but the boy thinks Jimmy is looking at him with pity. Ma's gonna whip you for sure.

Where does the idea come from? The boy can't say. It is just there, as fully formed as a slide projector image appearing on the blank wall of his mind.

You still carry around that penknife?

What? Yeah, why?

Give it to me, the boy says. And take your arms out of your sleeves.

Wha—

Up ahead the old man's voice reaches them, faint and warbling.

Oh my darling, oh my darling—

Just do it, the boy says. And hurry it up, unless you want to be out here all night.

Who knows why Jimmy complies? The conviction in the boy's voice or the constriction of his new shoes, or the way the old man had spoken to him as if he were almost his son? He digs the little knife from his pocket and hands it over, then slips his arms out of the sleeves of his undershirt, the white fabric bunching around his neck and narrow shoulders like a scarf.

Bend down.

Dale—

Oh my darling, oh my darling, oh my *dar*ling Clementine!

C'mon hurry, he's getting away.

Jimmy bends and the boy pulls his undershirt up over his brother's face the way Gregory had done earlier in the day. He uses the long tail to knot it snugly in place, then puckers a little piece of fabric out over Jimmy's right eye and saws it off with the penknife, then repeats the procedure on the left. Throughout the surgery Jimmy stands slightly stooped, the way he does when his mother cuts his hair in the kitchen, and it's only when the boy has cut the second eyehole that Jimmy stands up and blinks several times as if he is just waking up. His father was taller than mine, the boy thinks, looking up into his half brother's covered face.

This is a bad idea, Jimmy says then, but there is lust in his voice too. A bad, *bad* idea.

The boy does his own shirt quickly. It is hard to knot the shirt over his head with his eyes covered and the knife in one hand, but eventually he does it. The shirt is like a veil. No, like a caul: translucent but not transparent. It actually seems lighter in there than it is outside, as if—yes. As if his face is submerged in milk.

Quickly, jaggedly, he cuts eye holes in the stomach of his shirt. He looks at his half brother through them. Shirtless. Hooded. Knows that he is looking at a mirror of himself. Jimmy's skinny stomach is moving in and out rapidly, his breath ballooning the shirt over his mouth with every exhale. The boys pant in unison for a moment, as though they have already done it. The knife in the boy's hand is slippery and wet as if already coated with the old man's blood.

Oh my darling, oh my darling, oh my *dar*ling Clementine!

They seem to know not to speak, so instead they scream, their hyas! and whoops! and hi-yees! gradually melding into the Indian battle cry favored by suburban kids all over the nation.

Woo-boo-boo-boo-boo-boo-boo-boo, woo-boo-boo-boo-boo-boo-boo-boo!

They tear through the Barrens, scaly branches lashing at their bare chests with a pain that is luxurious, energizing, liberating. The boy imagines blood streaking down his chest and ribs, painting him like a true redskin. The fallen tree he leaps is the body of his brother brave, murdered by the white man ahead. He will avenge this and a thousand other misdeeds. He will right the wrongs of history.

The boys scream and run and whoop and holler their way toward the old man. They go faster as they get closer, their voices disintegrate into an unintelligible garble of high-pitched syllables. The boy is far ahead of Jimmy but he doesn't think about his form, about the placement of his feet or the rhythm of his breath. He isn't running a race, he is running from Vinnie Grasso and Bruce St. John and Robert Sampson, he is running after Julia Miller. He doesn't think about leaving Jimmy behind but rather about closing in on the old man, closing in for the kill. His arms fly out from his sides as though he were trying to beat back a swarm of bees, the knife still tight in his right hand, its exposed blade slicing through the air.

When he comes upon the old man it is as if he has grown three feet taller in his rage. The old man is a little thing that barely comes up to his waist, appearing suddenly out of the ground, arms upraised, mouth open, lips moving in frantic but silent supplication. The boy has time to realize the old man is kneeling just before crashing into him and rolling across a small clearing. In the night's one act of benevolence, the knife flies from his hand and disappears into the dark white sand.

The boy sits up, blind for a moment, dizzy, then adjusts the shirt over his face. He suddenly realizes the old man is screaming.

Mercy! Have mercy on an old man! Mercy, mercy!

The boy scrambles to his hands and knees. For a moment he thinks he is going to be sick and his head drops, but then the nausea passes and he looks up again. The old man is on all fours staring at him, his mouth quivering but silent. His gaze is so seeing that the boy thinks he must be able to look through the shroud covering his face. Then:

Please, the old man whispers. Please, I beg of you.

He reaches one hand out and open in front of him. It shakes in the air, the fingers spasming and twitching.

I'm just a drunk. A drunk who can't even make a fist to defend himself. Please. I beg of you. Have mercy.

And then Jimmy crashes through the trees. His foot carries the weight and speed of his sixteen years behind it. It catches the old man in the ribs and stretches him out on the sand. Immediately Jimmy is kicking him in the legs, the ass, the kidneys, his voice still screaming out of his mouth in a garble of hate and rage, and at the sight the boy finds himself running toward the old man on his hands and knees like a dog toward a downed deer. Still on his knees, he plants himself beside the old man and pummels his face. The old man curls himself into a ball, his face buried in his hands, his voice a constant stream of Stop! Stop! Stop! Stop! Stop! Stop! Stop!

And suddenly they do stop, the boy kneeling and panting at the old man's head, Jimmy standing and panting at the base of the old man's spine. They have not hit him particularly hard, or long. The old man is still conscious. He remains curled up with his face in his hands, his voice subsiding into a thin wordless mewl.

Down at the other end of him, Jimmy bends slightly, rests his hands on his knees. The boy too is suddenly exhausted. His rage is gone, even the memory of it fading. The old man looks so small on the ground, smaller than Lance or even Gregory, and the boy wants to do nothing so much as lie down beside him and sleep.

Jimmy comes down on one knee heavily, flips open the old man's jacket, reaches for the wallet in the inner pocket. There is a bottle there as well, and he throws it into the trees before taking the money from the wallet and replacing it in the old man's pocket, and then he folds the old man's jacket closed again, as if closing up his chest after surgery. He sits back on his heels. The shirt over his face is stuck there by sweat, taking on the shape of the skull beneath the skin. The money is a thin sheaf of bills in his right hand, and the boy stares at it in incomprehension. Is this what they were after?

He is still staring at the money when it, and Jimmy's hand, floats upward. Why is it floating? The boy's mind cannot process even the simplest information: it takes him several seconds to realize Jimmy is pointing at him with the hand that holds the money, several more to realize why: the shirt over his head has come unknotted, exposing the right side of his face. It is at that moment he realizes that the old man is not in fact whimpering wordlessly.

My own boy. My own and oldest boy. My one and only boy.

Holding the shirt in place with his left hand, the boy stumbles up and out of the clearing, Jimmy hard on his heels. They run without direction until suddenly they burst out of the Barrens onto a street—Sixth, the boy sees when they reach the first corner. There are no streetlights and only a few houses, so the street is nearly as dark as the forest. The boys tear off their shirts and stuff them into a trashcan in front of one of the houses. For a moment they look at each other's uncovered faces as Adam and Eve must have looked at each other after eating the fruit of the tree of knowledge, and then they make their way home.

They have walked all four blocks and are turning the corner onto Second before either speaks. Then Jimmy says,

What'll we tell Ma? About the shirts?

Tell her we got in a fight. Tell her I ripped yours.

She'll whip you sure.

She'll whip me anyway.

But it is later than they thought: their house is dark, and the boys climb up the fallen elm and sneak in through the loft window. Before they do, the boy pulls the ribbon off the elm sapling and stuffs it in his pocket. Upstairs, he and Jimmy pull off their pants and pull on fresh undershirts and climb onto opposite sides of the bed. Lance and Gregory sleep in the center of the bed, Lance already slipping into the crease between the mattresses, Gregory's arm thrown over him in a proximate transfer of affection. The boy and Jimmy lie down and turn their backs to each other.

The boy doesn't know what time it is when his mother's voice awakens him. Eyes still closed, he flinches, warding off a blow that doesn't come. When she speaks again, he realizes she is downstairs.

If you just wait a moment, officer. I'll get him.

When he opens his eyes he sees that it is still dark. He looks at the window across the room as he listens to his mother's heavy tread on the floor below him. The ladder rattles against the side of the loft, then creaks as she puts her foot on the rung. He could push it down before she got up here, but she would just stand it up again. He could probably make it out the window too, but then what? He is in his drawers, the police are downstairs. Even if he didn't dress, just grabbed Duke's cutoff pants and bolted out the window, they would beat him to the base of the dead but still condemned elm tree — twice tried, twice convicted and sentenced to death. And so he just lies there, listening to his mother mount the ladder behind him. The back of his head is only a few feet from the ladder and he imagines he feels her breath on the top of his head when her face clears the floor. But it is just her hand. Her finger, which she jabs into the crown of his skull. She hisses,

Get up!

He turns and looks at her. She is in her nightgown, her brown hair thick and curly and wild around her face, the gray strands catching the light from downstairs and glinting as though sparks were being generated by the malevolence of her mood. Nothing tempers the loathing in her face. Her nose is wrinkled, her lips curled back as though assaulted by a noxious odor. Her finger reaches out again and pokes him right between the eyes as though he were a dead mouse on the bed.

Hurry it up. The officers don't have all night.

By the time he dresses and gets downstairs she has taken her place on the couch. Two police officers stand just inside the closed door, thick and shapeless in their dark uniforms. There is an impatient expression on the face of the taller one, a bored look on the shorter, but there is something else on both their faces as well. A look of distaste, and something else. The policemen stand as close to the room's exit as possible, their hands in their pockets and their eyes focused determinedly on their shoes.

The policemen aren't unfamiliar to the boy—they have brought the old man home on more than one occasion—but for some reason he has never been able to remember their names. Even now, approaching them as slowly as possible in the tiny room, he reads their nametags and the names there disappear from his brain as if wiped away with an eraser. Then a sound distracts him, and he looks over and sees the old man curled in a corner of the room, half concealed by the couch and muttering to himself. He could be cowering or just sleeping. Both are possible. Both have happened before.

I'm sorry to keep you waiting, officers, his mother says then. But I thought the boy should see this. Let it be a lesson to him.

The officers look at his mother and then they look at the boy and then they look at their feet again, and the boy realizes the expression on their faces is shame.

I'm worried, you know, his mother continues. He's been a thorn in my side since the day he was born. Disobedient. A troublemaker. Getting held back in school.

Once—the boy starts.

You shut up! His mother's finger, the finger that had just awakened him, shoots straight out from her shoulder at the end of her arm. It flies across the room and pierces his throat, stealing his voice.

You see what I mean? she says, lowering her arm. The boy has to learn his place or he's going to turn out just like his father. She settles back on the couch. Don't let me keep you from doing your duty, officers.

The policemen stand by the door a moment longer. The taller one shifts his weight from foot to foot. Then the shorter one shakes his head and says under his breath,

Criminy. Lloyd! he says then, louder. Lloyd, c'mon. Wake up.

The old man waves a hand at the offending noise as though it were a fly tickling his ear, or a cat, or a child.

Lloyd, the shorter policeman says, starting across the room. C'mon now. Time to wake up.

The old man is waving his hand again when the shorter policeman grabs it and turns him roughly onto his back. His face, the boy sees, is puffy and red, his left eye slightly swollen and purple.

Let's go, Lloyd. We been here long enough as it is.

The boy looks over at his mother then. She is staring at him with a look of deep and abiding satisfaction on her face.

Don't be looking at me, she says. Look at your father. Look at what's in store for you.

But the boy isn't looking at her. He is looking at the pile of orange peels between her slippered feet. It looks as though she ate the whole bag. When his mother sees where he is looking she kicks the peels beneath the couch.

The boy figures out what's going on just as the shorter policeman grabs the old man by the lapels and pulls him into a sitting position. They have dragged him home and roughed him up before, threatened to lock him up if they find him sleeping in the Barrens or on someone's front lawn one more time, and in the past his mother has screamed at them to stop. But tonight, the boy realizes, tonight his mother has asked them not to stop but to wait. Wait until she could get the old man's eldest son out of bed. Not so they could arrest him for beating up his own father, but so he could watch the policemen do it too.

Still holding him by the lapels, the shorter policeman administers a couple of slaps to the old man's face.

How many times, Lloyd? How many times are we gonna have to go through this? This routine's getting old, Lloyd, how many times are we gonna have to go through it?

The old man makes a face and twists his head back and forth like a baby refusing food. His eyes and mouth are pinched tightly shut.

The shorter policeman smacks him again. Huh, Lloyd? Answer

me, how many times are we gonna have to drag your ass in off the streets?

Sleepy, the old man says then, still trying to twist his face away from the shorter policeman's blows without opening his eyes. Just lemme sleep.

That's what I'm saying, Lloyd. Why can't you sleep in your own bed instead of making us pick you up off the streets and drag your sorry ass back here week after week? We're tired of it, Lloyd. We got better things to do with our time. *Open your goddamn eyes when I'm talking to you, Lloyd!*

The shorter policeman administers a particularly vicious smack and the old man's eyes open. He stares up into the face of the shorter policeman with wide uncomprehending eyes. On the couch, the boy's mother sits back and pulls one of the cushions into her lap. She is staring at the boy and it seems to him that she is fighting to keep a smile off her face.

What's this? the shorter policeman is saying now. Looks like you got a bit of a shiner coming on here. Looks like someone got to you before we did. Huh, Lloyd, someone get to you before we did?

The old man blinks, swallows, but doesn't say anything.

What's that, Lloyd? the shorter policeman says. I didn't catch that. Got in a brawl with one-a your bar buddies? Or maybe someone dished out a bit of street justice, Lloyd? Someone else as sick of your drunk bullshit as we are? Huh, Lloyd? When the old man still doesn't say anything the shorter policeman shakes him by the lapels. Answer me, Lloyd. He presses his finger into the swelling around the old man's eye. He pushes his finger right into the bruise as though it were a rotten apple. Huh?

Mercy! the old man screams then. Mercy, please, have mercy! He flails out of the shorter policeman's grip and crawls away from him along the wall. Mercy, please! I beg of you!

For a moment it looks as if the shorter policeman is going to let him go. The old man crawls a few feet and the policeman watches him go with his hands on his hips. But then, almost casually, he begins walking along behind him.

Mercy, Lloyd? the shorter policeman says. We'll show you some mercy. As soon as you start acting like a man. When are you gonna start acting like a man, Lloyd?

The shorter policeman ambles along beside the old man as though he were out for a Sunday stroll. When, occasionally, he kicks the old man in the hip or ribs, it is as if he is returning a stray soccer ball to boys on a field.

Huh, Lloyd? When are you gonna start acting like a man? Take care of your wife, set a good example for your children? Huh, Lloyd, how long do *they* have to wait?

When he kicks the old man, the old man bounces off the wall and keeps on crawling. His jacket, split along its back middle seam, falls open around his torso like a pair of broken wings. His left shoe is missing, and a dirty gray sock hangs off his foot like a half-shed skin. Mercy, he says, but quietly, quietly. Have mercy, please.

And of course the room is an eight-sided circle: the old man crawls along, the shorter policeman kicking him occasionally, his head hanging below his shoulders, and when he bumps into a corner he turns to the right and keeps on crawling back to where he started. The boy is in the center of the room, and he turns slowly, following the old man's progress with his whole body. Around the kitchen table, behind the bed, and so on to the front door, where he bumps into the motionless legs of the taller policeman. For a moment he seems almost to be sniffing at them like a dog, and then he sits back on his heels and stretches his arms up toward the taller policeman's face.

Mercy, my good sir! I beg of you, show a poor man some mercy!

The taller policeman takes a step back from the old man, then stares down at him with his lips parted in a grimace, his head shaking back and forth. The old man's arms waver asynchronously, like the antennas of a grasshopper, and even as he sits there with his hands upraised a dark stain spreads out over his crotch and down the legs of his pants.

Mercy, sir, he pleads quietly. I beg of you.

The taller policeman licks his lips as though he has eaten something foul. Inside his pockets his hands are clenching and unclenching. The old man's urine trickles to the floor audibly.

Aw, Jesus Christ, the taller policeman says. C'mon, Sal, let's get the hell outta here before I throw up.

My own boy, the old man says as the taller policeman steps back and pulls open the door. His hands are still upraised, his urine a blotchy-winged butterfly staining the legs of his pants. My only boy. Thank you for your mercy.

The shorter policeman steps around the old man and heads out the door. Before he goes he says, Next time it'll be the lockup Lloyd. But his heart's gone out of it. He nods goodnight to the boy's mother and pulls the door closed behind him when he leaves.

The old man sits on his haunches for a moment, and then all at once he folds over, his torso on his knees and his arms stretched forward as if he is prostrating himself before his god. His face is in the puddle of his own urine, and his voice emerges wet and muffled beneath his flesh.

My own, my one and only boy.

The boy just stares at him. He does not know what he feels. He is so overwhelmed by emotions he feels numb, but then suddenly one thought emerges clearly:

He wishes he had never left the farm.

Isn't it funny, he thinks, how when he was on the farm he missed Long Island, and now that he's on Long Island he misses the farm? Isn't it funny?

The first blow is hot and wet. As if she has sprayed lighter fluid on him and lit it at the same time. The next catches him in the palm of his hand when he turns to ward off the blow. The metal coupling at the end of the hose bites deeply into the palm, and, despite himself, he screams. He turns then, protecting as much of his soft parts as possible, offering up instead the broad plain of his back.

Good for nothing sonofabitch. Goddamn worthless piece of Upstate trash. I never should-a married you! I should-a lived on the streets and raised my three orphans in the gutter rather than subject them to you! Goddamn you Lloyd! Goddamn you for ever and ever!

She is beating at him with one hand and ripping at his undershirt with the other, and because she is so close to him she can only catch him with the root of the hose and so it doesn't really hurt. But then her fingernails dig so deeply into the fabric of the shirt that they rip right through, and she pulls it up and over his head. When the white fabric covers his face the boy suddenly screams.

I'm sorry Dad! I'm sorry, I'm sorry!

The hose whistles through the air, comes down on his back again and again.

You'll pay, you goddamn sonofabitch, you'll pay for what you've done to me and my children!

I'm sorry Dad. I didn't mean it, I'm sorry!

Again and again the hose comes down on his back. Again and again the boy calls out, begging for forgiveness.

I'm sorry! I'm sorry, I'm sorry!

Then, all at once, it stops.

The boy remains bent over his knees for a moment, then lets himself fall over to one side. His arms are still upraised, the undershirt still over his face. Through the opening at what should be the bottom of the shirt he can see his father, asleep on his side. Then a shadow darkens the shirt.

Take a good look, she says. Take a good long look at your future.

He doesn't move until the lights go out and he hears her settling into bed, and then all he does is pull the shirt off his face. He waits until his mother's snores penetrate the thin screen of quilts before standing slowly, his back so sore that he cannot straighten completely. He stands there for a moment, his back hunched, fighting back a wave of nausea. His mouth stretches open as dry heaves seize his body, nearly knocking him over, and the old man lies on the floor in front of him with his hands pressed between his wet thighs, looking for all the world like something the boy has retched up.

When the nausea passes the boy eases outside. The ocean air is wet and cold on his stomach, but his back is burning, burning with a heat so intense he wants to cry out. But the heat is also familiar somehow. It is the heat of the cow he killed, the boy thinks, come back to remind him of all the reasons he couldn't stay on the farm.

He looks around for a moment, wondering where to go, then heads toward the garage. He has to duck under the fallen elm to get to the side door. His father had built the garage in an industrious week five years ago. He had avoided his cough syrup and limited himself to occasional shots of whiskey in coffee throughout the process, working every morning after he got home from work and keeping at it well into the night. On the night he finished though, he had gone out to celebrate, and when he got home in the wee hours of the morning he announced his presence with an axe. The family had awakened to the sound of the old man chopping down the elm tree that grew in the front yard. One by one they had stumbled out to see what was going on. It was a precautionary measure, the old man said, to keep it from falling on the garage. His mother was afraid it was going to fall on the house, but what can you say to a drunken man with an axe? Duke was the only one of them who might have been big enough to do anything, and Duke just laughed and laughed. The rest of them had stood there and watched the old man chop until, with a crack like a thunderbolt, the tree had gone down. For a drunk the old man had pretty good aim: one branch took out a window, another knocked a hole the size of a man's fist in the roof, but that was the extent of the damage. The tree fell directly in front of the garage door, and there it stayed. Forever.

Inside the garage, the only light comes through the solid and broken panes of glass in the door. It takes a while until the boy's eyes adjust to the gloom, and then he walks to the car that has been trapped in the garage ever since it was built. He cracks open the driver's side door and leans across the seat and pulls from the glove compartment one of the three bottles of the old man's cough syrup he hid there when he got back from the farm. He uses the bottle as the old man had used the axe, except the boy breaks out the remaining panes of glass in the garage door. There are eight left. As many children as there are in the family, if you still count Duke. The boy smashes the panes one by one, pausing until the echoes of one pane of glass falling to the ground have faded before going on to the next, half expecting someone to come out and stop him, or for the bottle in his hand to break. But no one comes and the bottle doesn't break and after he has knocked out the eight panes of glass he throws the bottle on the earthen floor of the garage, but it only bounces a couple of times and rolls against the wall opposite the garage door.

The boy stares at it a moment. It gleams in the light, as benign as a tiny spool of wire. But the boy knows what even one piece of wire can do, so he walks over and picks the bottle up. It only takes a moment for his hand to remember what his brain has forgotten. The shape of it, the heft. The warmth against his palm. The bottle is wet in his hands and at first he thinks it has come open but then he realizes it's his blood. His hand is bleeding, though whether it was cut by his mother's hose or by one of the panes of glass he doesn't know.

It's the blood he's after, at first. His own blood. He licks it first from his hand and then from the bottle itself, and as he licks it he cannot stop himself from thinking again that the bottle is like an udder in his fingers, eager, insistent, desperate to be drained. Even before he unscrews the lid he is aware that it is milking time. Dawn's early light glimmers through the broken panes of the garage door as his hands do what they have been trained to do at this hour, twisting open the bottle and bringing it to his lips and holding it there until it is drained. The boy burps when he finishes. His breath comes out of his mouth in a ball of fire, and finally, finally burns away the world.

PART 2

SOMETHING ABOUT SNAKES.

In the garden.

Garden snakes? No. No, but they *were* green.

She could almost see them in front of her, their pointed heads poking a few inches out of the earth. Snakes as green as grass, dozens of them, scores, hundreds, their green heads sprouting from the ground in a grid as neat as an orchard grove.

Sprouting? Grass? Grove? *Something* about planting, growing. Planting snakes, growing them—*what?* She can see them in front of her, practically hear them calling her. *Gloria . . . We're waiting . . .*

And then it hits her: the asparagus. The asparagus would be ready today. Should be ready. *Finally.*

The shock of her old room after a month at Justin's: when the girl opens her eyes the sloped ceiling seems practically pressed to her nose, the tattered map of the heavens stretching out on either side beyond her peripheral vision. Of course, without her contacts it's a little blurry, a field of midnight black and blue. But she culled the map from a *National Geographic* when she was twelve—the same eight pieces of tape have been holding it up for a decade—and she doesn't need to see it to know what it depicts. The hemispheres, the relative size of the planets, the faint spatter from an exploding Diet Coke like an extra constellation between Sagittarius and Scorpio.

July 19, 2001. Sun in Cancer, cusp of Leo. By rights the first crop of asparagus should have been on the table last month, but spring was late this year, late and dry and cold, and she hadn't even cut back the feathery bushes until two weeks ago. In the time since then the stems seem to have grown thicker rather than taller, and even if they haven't pushed through their protective straw matting she's going to have to harvest them in the next day or two, or they'll end up tough as the pit-trap stakes they resemble. Or snakes. Pale green snakes, hiding just beneath the straw. But tasty snakes. She's been wanting to try a recipe Justin's mom gave her for barbecued asparagus all summer, but at this rate her crop is going to end up *in* the fire rather than on it.

It's hot enough today, though, especially up under the eaves. The sun beats against the checked blue curtains, which seem to fade visibly beneath its onslaught. Too hot to sleep, too hot to stay in bed. The girl sits up languidly, pulls on yesterday's cutoffs, exchanges Justin's old T-shirt for the white halter top with the blue embroidery on the sides, the one he calls her hippie halter top but loves anyway, she knows—knows from the way he comes up behind her and wraps his arms around her, folding them one over the other on the slice of bare skin between the halter top and her shorts. *Hey, hippie chick,* he says whenever he does that, *how's about giving me some-a that free love?*

She sorts through the jumble of brushes and combs and picks and products on top of her dresser, the endless bottles and tubes of mousses and gels and sprays that seem to proliferate like buildings in a crowded city—and this is just the stuff she left behind when she moved out. Sort of moved out. Whatever she did. At any rate all she wants is a hair tie, but though she finds loose coiled hairs in plenty there's no sign of a rubberband amid the skyline of beauty products. How *can* one person have so much hair? she thinks, looking at her unruly blond spirals in the mirror. She pulls it back off her face with one hand, wonders yet again if she should cut it all off. Oh, but Justin loves it, she thinks. Loves the halter top, loves the hair. Well, what boy doesn't love long curly blond hair? Yes, but Justin *loves* it.

Something catches when she goes to pull her hand away, and she feels yet another strand detach itself from the million or so remaining on her head. Her engagement ring. Oh yes, that's right. She's engaged. Even though she's alone in the room, she blushes.

She holds the ring up, examines for the thousandth time and the first time the pale square-cut stone and the diamond-flecked loop that binds it to her hand. It seems like a particularly elegant hand for so early in the morning—hard to believe she'll be waking up with that hand for the rest of her life. She looks now at the translucent filament hanging from it. It's not the first time her hair's gotten caught in her jewelry, won't be the last either. She's always liked rings, and always had problems with them—in high school her friends joked she had more hair on her palms than a Catholic choirboy. But the engagement ring with its quarter-carat pronged setting is particularly lethal. She could make a voodoo doll with the hairs it's pulled from her scalp. By now she's used to it though, not just rings, but bracelets and necklaces. Her mother's pearls—double stranded, with an ornate gold clasp. She wore them to the prom with that black dress she lost five pounds to get into, and it was practically a sadomasochistic experience when Justin pressed her to his chest during the slow songs. An auger would have done less damage to her head. But even as she thinks that she suddenly remembers: she didn't go to the prom with Justin, but with Billy Atwater, and, a little guiltily, she untangles the hair from the ring and lets it drop to the dresser. She slips a few thin silver bangles on her wrist—three, to hear them jingle. She jingles them, then lets her hand fall to the dresser.

Billy Atwater. She can hardly bring his face to mind—when she tries all she gets is Justin's. Is that what married life will be like? The filling in of all those murky faces in your memory by your spouse's? Or is the replacement simpler? She looks around her old room again. God, it's so true what they say. It really does seem smaller since she moved out.

Meanwhile her hair's still hot and heavy on the back of her neck, and not even a barrette on the dresser. She steps into her Tevas, finds even their thin straps too constricting in this heat and kicks them off, then heads into the hall. The floorboards are worn smooth as a baby's bottom beneath her feet. She hasn't noticed that in years.

Twins! she calls, skiing her feet over the soft planks, avoiding by instinct the domed nailheads that rise a little out of the warped old wood. Christine, Carly! Have you been in my things again?

She looks into their empty room and the first thing she notices is the clock between the unmade beds. It's after ten. She whirls around then, looks in her parents' bedroom, and there on her mother's half of the crisply made bed is a rectangular outline impressed into the taut bedspread with its repeated motif of a basket of violet irises. Her mother's suitcase, she realizes with a pang.

She turns and heads toward the stairs.

Twins! she calls again. Are you guys in here?

What is it about those two? She calls them twice more as she heads down the steep narrow staircase—it's almost like a ladder, she thinks, nearly tumbling, has it really only been a month since the last time she slept here?—but it's not until she goes into the living room and pulls the rubberband out of Carly's palm-treed pigtail that they actually look up at her.

Um, sleep much? Christine says.

Yeah, what time did you get in anyway? Carly says. She makes a production of blowing away the pale brown bangs that have fallen in her face even though they barely graze her eyebrows.

The girl walks to the mirror set in the ornate Victorian hat stand by the front door, begins the elaborate process of twisting her hair into the rubberband. It takes both hands to do it, and she can't help but notice how her breasts press against the halter top when her arms lift up to frame her face. It seems slightly vulgar all the sudden, and she finishes her hair quickly and turns from the mirror.

What time did Mom and Dad leave?

Um, like *seven*, Christine says.

Did Mom do the pot thing?

Practically cymbals, Carly says, pantomiming.

Shit. I can't believe I slept so late.

How *was* the movie? Christine says, smirking. Did you even *see* it?

For the first time the girl notices the scattered magazines and piles of little bits of paper all over the floor and coffee table. The piles are color-coded, red, blue, green, black. It looks like her sisters are making confetti by hand.

Um, what *are* you doing?

Carly makes a face.

We have to make these like *collage* self-portraits for camp. It's the stupidest thing ever.

What are you guys going to be, airheads?

No, no, it's totally cool, Christine says. She reaches around behind her and holds up a big piece of glossy white cardboard. There are lines drawn on it—some kind of sketch?—but it takes the girl a moment to realize it's the twins' faces because she forgot to put her contacts in and because the white spaces of the drawing seem to be filled with writing. When she squints she realizes the sketch is based on the picture they took at the fair last year, the one they had scanned onto matching T-shirts.

Christine points with her finger: First we like projected that picture we took at the fair last year on this cardboard, you know, the one we had scanned onto T-shirts—

Christine like *totally* took her shirt off.

Christine blushes.

I had my swimsuit on.

Barely.

Anyway. Then we like traced the picture, well, not the whole picture, just like the outlines of the major color groups. It's not as easy as you'd think because your hand keeps like making a *shadow* and then you can't see the lines, and then when you *do* get it done you have to write in how you're going to lay out all your colors and whatever.

She just did it just to flirt with this boy.

Did not!

Did too!

Whatever, Christine says, blushing even more hotly. *Anyway.* After you've finished the *picture.* You cut out all your colors from magazines and glue them in *place.*

Paste by numbers, Carly says, blowing at her bangs. It's like *so* eleven years old.

And what are you, twelve?

Thirteen! the twins protest in unison.

The girl blinks.

Well, all I have to say is, if that's this month's *Redbook* you shredded Mom's going to murder you. She starts toward the kitchen then, then veers toward the stairs. What do you want for lunch anyway? she says, ducking instinctively at the third step, which is only six feet below the landing above. I was thinking I might barbecue asparagus. Justin's mom gave me a recipe.

Ew, stinky pee! the twins say at the same time, falling into a paroxysm of laughter.

Upstairs the girl rummages through half-empty drawers, eventually trading the suggestiveness of the halter top for a more demure T-shirt, orange, blousy. She tries it tucked and untucked, then decides she doesn't like the way it goes with the cutoffs and finds the ancient pair of olive cargo shorts she got at the Army-Navy in Albany. She tucks the T-shirt in and slips on her Tevas again.

I was thinking chicken shish kebabs, she says as she descends the stairs. Or beef. Onion, cherry toms, some pineapple. I think there are green peppers in the garden too. She is in the doorway to the living room. How's that sound?

Carly pushes her hair off her forehead.

What?

Never mind, the girl says. I'm going to the grocery store, I'll be right back. You want anything? she calls as she leaves the room, but they are already absorbed in their picture.

That is *so* the color of poop, Christine is saying. And it is *not* going to be *my* shirt.

A magnet in the shape of a milk bottle holds a twenty-dollar bill to the refrigerator, and the girl grabs it on the way out. Outside, it's a perfect day. Just perfect. Not nearly as hot as her south-facing bedroom, thanks to the shade of the two maples that flank the front walk and a breeze that carries the smell of phlox and manure and fresh-cut grass. Not theirs though. It looks like her father hasn't gotten to the lawn in weeks. The grass is so long it folds over and brushes the tops of her feet in her sandals. That *is* something she noticed even before she moved out, the slight deterioration in things since Brian and Darcy left. Unmown grass, untrimmed hedges. When she got in last night her headlights had glinted over something shiny in the ditch in front of the east pasture: a six-pack of empties someone must have tossed out a window. That's the kind of thing that wouldn't have lasted an hour when Brian still lived here. Either he or their father would have picked them up immediately. But with Brian gone most of her father's time is taken up with the cows and so little things slip by. The cans have been there long enough that the grass has folded over them—it looks like the ditches haven't been mowed at all this year—and the girl had fished them out and tossed them in the back seat before parking in the driveway and sneaking into the house, and when she pulls the door open this morning the first thing she notices is that her car reeks of stale beer. It's an oven too, and she rolls down the window and takes the six cans to the recycling barrel before she starts it. Or, rather, tries to.

One, two, three, *start*, she says, and turns the key on the LTD. The engine turns over easily, jauntily even, just refuses to catch, and she turns the key off, gives it a little gas. Okay, two, two, three, *start*, she says, and this time the engine coughs a little at the end of its cycle, then goes quiet again. She pumps the pedal one more time, then, Three, two, three, *start*, she says, and the engine groans, coughs, splutters, and catches. She guns it a little, pats the dash-board. That's it. That's my girl.

At the Shop-Rite in Greenville she can't choose between chicken or beef and picks up a package of each. It looks like a lot of meat for only four people, though, but then she remembers the boy, who always eats as if it's his first and last time. Okay then. Canned pineapple, two big white onions, a net bag of cherry tomatoes—why her mother only plants beefsteak she'll never know. A package of butter and a head of garlic for the asparagus. She counts the stuff in her cart. The express lane in the Greenville Shop-Rite recently went from eleven items to nine. You wouldn't think it would make a difference but it does. She still has room for salad dressing though, and she grabs a bottle of Lo-Cal Thousand Island on her way to the front of the store. And what was that spice Justin's mom told her to get for the asparagus? Thyme? Parsley flakes? Something green and—marjoram, that was it. She grabs a bottle. With the marjoram she has ten items in her cart, and she transfers them all to the baby seat as if to emphasize the smallness of her load. If the checkout girl says anything, she'll say she thought the onions counted as one thing. Like the tomatoes, she'll say, if it comes to that.

Back at home she kicks off her Tevas outside the side door. *Of course* no one cleaned the ashes from the barbecue the last time they used it, so she has to get the shovel and bucket from the living room fireplace before she can light the coals. The twins are still in the room, which is awash in bits of paper.

I thought you were making a portrait, not a mural.

Carly frowns.

"Choices," she says. She makes the quotation marks with her fingers.

Christine looks up. Looks at the girl, then at Carly. They frown in unison, then smile.

Right, Christine says, Justin called, even as Carly says, This guy came by.

The girl's eyes rally between her sisters, settle on Carly.

Who came by?

I don't know, Carly says. Christine talked to him.

The girl looks at Christine, who shrugs.

I don't know. He said he was looking for Donnie. His dad knew him or something. I sent him to Junior Ives'.

Donnie's not at Junior's today, is he? I thought he was at Walsh's.

Christine shrugs. I don't know. I thought he was at Junior's. That's where I sent him.

Right, the girl says. Dad didn't call, did he?

Carly shakes her head. He said they probably wouldn't know

anything until this afternoon. Justin called though. He said he *misses* you.

Oh, grow *up*.

On the way back out the girl grabs her mother's garden shears from the mudroom. Hercules, drawn by the activity around the grill, has stretched out in the sun on the driveway, and the girl stoops down to scratch his swollen belly.

Herc, you're a fat old man, aren't you? Yes, you're my big fat baby.

Hercules lifts his head a little, licks the girl's hand, then stretches out again. His tail thumps the ground in little puffs of dust.

The girl approaches the garden warily, as if she is sneaking up on her asparagus. As if it might shrink at her approach, a defense mechanism like a bull snake's feigning death. Her dream flashes in her mind again and she shudders, almost afraid to unlatch the gate. When she does she disturbs a rabbit—in the carrots, thank God.

As she walks down the rows she can't help but think the garden looks a little ragged this year. Just like the lawn. The earth under her bare feet is dry and flaky—it must have been a week since it was watered—and the weeds in the onions are taller than the onions themselves. The radishes weren't replanted the last time they were harvested, and what was that, two weeks ago? She was home for dinner that night—it was the last time she was home for dinner—but she can't quite remember when it was. The two hollow rows look like a pair of parallel mole tunnels, half collapsed. Actually, she sees when she gets closer, one of them *is* a mole tunnel. Her mother would go *ballistic* if she saw that. The three of them used to be so diligent about the garden. She and Darcy and their mother. But it seems like her mother went at it half-heartedly this year, alone—planting late, tending haphazardly, not bothering with any of the flower borders she and the girls used to set down every spring. Now there are only a few marigolds that managed to reseed themselves from last year. The geraniums are still wintering on the sun porch and the pink and purple impatiens the girl picked up from Story's nursery hang off the fence where she left them a month ago, stifling in their white plastic pots. The only thing that looks healthy are the wild pink roses that cling to the supposedly rabbit-proof fence—*not!*

But her asparagus is fine, she thinks. A few scattered green tips actually poke through the straw bedding. Not as many as she'd like maybe, but when she peels back the straw she sees there are dozens more hiding just out of the sun. More than enough for lunch, especially with only five at table.

It's a funny thing, harvesting asparagus. Delicate and brutal at the same time. Like an operation. First you peel back the straw carefully so you don't snap the stalks in the middle, but then you drive a pair of garden shears right into the earth at the base of the plant to sever stalk from root. The metal blades grit against the grains in the dirt with a faint sound that sets your teeth on edge if you think about it, and the girl tries not to think about it, peeling and cutting, peeling and cutting, laying the stalks out on the ground like a picket fence. It's like an operation, she thinks, like cutting ribs out of the scarecrow's chest, and suddenly the girl drops the shears to the ground and presses the back of her hand to her mouth. Her left hand, of course. The one with the ring. How *could* she have overslept, today of all days? Gone out to that silly movie with Justin and then slept straight through to ten o'clock as if she hadn't a care in the world?

She gives herself a moment, half sadness, half reproach. She has no idea why she's so upset. It's not like it's a serious procedure. What was the word her father used? Precautionary? Exploratory? But still. She could've at least dragged herself out of bed to have breakfast with her mother before she went to the hospital. When she's caught her breath she takes her hand from her mouth, looks at the ring again. The finger it's on is flecked with dirt. It doesn't look elegant as much as it looks like a banded bird leg, a tag to remind her that no matter how far she migrates everyone will always know where she belongs now.

She takes a deep breath then, finishes harvesting the asparagus. One of her mother's old bandannas is knotted and hanging on the gate, and the girl unties it as gently as if it were a snarl in her mother's hair and smoothes it out and lays the asparagus in it and carries it up to the house that way, like a baby in its carrier. She sets the shears and asparagus down on the picnic table and is just checking on the coals when she hears gravel crunch in the driveway. Surely Donnie can't be here already, she thinks, it's not even noon. But when she glances at her watch she sees that it is in fact ten past, and then she looks up and sees a white Lincoln sitting in the driveway.

There's glare on the windshield and she can't make out who's inside. The license plate's a kind of tan noncolor—not New York. She squints, but can't make it out.

The car idles a moment, then shuts off. There is a little ticking noise as the hood immediately cools and shrinks, so distinct in the quiet afternoon she can hear the sound bounce off the wall of the dairy barn and echo across the yard. Then, slowly, the driver's side door opens and a young man gets out of the car. Thirty-something, baby blue pants, short-sleeved brown shirt. Not quite old enough for such a car, she thinks. Her first thought is that it must be his father's, and when a moment later the passenger's side door opens and an older man gets out, she nods her head. The older man is a little shorter than the younger and big around as a barrel, and his calves where they stick out from his denim shorts are white as the base of the asparagus plants she just cut. But you can see the resemblance in the softness of cheeks and nose. A fringe of beard like Abraham Lincoln's outlines the father's jawline, the son wears a soul patch beneath his lip. But give the boy some time, she thinks, his face will get as florid as his father's, as soft as a carnation past its prime.

Meanwhile, the coals aren't quite ready, and she uses the ash shovel to spread them over the bottom of the grill to make them burn faster. She's thinking she really should take the bucket down to the ash pile and dump it, but if she doesn't get inside and cut up the meat and vegetables and get them on the skewers she'll never have lunch ready for Donnie and the boy when they come in. But for the moment she's stuck there waiting for the two men, who walk up the driveway slowly. Shyly? Nervously? She can't really tell. The older man looks a little uncertain but even without her contacts she can see the big smile on his face. There is a slowness to his step that seems unrelated to his weight, as if he is trying to set his feet down without hurting them, and she's willing to bet he's bald under his brown suede cap, which is *way* too hot for a day like today. The younger man does look nervous though, and he has a hard time holding to his father's pace. He gets a few steps ahead, then drops back, then gets a few steps ahead again. He has a crewcut, and even though it looks cool she's willing to bet it's probably just because he's losing his hair too. *Men.* Justin already frets over his temples, asking her if she thinks his hairline's receding. Like the tide, she says. It'll be gone in an hour. She can feel the sun beating down on her own head, and if she had a razor in her hand she'd shave her hair off in a heartbeat.

The men stop when they are a few feet away from her, on the other side of the grill.

Hi there, the father says. He has a deep voice, as friendly as his smile.

Hi.

The son sort of waves.

There is a silence then, and the girl realizes the car's hood has stopped ticking.

We came by before, the son says after a moment. I think I talked to your sister.

The girl nods. She is putting the rack on the grill. It's a little greasy, and she tries to handle it with only the thumb and forefinger of each hand. She should probably clean it, she thinks, but it's late. The fire will kill any germs.

We're looking for Donnie Badget, the boy says now.

No, Dale, the father says, turning to his son. I keep telling you, the man who worked for Uncle Wallace is Donnie *Sutton.* Donnie *Badget* is the guy who built my car.

I thought the guy who built your car was Donnie Arnold.

The father shakes his head.

I don't even *know* anyone named Donnie Arnold. Donnie *Badget,* Dale. He built my car. Donnie Sutton worked for Uncle Wallace.

The girl watches their banter. They remind her of the twins, and she tries not to laugh. She closes the grill, takes another look at the car. Looks like a Lincoln to her.

The father sees her looking at the car.

Oh no, not that car, ma'am. That's a Lincoln Town Car. I had a man named Donnie Badget rebuild me a 1931 Chevy street rod. Real pain in my ass but he did a nice job, pardon my language. Won a prize at every car show I've taken it to.

He grins then, easily, and she grins back at him. The way he calls her ma'am reminds her of her customers at the restaurant, the ones who start out calling her ma'am and end up calling her honey by the end of the meal and press their tip in her hand rather than leave it under a saucer. *This is for you, honey,* such men say, surrendering a few wrinkled singles as if they were gold coins. *Don't spend it all in one place.*

Throughout his father's speech the son has looked around the farm. He turns all the way around, takes in the dairy barn and barnyard across the road, the garden, the garage. He spends a particularly long time examining the house, as if appraising it. She can see his eye following the line of the eave, up and around each dormer, and as his eye passes over her own bedroom window she wonders if they're just a pair of house hunters up from the city. If her grandfather were around he'd chase them away with a stick. But then she thinks, how would they know about Donnie?

Her eye is caught by the eaves again—the flaking paint, a gap where the gutter is coming unstuck from the side of the house—and then she realizes the father is holding out a picture.

There it is, at the Sedgwick County Car Show. That's the Audience Favorite trophy next to it. That's Sedgwick County Kansas, he adds.

She looks at the picture, but between the distance and the heat waves rising off the closed barbecue she can make out little more than a shiny blue blur. She really *has* to get lunch going.

She nods at the Lincoln again.

You drove all the way from Kansas? To find Donnie?

Well, actually we come down from Rochester. Every summer we have a family reunion at my uncle's house, that's my mother's brother's house up in Rochester, but this year Dale and I thought we'd come down here. Check out the old farm, see if we could track down any of my old acquaintances. Dale here actually thought Donnie was dead, but when we saw Flip Flack at the Greenville barbershop he told me Donnie worked for you, so I guess he was mistaken.

The girl smiles.

Well, he works for my father, but he's been here so long he seems like family. He's still going strong, she adds. I wish I had half his energy.

It's a beautiful farm you have here, the father says, glancing around casually. Not like the son, who seems to study everything, but like someone who already knows what he is looking at. He looks back at her. It's a hard life, dairy farming, but it's a beautiful farm you have here.

For the first time the father's words carry a hint of something other than history, a tinge of loss or maybe even regret, and despite her duties and distractions the girl's curiosity is piqued. It occurs to her that she should shake their hands, but hers are covered with grease from the grill. She tries wiping one palm on the other but it doesn't really help.

Christine said she sent you over to Walsh's.

The men look at each other.

Walsh? the father says. I think she said Ives. Junior Ives?

On 81, the boy says now, about two miles east of Oak Hill?

That's Junior Ives. I didn't realize Donnie was there.

He wasn't.

I think he's at Walsh's. It's off 32, almost all the way to Cairo.

Now that they are talking directions, the son seems to be asserting himself.

Can you tell us how to get there?

The girl is about to, but then she sees the asparagus wrapped in her mother's bandanna. The men have aroused her interest to say the least, but if she doesn't get the skewers ready lunch will never be done on time. And she's already messed up enough for one day.

It's kind of hard to find if you don't know the roads, she says, reaching for the asparagus. But he should be here in about an hour for lunch.

My father used to work with him, the son says then. On a farm over in Greenville.

Wallace Peck, the father says. Did you know him?

She shakes her head.

Well, yes, that was before you were born probably. Let's see, Uncle Wallace died in seventy-five or seventy-six, what year did I marry Pam, Dale?

Seventy-six.

Okay then, so Uncle Wallace died the year I married Pam, so he died in seventy-six, so he probably died before you were born. He had a stroke, it was terrible to see.

I'm twenty-one, the girl says after what seems like a respectful pause. She suddenly realizes she is unwrapping and rewrapping the asparagus, and sets it down on the picnic table again. Donnie's been here since I was about three. She glances at her watch. He should be here in about forty minutes.

Twenty years, the father says, and again his voice deepens with emotion. I bet he worked for Uncle Wallace for at least that long. Longer even. My God, twenty years.

The girl nods now, remembering. Her words tumble out of her mouth as she tries to speed the conversation along. I know he worked for someone just north of Greenville for a really long time. Wait, isn't that how he got his house?

Well, my uncle left him a piece of land when he died. He left a piece to Donnie and a piece to my Aunt Bess and then I guess the rest of it he just let be sold off when he died. He was going to leave it to me once but that's a whole other story. He had a stroke and he lingered for about a year I guess, never did recover his senses from what

I understand, and then he died. I come up to see him once, it's a terrible thing to see an active man struck down like that. The father pauses for a moment, then goes on. Well, then Dale here come up last year. He come up with his friend and he talked to Flip Flack who was my neighbor when I was a boy. Dale says Flip told him no one lived on the farm for a long time but then I guess a young couple bought just the house. They tore down the barn even, I guess they just wanted a place to live. I thought they cut down all the elms in the front yard too, but Flip Flack told me that was the Dutch elm disease. Said they were gone before Uncle Wallace actually, which if they were I don't remember from my trip up here to see him. The father pauses, then shakes his head. Nope, I seem to remember them being there, six of them right in a row, hundred-year-old elm trees. But Flip said they cut em down in seventy-two, seventy-three. The father shrugs. I guess the land was still for sale when Dale was here last year, but we just come from there and there's a house up on the hill at the top of the pasture now, right where I always wanted to put one. Yes, ma'am, the father says, whoever they are they've got the best view of the Catskill Mountains in the whole county, up there on that hill.

The girl nods again. She reaches for the asparagus.

Well, he should be here soon. Not even an hour. I'm sure he'd love to see you.

The son has a look on his face, like he is trying to say something nice and doesn't know how — not to her, but to his father. He looks at her hands fiddle with the asparagus, and all at once he says,

Well, if you could maybe suggest a place to eat, we could go have lunch and then come back. We stopped by the kitchen in Oak Hill but it wasn't open yet. Do you know of someplace else?

Something in his tone. It's almost plaintive — almost like his father's, when he'd talked about the farm. Her eyes fall to the tiny pile of asparagus in her hands. If nobody is greedy there'll be enough to go around.

Well, why don't you eat with us? she says. It's just shish kebobs, but there's plenty.

192

Oh, we don't want to put you out, the boy says.

The girl looks at the asparagus again, wrapped up in her mother's blue bandanna like a gift and capped by the shiny diamond of her wedding ring. It's as if all her preoccupations—all her history—are contained in that little tableau. She's not sure if she should cook it or bronze it.

It's no trouble, she says, suddenly wanting to do this thing. I'm already cooking, all I have to do is put a couple extra plates on the table.

I feel like we're imposing—

Pipe down, Dale, the father says then. I haven't been asked to lunch by a girl this pretty in thirty years.

You've only been married to Pam for twenty-five.

Oh right. The father laughs a little. Has it been that long? Sorry honey, he says then, but the girl can't tell if he's talking to her or to his absent wife.

The boy asks to use the bathroom as they go inside and she directs him to the WC and then leads his father into the kitchen, where he immediately goes to the far side of the table and sits down.

Pardon me honey, he says. I have a little gout in my left foot, it's been acting up lately. He sits with his back against the window so he can watch her, his knees falling open, his stomach spilling between his thighs. With his thin white beard, he looks a bit like an off-season Santa.

Go right ahead, she says, puncturing the shrink-wrapped package of meat with a fingernail. Can I get you something to drink? Even as her nail pierces the plastic and drives a little into the top steak, she realizes she hasn't washed her hands since she harvested the asparagus.

Well, thank you. I'll take an ice tea with lemon if you have some. She can feel his eyes on her as she takes the meat to the sink, washes the dirt from it and her hands. When she glances at him out of the corner of her eye, the smile on his face is almost beatific.

Sure. Twins! she yells. I need you in here!

The son comes in from the bathroom, still with that slightly nervous look on his face. He hesitates in the door a moment, then makes his way to the table and sits opposite his father, turning the chair around to face her.

I love your house, he says.

Something funny about the way he says it. Wistful. Again she wonders if they just want to buy it, turn it into a weekend place. Sell off the cows, tear down the barns, parcel out the land to developers — do, she realizes, exactly what was done to the father's uncle's farm. But she's too focused on the meat in front of her to give it more than a passing thought. She's made kebobs a dozen times before, but it's always been with her mother right there, not in a hospital drinking radioactive fluid. She shakes her head a little, focuses on what's in front of her. How big should the pieces be? Should the chicken be the same size as the beef? Maybe it should be smaller, to make sure it cooks through?

It's old, she says absently, the house. Then: Twins!

My Uncle Wallace had a old house too. They're hard to keep up, these old houses. Uncle Wallace kept one whole half of his house closed off just to save on heat. The father laughs. You don't need a plumber, do you?

The girl laughs too, even as she realizes the father must be a plumber.

No, I'm in Kansas now, the father is still saying. Been there for thirty years, don't do that much repair work anymore. The real money's in bigger jobs, I specialize in trenchless sewer line replacement myself. Are you familiar with that procedure?

The girl shakes her head.

I'm sorry, would you excuse me for a moment?

The girl goes to the living room, where the twins seem to have spread their collage materials over every available surface in the room and then abandoned the project. They sit side by side on the couch watching *The Young and the Restless,* the left side of Christine's calf pressed into the right side of Carly's as if they were Siamese twins, not just identical.

I need you in the kitchen, she says. Hello? *Hello?* Earth to Carly and Christine. I need some help getting lunch ready.

Christine looks up blankly.

What?

When Christine stirs, her calf flesh peels off Carly's with the same sound the plastic wrap had made when the girl pulled it off the meat. There is an identical egg-shaped patch of red on each of their legs. The girl stares at the marks for a moment, loving her sisters fiercely, then rouses herself with a shake of the head.

Kitchen, she says. *Now.*

Kitchen, Carly says. Now. She blows her bangs off her forehead. I can't *wait* till Mom gets home.

The girl hurries back into the kitchen. As she comes in, the son is registering the four corners of the room as if he is measuring it, taking stock of the crooked cabinets and warped floors, the mismatched chairs that crowd the table. The father sits with one arm resting on the table, smiling so pleasantly into the distance that she doesn't want to disturb him. She pauses in the doorway.

Sorry, she says then, then comes the rest of the way into the room. Sometimes it's like pulling teeth with those two. You were saying something about pipes?

The father nods, his smile widening so much when he looks at her that she almost blushes.

Trenchless sewer line replacement. Are you familiar with that?

She shakes her head, picks up her knife, starts cutting the meat. She decides she'll cut the chicken and beef the same or else someone will complain they got gypped.

Well, with traditional sewer line replacement you have to get out there with a backhoe and trencher and rip up the customer's lawn in order to get the old line out.

Christine and Carly finally trundle into the kitchen, then stop when they realize there are strangers in the room.

These are my sisters, the girl says. She points with the gristly knife. Christine, Carly.

Hello there, the father says. I'm Dale Peck. This is my son, Dale Jr.

The son stands to shake the twins' hands. Christine almost giggles. Then he turns to the girl.

We never introduced ourselves actually.

We didn't? the girl says, and then she gets it. Oh right. I'm Gloria. Gloria Hull.

Dale, he says.

He holds out his hand but the girl just waves her greasy fingers at him.

Carly, would you see if there's some ice tea for lunch? Christine, I need you to cut onions.

Onions!

The son sits down again, slumping just a little, then sitting unnaturally erect.

Carly pulls open the fridge.

There's no ice tea.

Well, make some, dummy. Yes, Christine, onions. Wedges, for kebobs. Oh, wait. First go see if there are any green peppers in the garden. I think I saw some yesterday.

Christine sighs dramatically, then trots down the side hall. Carly looks at the two men at the table, then up at the girl.

What should I make the ice tea in?

The fish tank, the girl says. A pitcher, duh.

I just thought—She looks at the men again.

You can always make more. Come on now, get a move on. Donnie and the boy'll be here in half an hour.

Carly bangs cabinet doors as she rummages up a pitcher, a spoon, the ice tea mix.

So like I was saying, the father says over the noise. When you replace your sewer line the old-fashioned way you have to dig up the old line, completely destroy your lawn, driveway, utilities, whatever's in the way.

The girl nods. My fiancé's grandmother had to do hers last year. It was a mess. She had a beautiful blue spruce in her front yard, the roots got so damaged Justin had to cut it down. Justin's my fiancé, she adds, and smiles.

I saw the ring, the son says, and the girl is about to hold it out to him when the father says,

Exactly. But with trenchless sewer line replacement, he continues, even as his son makes a sorry-for-the-spiel face, my men just dig one small hole at the beginning of your sewer line and another hole at the end, and then they pull a new pipe through the existing tunnel. You can pull it under anything, lawns, trees, swimming pools, garages, without disturbing what's on top. With my equipment I can even send a camera down the line, video the whole thing, show you exactly where the blockage is and how my drill bit is going to bore through it. Yes, ma'am. Plumbing's coming into the future just like everything else.

For a moment the girl finds herself imagining it. The incision, the drillhead inching down the tunnel like a mole and flashing blurry pictures on a TV. She imagines it is not unlike what they are doing to her mother right now.

The father is still talking.

Now, you've got this rocky Upstate soil here, don't you?

Hmmm? Oh, yes. Full of rocks. Stir it, Carly, don't break the pitcher.

I know it. I know this land. My Uncle Wallace's farm had that same soil. Backbreaking work just clearing a garden or laying a fence. He smiles again. Yeah, I'd have to charge you a bit extra for wear and tear on my drill heads, but I'd give you a good price. When I was finished you'd have a sewer line guaranteed for the life of the house and you'd never even know we'd been here. So when do I start?

She catches the son's eye then, realizes he is as afraid as she is that his father is serious, but then the older man laughs.

Damn, I almost sold myself.

The father is still chuckling when Christine comes back in.

Peppers, she says, dumping them on the counter and then just standing there. Two green ones, one red.

You know how to use a knife, don't you? Come on, you've helped me make kebobs before.

Who wants ice tea? Carly says.

I will, thank you, dear, the father says. Dale, want some ice tea?

No thanks.

Oh, that's right. You never did like ice tea. Too Kansas for you. Too country. My son's a city boy himself. Lives down in New York City, works as a writer.

The girl tries to smile as she cranks a can opener into the sliced pineapple.

My older brother lives down there. You'd think I'd go more often, but I never do. He wants lemon in that, Carly, I think there's a bottle in the fridge.

Ah, the son shrugs, it's not all it's cracked up to be.

My son's a very famous writer, the father says now. Perhaps you've heard of him. Dale Peck. Tell her the names of your books, Dale.

The girl dumps the pineapple juice down the sink, empties the sliced rings onto the cutting board. With a few swift strokes, she cuts them into evenly sized chunks.

Carly, grab the skewers would you?

She already has them.

Aren't you supposed to marinate the meat? In the pineapple juice?

Oh shit.

The girl looks up and realizes the son has said the names of his books and she hasn't heard them.

I'm sorry, I don't really read much besides school stuff.

That's okay, he says smiling. No one really reads them much.

You could get them off the Internet if you were interested, the boy's father says. Do you get on the Internet much?

We'll just put barbecue sauce on them, the girl says to Carly. Then, to the father: I know you're not going to believe me, but I've never used the Internet. I don't even have email. Even as she says this she is grabbing the aluminum foil for the asparagus. She peels off a big piece and spreads it flat on the counter. Christine and Carly are assembly-lining the meat and peppers and onions and tomatoes and pineapple onto skewers.

Just a country girl at heart, she hears the father say, and despite herself she makes a little face.

Just lazy really, she says, spreading the asparagus heel-tip, heel-tip on the foil. Or not interested. I'm studying to be a schoolteacher so I guess I'm going to have to learn how to use it eventually. She cuts several chunks of butter and drops them on top of the asparagus. It's the future, right?

My son teaches.

Writing, the son says. He shrugs.

That makes sense, the girl says absently. She has just folded up the foil when she realizes she's forgotten the marjoram. She unfolds the foil and sprinkles the marjoram on, adds salt and pepper and kind of crimps the foil back together. Christine and Carly have finished the skewers in record time. She glances at her watch. It's a quarter to one.

Would you excuse me? I have to get this on the grill.

Of course, of course, the father says. Smells delicious already. He smiles at her like a teenager.

Christine and Carly follow her outside with the kebobs and the asparagus.

Okay, so, like, who *are* they? Christine says as soon as they're outside.

The girl opens the grill.

I'm not really sure. I guess the dad knew Donnie or something, when they were kids.

The coals are still flaming a little, but she doesn't have time to let them burn down. As she lays the skewers on the rack the meat juice causes them to flame even more, and she has to drop the skewers from a couple of inches to keep from getting burned.

Carly laughs a little. Do you think the son's gay?

That was it. That was how the son was looking at the house. He wasn't appraising it. He was decorating it. But all she says is Oh hush.

You're too young to know about these things, and then she sets the foil-wrapped asparagus at the end of the grill, as far from the flames as possible.

Um, our own *brother*, Christine says.

And sister, Carly says.

You know about Brian? And Darcy?

Um, *duh*, Christine says. You didn't think we actually fell for that *roommate* line did you?

Like, *twice?* Carly says.

The girl shakes her head. You kids these days, she says, you're growing up too fast, but by now she is distracted by the barbecue. She's afraid the coals are too hot and everything will burn. Already butter is seeping out of the aluminum foil that holds the asparagus. She reaches for the tongs.

The phone rings inside.

I've got it! Christine says, but Carly is closer to the door. She dashes in, reappears a moment later with the cordless.

I *bet* it was fun, she is saying. Gloria didn't sneak in until *two o'clock*. She covers the mouthpiece with her hand. It's Justin, she whispers. Then, into the phone: So, how much is my silence worth to you? What? Well, just because she doesn't live here anymore doesn't mean Mom can't ground her. Huh? Oh, I guess you're right. It does.

The flames are licking the kebobs and the girl is afraid they're going to be burnt to a crisp, so she goes down the line, using the tongs to turn them over. She nudges the asparagus further toward the edge of the rack.

Give me that, she says then, grabbing the phone from Carly and passing off the tongs to Christine. And keep turning them or they'll get all black. And you, she says to Carly. Go grab the barbecue sauce and baste baste baste.

The girl presses the phone into her ear and wanders up the driveway and around the garage.

Someone stole the C again, Justin says, and she laughs.

You should just make it official. The Winter Love.

I don't think that's the kind of resort my parents want to run, Justin says, and they both laugh.

When she gets to the woodshed she dusts the cobwebs and sawdust off a low stack and sits down. Justin's voice is a low soothing drone in her ear, her own voice sounds silly and giggly when it bubbles out of her mouth. She lets him talk, and somehow she doesn't quite get around to mentioning oversleeping and missing her parents before they headed off to the hospital or the two men who are sitting at her kitchen table waiting for her to cook them lunch. She only tells him the asparagus was ready today, that she is trying his mom's recipe. When he says, Yum, I wish I could be there, she says, I wish you could be here too, and it seems like they've only been on the phone for a few seconds when Christine comes running around the garage.

It's on fire! It's on fire!

The girl panics.

I'll be home tonight, she says, practically hanging up on Justin at the same time. She runs after Christine, half expecting to see flames spouting from the roof of the house. But it's worse than that.

My asparagus!

Flames are coming out of either end of the shiny foil bundle, as if the asparagus were a flaming baton.

It just like *burst,* Carly says.

You were supposed to be watching it, the girl says, grabbing the flaming bundle and pulling it off the fire. But even as she grabs it she is thinking, I called Justin's place *home.*

You just said to turn the kebobs, Christine said. You didn't say anything about the asparagus.

The girl shakes her head.

I didn't tell you to get that haircut either, but that didn't stop you — ow!

With the tongs, she tosses the asparagus onto the wooden table, even as she swats at what feels like a bee stinging the back of her neck. Her loose hair clues her in: the rubberband has snapped, leaving her hair free to fly around her neck and cheeks and forehead.

Meanwhile the foil bundle has landed on the picnic table in a shower of sparks and now smokes desultorily. It could almost be a baked potato fresh from the oven. *Please* let it be a baked potato, the girl thinks as she pushes her hair off her face with one hand, holds the tongs in the other and prods at the foil. Just a small miracle. That's all she's asking for. Just one little act of transubstantiation.

She has to use her fingernails to pry open the blistering bundle. When she finally pulls the foil apart she sees that the stuff inside has indeed been transformed: it looks like a pile of spent logs in the fireplace, and as the girl looks at it she realizes that she forgot to put the garlic in. Her cheeks burn, and for a moment she thinks she might cry.

Oh damn it, she says quietly, and just then Donnie's truck pulls into the driveway.

She waves at him, but as soon as he gets out of the truck he trots across the road to the barn, the boy clambering out of the passenger's side and running after him without bothering to close his door. She can hear a buzzer in the cab faintly, reminding Donnie he's left his keys in the ignition.

The girl looks down at the smoking mass on the picnic table, then back up at Donnie and the boy. For a moment everything seems far away, like a painting at the other end of a gallery: the tiny rectangle of Donnie's truck, dun colored, the bigger rectangle of the barn, red and listing slightly to the east, and then the pale blue sky framing the scene on three sides and reaching out endlessly in all directions. Measured against that sky, the barn and Donnie's truck and Donnie and the boy himself seem impossibly small and fragile. What was it the father had said? *They tore down the barn. I guess they just wanted a place to live.* The barn seems insubstantial, but all at once the men in the kitchen—well, the father anyway—become hard. Real. She can see them sitting at the table as if they were right in front of her, waiting patiently for her to serve the lunch she promised them.

The girl looks down at the burned asparagus. She grabs it with the tongs and dumps it in the ash bucket with the spent coals.

Right, she says. You, and she points at Christine. Get the kebobs off the grill before they burn up too. And you—she grabs Carly by a loop of her shorts—come help me inside.

Ow, *pinching!* Carly says as she shuffles along behind the girl. Glori*a!*

As they come down the hall she can hear the father's voice in the kitchen.

Well, I don't know, Dale. I spoke to him last Friday. You know he's retired now and he says money's a bit tight but he's gonna try to be there. It sure would be nice to meet my own brother after all these years. But hell, I almost didn't come myself. Can't hardly afford to miss the work. Well hello again, he says when he sees the girl. Either the sun just came out from behind a cloud or a pretty girl just walked into the room.

The girl can't decide who blushes more: her or the son. Of *course* he's gay, she thinks. I mean, baby blue *pants?*

Looks like someone let her hair down, the father says, and she definitely blushes more than the son.

Donnie just got here, she says, pushing at her hair, rummaging through the canned goods in the cabinet. He's out in the barn, should be right in. To Carly she says, Set the table. Make sure to put out a plate for the boy. She finds a dusty can of asparagus at the back of the cabinet.

My God, the father is saying as she turns around, and she pauses, caught by the awe in his voice, the look of wonder on his face. Donnie Sutton. I haven't seen him in forty-five years. She can see the barn through the window behind him, rendered even hazier by her mother's gauzy white curtains. She can hear the son shift in his creaky wooden chair, but he doesn't say anything. She realizes then that the emotion in the father's voice is as mysterious to the son as it is to her. She has never met the father before, the kitchen table that separates her from him could as well be a brick wall. But what, she wonders, divides this son from his father?

Suddenly the father turns. He looks her full in the face but doesn't quite seem to see her.

My God.

The girl feels a blush rise to her cheeks as if she has been caught peeping.

I, I'm sure he'll be pleased to see you too, she says, practically hiding her face in the drawer as she hunts for the can opener. Forty-five years is a long time, she adds, feeling the need to keep talking against the father's blank gaze, the son's strained silence. You should have a lot to say to each other. Is there any of that macaroni salad left? she says to Christine, who is walking in with the kebobs on a platter.

How should I know?

By opening the fridge and *looking*, the girl says, brandishing the can of asparagus like a grenade. Come on, we're late enough as it is.

There's macaroni, Carly says now. And it looks like Mom made a regular salad too. Should I put them both out?

Might as well, the girl says. She is emptying the canned asparagus into a pot on the stove and trying not to think about the fact that it is the color and consistency of snot. On an impulse she cuts up a few cloves of raw garlic and drops them into the soupy mixture, sprinkles some marjoram on top. It floats in the briny liquid like fish flakes.

Is that asparagus? the son says now.

She looks up guiltily.

Yup!

Yum! the son says.

You like asparagus? the father says.

I love asparagus.

You hated it when you was a kid.

Dad, the son says. *I'm thirty-four.*

When the father nods his head, his chin disappears in a cowl of loose flesh and gray beard. The weight of time seems to be particularly heavy on his head. It takes a moment before he looks up, smiles brightly.

A home-cooked meal, he says. If I'd known I was in for such a treat when I got up this morning I'd've dressed better.

The girl smiles back at him, stirring the canned asparagus a little viciously. The colorless stalks tangle around her spoon like ropy pasta.

The screen door bangs down at the end of the hall.

Go wash up now, she hears Donnie say. His boots clump down the hall. Seventy years old, and he never has learned how to comport himself inside a house.

She steals a look at the father, sees the son is looking at him as well. He is sitting very still in his chair, a half smile set into his face like you give to a dog in a strange yard.

When Donnie reaches the doorway he pulls up short, and for the first time the girl considers the reunion from Donnie's point of view, realizes she has no idea what kind of effect it will have on him. Maybe he hated this man, forty-five years ago?

Hey Donnie, she says, trying to keep her voice light. You've got a visitor.

She realizes, again, that she has excluded the son from the scene. Donnie does the same. His eyes pass between son and father, settle on the older man.

Howdy, he says warily.

A grin cracks the father's face.

Well hey, Donnie, how are you doing?

There is a pause before Donnie answers, his voice still cautious, quiet. The girl is acutely aware of the fact that she and Christine and Carly have all stopped what they are doing and are staring at him, as is the son.

I'm pretty fine, and yourself?

Oh, I'm doing great, Donnie. Just great. You don't remember me, do you?

Donnie takes hold of the doorframe with one hand. Pinches the trim like a woman scrutinizing dress fabric, speaks to it instead of the father.

Can't say as I do, no.

There is another beat then. It goes on a moment too long, and the girl feels genuine tension fill the room. She looks at the son again, and he makes a little face at her like, *Uh-oh*. But there is a half smile on his face as well, and as the girl looks at the son she suddenly feels the drama of the moment as he must, its simultaneous uniqueness and universality, the stranger who turns out to be a long-lost friend. God, she hopes he was a friend. For a few seconds she understands what it is to feel like a character in a book, and then:

Donnie, the father says, almost chastising the man in the door.

The girl looks back at Donnie, sees him clearly for the first time in years. A tiny man, shorter than she is, with bowlegs and worn jeans that ride too low on his waist and a little potbelly that spills over his belt. He toes the floor with a boot that seems composed of equal parts dirt and leather.

Can't say as I remember you, he says to the floor. No sir, I can't.

Just then the boy appears, squeezing between Donnie's hip and the doorframe and slipping into the room and then stopping dead in his tracks. The upright bodies crowding the tiny kitchen remind the girl of something—the hair products on her dresser, crowded together like a city skyline. Now why is *that*?

A sizzle distracts her: it's her asparagus, starting to burn in the pot beneath her face. She yanks it off the stove and turns toward the sink as if she is going to run cold water on it, but even as she turns she hears the father speak.

It's *Dale*, Donnie. Dale Peck.

The way people say their names sometimes: not *I'm Dale Peck* but *It's Dale Peck*. Of course it's Dale Peck. Who else would it be?

She pauses then. Holding the sizzling pan over the sink with both hands, she turns and looks at Donnie.

Well I'll be, Donnie says then. He doesn't say it very loud. A smile cracks his face, and the girl practically sighs with relief. I'll be. It is Dale Peck.

Chairs scrape then, hands are shaken, introductions made. This is my son, Dale Jr., the girl hears even as she turns back to her pan, peeks in. The asparagus is a little dried out but not burned, she sees, although it looks a bit like something you'd eat with a spoon instead of a fork.

She is just turning back to the table when the son says,
And what's your brother's name?

Brian, what? she says, then realizes he means the boy. Oh, that's, um, that's Tommy, she says, having to think for a moment. He's not our brother, she says. He just showed up here one day wanting to work. Isn't that right, boy?

The boy's eyes dart between hers and the son's, not sure if he is being mocked.

Yep, he says warily.

I call him boy because there was another one before him, they come and go. But this one's a good one, Donnie says he works hard. Isn't that right, boy?

Now the boy looks between Donnie and the son.

Yep.

Boy, why don't you sit on that end by Christine and Carly. We'll put Donnie there next to Dale Jr.

Oh God please, the son says. Coming from your lips that makes me sound so *old*.

The girl smiles.

We do have a brother. Brian. He lives down in the city too. In Queens. She looks at the table separating the son and his father, set with empty plates and full dishes of food. Oh. *Duh*. Eat, please, she says then. Come on, it's getting cold.

Thank God for Tommy. For a moment it looks like nobody is going to touch the food, then he reaches across the table and grabs a kebob. Grabs *two* kebobs. In a moment there is the pleasant sound of forks scraping dishes, things being passed. Bowls empty, plates fill up in hourglass exchange.

The girl puts the asparagus in a bowl and brings it to the table when she sits down. The son is just to her left and she hands it to him.

Asparagus?

Love it, he says. He spoons all of two pieces on his plate, where they lie gray and limply crisscrossed like shoelaces that have come untied.

The girl pushes at her hair.

Please, eat up, she says.

Just want to make sure there's enough to go around, the son says, passing the bowl to Donnie.

Eh? Can't stand asparagus, Donnie says, handing the bowl on to Christine, who spoons some onto her plate without looking and hands it off to Carly.

So Donnie Badget, the father says then. My God.

Sutton.

What's that, Dale? Oh right, Sutton. You're confusing me. Donnie Sutton, he says again. It must've been forty-five years since I seen you.

Donnie is holding a beef kebob in both hands as if not quite sure how to eat it.

Yep, he says, raising one end of the skewer and then the other, like a seesaw, or scales. The girl is about to tell him to just bite it when she notices the son fastidiously removing the meat and vegetables from his own skewer. He removes them one piece at a time with his fork, straddling the tines over the skewer and sliding the pieces of food off the end. Tomato, pineapple, beef, pepper, onion. He slides the bits of food off his skewer and aligns them as though he were setting up a chessboard.

So Donnie, the father says now. You certainly have a nice situation for yourself. Steady work, surrounded by pretty girls. He grips a piece of chicken with his teeth and slides it off its skewer. Meals included. Aunt Bess never fed you this good.

Donnie is working a cherry tomato off his skewer with his fingers. Been here twenty-five years, he says distractedly. Bess's been dead going on twenty.

She was a good woman, Aunt Bessie.

Yes she was.

The father sets his skewer on his plate. You remember when they got married? Everybody in the neighborhood come around in the middle of the night, gave them a twenty-one-gun salute. BOOM!

BOOM! BOOM! BOOM! the father says, making the sound of gunfire so loudly that everyone at the table jumps. He laughs a little. I never been so scared in all my life. I thought the world was coming to an end.

Well, who do you think rounded everyone up?

No kidding, the father says. That was you? I thought the Russians were coming.

Would you like some asparagus, Mr. Peck?

Oh, please, please, call me Dale. Thank you, honey, I will.

It's just there to your right.

Thank you, honey, he says, spooning half the bowl absently on his plate and passing the rest on to her. Here you go. So Donnie, he says then. We drove by your house, saw two names on the mailbox. You living with someone?

You ever know Geraldine Murphy? Donnie says. She lived over in Westerlo, married to Adam Murphy?

Questions and answers come slowly, naturally punctuated by chewing, swallowing. The girl is relieved that everyone is getting along, but vaguely disappointed too. It is not exactly as *dramatic* as Donnie's entrance into the kitchen might have promised. No tears, shouts, revelations. Just bits of biography salting the meal like a condiment.

She looks around the table again, makes sure everyone is eating, then allows herself to begin.

Adam died of liver cancer, Donnie is saying now, oh, gosh, a long time ago. Geraldine and I been together a while.

Married? the father says.

Yep, finally. Lived together a pretty long while first.

Any children?

She's got two from her first marriage and then we got two boys of our own.

The father nods his head. He puts his fork down, then picks up his half-eaten kebob with both hands.

Donnie Sutton, he says just before grabbing a piece of chicken

209

in his teeth. The name seems to start and stop his memory. He chews, swallows. Still bringing in the cows. What are you, Donnie, seventy-five years old?

I'm just seventy.

The father dispatches a tomato, a piece of pineapple, another piece of chicken.

Seventy years old and you look better than I do. I'm fifty-eight.

Yeah, I guess you was about thirteen, fourteen when you lived with Wallace.

I'm thirteen, Tommy says now.

So are we, Christine says.

The girl realizes the son has not touched his food in a few minutes. He is looking at the boy sitting next to his father. There is field dirt on the boy's face, on his wrists above his washed hands. His undershirt is dirty too, and too big for him, as if it is a hand-me-down. The son is wearing powder blue pants and a cabana shirt, but he seems almost to be looking at Tommy's clothes with envy.

Would you like more asparagus, Dale?

Hmmm? father and son say at the same time. And then the son, tearing his eyes from the boy: Oh, no thank you. I'm still trying to clean my plate. Is that Thousand Island dressing?

It's the diet kind, the girl says.

Perfect. He pours some on his salad but doesn't pick up his fork.

It just about broke my heart, the father is saying now. When I had to leave the farm. Biggest mistake I ever made in my life. I tell you, Donnie, two weeks after I left I called Uncle Wallace and begged him to take me back but he was a hard man, he wouldn't do it. The father looks at the empty skewer in his hands, then licks it clean. You broke my heart, Dale.

What? the son says.

The father looks at his son.

That's what Uncle Wallace said to me. You broke my heart.

Oh, the son says. His smile seems a little sad to the girl. I thought he broke yours.

The father doesn't say anything for a moment. Then:

He did love me. He said I was the son he never had.

Donnie is nodding slightly.

I think he took it real hard that you left.

He wouldn't even let me come visit, Donnie. Only other time I saw him was after he had his stroke.

There was that time when we were kids, the son says. After Mom died. You took us to the Catskill Game Farm.

Oh, that's right, the father says. We did stop by, didn't we? He gazes off in the distance. And he didn't even invite us to dinner, did he?

The son shrugs. I think I tried to milk a cow.

The father's eyes are still soft.

It's a hard life, dairy farming. You were better off, believe me, he says to his son, as if he'd made some long-ago decision with his progeny in mind. He turns to the girl. What do you got, sixty, seventy head of cattle here?

The girl smiles, shrugs.

I think so? Eighty?

Probably pays just enough to keep it going, right?

It's not making my folks rich, that's for sure. But it sent three kids through college.

The father nods his head.

Yeah, if I'd've stayed on the farm I might've been happier but I never would've learned a trade. Would've been dirt poor all my life, never had nothing to give you kids. You can't imagine, Dale, the father says, returning to his son. I know we wasn't the richest but you can't imagine what it was like on that farm, up at four-thirty in the morning, in bed by eight, nine o'clock at night, carting milk buckets by hand, hay bales, wheelbarrels full of—

Wheelbarrows.

What's that Dale?

It's wheelbarrow. Not wheelbarrel.

There is a pause. The girl watches the father and son stare at each other for a moment. There is a half smile on the son's face, the father's too. She can see this is some sort of game they play, although she is not sure what it means.

Dale, the father says at length, emphatically. Uncle Wallace used to pull rusty nails out of old boards and drop them in a *jar*. He kept half-a that tiny little house shut up to save on *heat*.

I know, the son says, winking at the girl. You already told me. Today in fact.

Well I just wanted to make sure you didn't *forget*, the father says, a little indignantly, but then he laughs at himself. He turns back to the girl.

You said you had a brother?

Brian, yes.

Is he going to take over the farm?

Brian's not really interested in farming actually. He lives down in the city, she says one more time. She turns to the son. *In Queens.*

The son smiles blankly.

I'm in the East Village.

I understand, the father is saying. That's kids today. They don't want to do what their parents did. They want a better life.

Brian's not really sure what he wants to do. He's working as a trainer right now.

The father nods. I make my living as a plumber, he says, turning back to Donnie. Living out in Hutchinson, Kansas.

Good living, Donnie says. It's hard to tell if it's a question or a statement.

Well, you know, when I graduated from high school I had to choose. Carpentry or plumbing. I was good at both. I supposed I liked carpentry a little more but I figured people always need a plumber regardless of the economy. It's seen me through. I'm mostly into pipe bursting now. Are you familiar with that procedure?

Pipe bursting?

Trenchless sewer line replacement.

Trenchless?

No trenches.

Dad, the boy says.

What, Dale? Sorry, he says to the table. I'm a little hard of hearing. What did you say, Dale?

I was about to say that you've already told everyone about pipe bursting.

Well, I haven't told Donnie.

Donnie, the son says. You don't happen to need a new sewer line, do you?

What? Donnie says. He looks completely confused. My sewer line's fine?

I'm not selling it to him, Dale. I'm just explaining to him how the procedure works.

Father and son look at each other for a moment, and then the father laughs.

Pardon me, the father says to the girl. I get a little carried away sometimes. A man likes to talk about his work.

The girl smiles.

My grandpa and my dad and Donnie can talk about the farm for hours.

Forever, Carly says from the other end of the table.

The father nods. He is staring so intently at the girl's face that she has to drop her eyes to her plate. Her asparagus is still sitting there, cut into bite-sized pieces but uneaten.

The girl almost jumps when she feels the father's hand on her hair.

Here you are, honey. You had something in your hair.

It is the broken rubberband.

Oh. Thank you.

She takes it from him, holds it for a moment then drops it on her plate.

And where are your parents? the father says. Are they around?

Oh, she shrugs. My father had to take my mother to the hospital in Albany this morning. That's the only reason I'm here really. I live with my fiancé now, but I promised I'd look in on the twins, make sure the men got fed.

What? Christine looks up blankly at the other end of the table.

I'm sorry to hear that, the father says. I hope she's okay.

Oh, it's nothing serious, the girl says. Just one of those procedures. Precautionary, exploratory. She should be home tonight, but she packed a suitcase just in case. Said it'd be her first vacation since she married a dairyman.

The father and Donnie laugh a long time at that.

The girl smiles brightly.

Did I hear you say something about seeing your brother?

The father smiles back at her. My half brother. Now there's a story. Dale should tell it, he's the storyteller.

The girl turns to the son.

The son makes a little face. He looks at the girl, his father, back at the girl.

God, where to start. Okay. So my father's father was married before he married my father's mother.

She was called Nancy Mitford, the father says.

Right. My grandfather's first wife. Nancy Mitford. Anyway, Nancy and Floyd, that was my grandfather, Floyd—

Lloyd, Dale. My father's name was Lloyd.

The boy shrugs at the girl.

You see we have a bit of a generation gap in this family. Anyway, Lloyd and Nancy had a son together, and they named him Dale Peck.

The girl turns to the father.

Nope, not me. My father named me after his firstborn son.

The girl is confused. Did he die?

No, the father says. His mother took him. Nancy Mitford. She hid out in the fields one day, waited till my dad left, and then she took off. My dad was a incorrigible drunk, you see, I guess they couldn't make things work out. So she left and took her son with her, and then when my dad got married to my ma he named me after his firstborn son. My ma always hated the fact that he did that.

The girl is completely lost, but she just smiles. There is a pause, and then the son says,

214

Well, what would she have named you?

What was that, Dale? The father cups a hand over his ear.

What would your mother have named you? If your father hadn't named you Dale?

Why, I don't know, Dale. She named my older brothers Duke and Jimmy. James. I guess she would have named me something like that. Then my little brothers, Lance, he's named after my great-grandfather on my dad's side, and Gregory, he was named after the movie star.

Gregory Peck, the girl says.

He got hit by a bus, the father says.

Gregory Peck got hit by a bus?

No, my little brother. He was killed by a bus when he was fifteen years old. My mother looked me right in the face and she said to me it should have been you in front of that bus. Not my baby. Not my baby boy. My mother always hated me for being my father's son, see, she wouldn't have married him otherwise. My brother Lance, he named his first son after Gregory.

The girl realizes her smile has gone a little rigid on her face.

You, um, you were saying something about meeting him. Your brother? Your half brother?

Oh right, the father says, suddenly smiling again. Tell her, Dale.

Well, the son says, I got a call last winter, this guy was practically screaming into the phone, Are you Dale Peck? Are you Dale Peck? And when I said yes he said, I'm your brother! And of course I knew the story, so I said, No, you're my uncle, and he was like, What do you mean, your uncle? Why did you call me? He was so confused and excited he thought I'd called him. The son shrugs. I guess he'd had a friend over setting up his computer, and his friend showed him how you could get phone numbers off the Internet. So they put in our name and New York State and the rest is history. My number's unlisted, the son said then. But it came up anyway.

I tried looking up my brother one time, the father says, but I didn't find him because his mother gave him her second husband's name. Gorman. Dale Peck Gorman. But you should get on the

Internet. You never know who you might meet. Maybe you've got a long-lost brother or sister out there.

Carly looks up from the other end of the table, where she and Tommy are thumb-wrestling.

What?

Never mind dear, the girl says. Go back to your game. She looks around the table then, suddenly realizes that everyone has finished eating. She turns to the son, the father. Anybody want seconds?

Everyone is full.

Christine, check and see is there any of that apple pie left?

Uh—

Now.

There's cherry, Carly says. Mom made it yesterday.

Good, the girl says. Go get it, would you?

Christine gets the apple pie from the fridge and Carly gets the cherry from the pantry while the girl gets plates and forks—no, spoons, she decides, and grabs a quart of vanilla ice cream from the freezer. She is aware that the meal has gone on longer than it usually does and she still has to wash up. But it doesn't feel finished yet.

Hey, Donnie, the father says now. Would you mind giving Dale a little tour after we're done here? Show him the barn? I'd like him to see what his old man did once upon a time.

Donnie looks up from the plate of cherry pie Carly has put in front of him. Well, I guess we could spare a few minutes. Ralph'll be wanting us back out in the fields before too long.

That's my grandfather, the girl says, putting a plate in front of the father. I gave you a little of both, she says.

Well, thank you, darling, the father says. Eat up, Dale, he says to his son. Homemade apple pie.

Just a little, the son says. He pats his stomach, though whether he's indicating he's full or watching his weight the girl doesn't know.

Spoons scrape rhythmically over china. Slices of pie disappear from the plates. It seems that almost as soon as she has served everyone they are done eating. Already Donnie is fidgeting in his chair.

Was you still wanting to see the ladies?

If it's not too much trouble? the son says.

Nah, nah.

Donnie pushes back his chair so quickly it almost falls over.

As they walk down the slope of the driveway the son lags behind a little, letting his father and Donnie walk on ahead. The girl thinks of how he'd had trouble keeping to his father's pace when they first arrived.

I just wanted to say thank you for lunch.

Oh, it was no trouble. I was already cooking.

Not just for the food. The son opens his mouth, closes it again. There is half a grimace on his face, as if saying these things is difficult or even painful for him in some way. The girl tries to set her face into an expression of calm welcoming, as she does when one of her kindergarteners gets nervous during show and tell.

My father and I have been through some tough times, the son says finally. It's nice to be able to spend a pleasant afternoon with him. Doing something that's important to him.

Oh.

The word comes out of the girl's mouth without premeditation, and it seems somehow adequate as a response. Round, and full of feeling.

If you're ever in the city, I'd love to repay the favor.

Well, I really need to get down there to visit Brian and his boyfriend. If I do I'll be sure to look you up.

I'd like that, the son says. The blandness of his smile suggests that he hasn't heard what she said, or perhaps he doesn't think the coincidence as significant as she does. But it seems he's just distracted. What's this? he says.

It's called a Century Farm plaque. The state gives them to farms that have been in the same family for more than a hundred years.

The son kneels down in front of the big slab of granite. He uses his hand to sweep back the unmown grass that has folded over the edges of the plaque mounted in the stone. Hull Farm. 1887–1987.

Cool.

He looks up at the farmhouse at the top of the lawn then. His

217

hand is still on the Century Farm plaque, and there is that look on his face again, and the girl suddenly realizes he's not decorating the house but imagining himself in it. It's as if he is giving himself her house's history, her family's past. As if he doesn't have one of his own.

He stands then, and the girl steps back, feeling for the second or third or fourth time like a voyeur in her parents' home.

Guess we'd better go see the "ladies," the son says.

There are only half a dozen cows in the barn. Donnie's tour is cursory, and already almost over: he has walked from one end of the milking alley to the other. The son follows his father and the girl walks behind, single file. She is barefoot, and she takes care not to slip into the manure gutters.

At the far end of the barn Donnie turns, pauses. The father turns, looks again at what he's just looked at.

It's all automated now, huh Donnie?

Yup.

The father turns to his son.

When I was up here we still had to carry the milk in pails to the holding vat. Eighty pounds those buckets weighed. I used to carry two at a time, they weighed more than I did.

Donnie says, Yup, again. He does a little soft-shoe sidestep. You used to sway between em like you was drunk, but you never did fall over.

Well hell, Donnie. Uncle Wallace would've kicked me square in the ass if I'd done something like that. He'd've put his boot right through the seat of my pants and had Aunt Bessie charge me for sewing up the hole.

Donnie nods his head. Wallace was a thrifty man. There is a pause, and then he says, Silage is automated too. He presses a button on the wall behind him, and a few grains of corn and ground stalks spew into the end of the trough.

One of the ladies lows.

Well look at that, the father says. Is that corn?

Corn, yeah.

Just then the door at the other end of the alley opens, and the girl's grandfather walks in. He limps only a few steps into the barn on his lame hip, spots Donnie, and waves a hand.

That's Ralph, Donnie says. I gotta get going.

He trots down the alley. The grandfather has already left the barn.

That's my grandfather, the girl says to the son. Donnie's always been a bit afraid of him.

Donnie pauses in the barn door.

Bye Dale. Good seeing you.

Bye Donnie, the father says to the closing door. He laughs. Donnie Sutton. Seventy years old, gotta get to the fields.

On the way out of the barn the father scratches one of the ladies on the forehead, then cups her head in both his hands.

Well, hello there baby. Yes hello there beautiful. Those are just the prettiest brown eyes I've ever seen, yes they are.

The son watches his father with a soft smile on his face, full of wonder and love, and longing too. He looks at his father with the same expression he'd looked at the girl's house a moment ago. The father continues to hold the cow's face in his hands, his face blank again, lost to memory, and all at once the weight of the afternoon settles on the girl's shoulders, the significance of what is passing between these two men. The father holds the head of the cow in his hands as though it were something delicate, precious, crystalline—and already broken—while his son watches him with a look on his face that seems to say, If I had a tube of superglue in my hand, I'd put it all back together for you. But the father has eyes only for the cow in his hands. The years seem to melt off his body for the few moments he holds her, the thin limbs of a boy emerge, eyes innocent of a loss he can only acknowledge by pretending it didn't happen. All at once the girl looks around at the spindly walls of the dairy barn, the vertical slices of light that come through the boards where the battening has fallen off. She sees the straggly lines of the unkempt garden, the unmown lawn, the grass obscuring the edges of the Century Farm plaque. She realizes that loss belongs not just to these men. It's all she can do not to take the son's hand in hers and squeeze it.

The son puts his hand on his father's shoulder.

We'd better get on the road if we want to make it back to Rochester tonight.

The father looks up with a start. Looks at the girl, and then at his son.

I tell you what Dale. There was a time when all I wanted was to be a dairy farmer. I called up Uncle Wallace and begged him to take me back, but all he would say was, You broke my heart Dale, you broke my heart. I told him Ma beat me and Dad was drunk but all he'd say was, You broke my heart. But his heart was too hard to break. It's a hard life, dairy farming. It's no life for a man.

No one says anything, and after a moment the father turns back to the cow in his hands.

But you're a pretty thing anyway. Yes you are. But not as pretty as Gloria Hull.

As they leave the barn Donnie and the boy are pulling out of the driveway in Donnie's pickup. Sand spurts from under his tires as he races after her grandfather. The father laughs again.

Seventy years old and still raring to work. Donnie Badget. Sutton, I mean. He laughs at his son. Donnie *Sutton*. Hey, he says then, to the girl. Would you mind if I took a picture of you and Dale? Nobody's gonna believe me at the reunion when I tell them a sexy blonde made me lunch, I'm gonna need proof.

The girl feels her blush on her cheeks like a prickly brush. She pushes her fingers through her hair.

Sure.

She and the son stand side by side with their backs to the barn. She feels it behind her like a backdrop, sees the farmhouse over the father's shoulders as similarly two-dimensional, unreal. She and the son sling their arms over each other's shoulders. She tries to pinpoint a moment when this understanding was forged, this connection, but can't. Still, it feels natural, and she squeezes his shoulder a little.

Now it is the father's turn to beam at his son.

Look at that, he says. Dale with his arm around a pretty girl. He guffaws, but lightly. Oh well.

The camera clicks audibly in the quiet afternoon.

They linger by the Lincoln, hug. Linger a moment longer. The girl wants them to stay, and she wants them to go too. The moment is full, and she feels it would become distorted if anything else were added to it. Then the father and son get in the car. The girl watches the car as it drives away—it's what you do, after all, at a leave-taking. The son backs out of the driveway slowly, the gravel crunching under the Lincoln's big wheels, then pilots his father's car a little too quickly around the curve by the creamer and shoots up the hill toward the bridge into town. Then the car crests the hill and is gone as suddenly as it appeared. The girl watches the empty space for a moment until it occurs to her that she will probably never see it, or its occupants again, and then, with a small, nebulous sadness, she walks toward the house to do the dishes before heading back to Justin's. Within moments she's distracted by the prospect of hand-washing seven plates (why *won't* her mother buy a dishwasher?), scrubbing the burned residue of canned asparagus from the bottom of the pot, taking a wire brush to the barbecue grill. She should dump the ash bucket too. Maybe she'll even plant those impatiens. But Justin's mother had talked about roasting a chicken tonight, and she doesn't want to be late. She looks at her watch. It's coming up on three-thirty. A two-and-a-half-hour lunch. Her grandfather would have a *cow*.

The twins have returned to their collage in the living room. There seems to be more paper stuck to their skin than to the piece of cardboard between them. The place is a mess, and she feels a surge of anger. She is almost ready to deliver a lecture about how the twins don't care about their own home when Carly says,

Dad called. She doesn't look up from her work.

The girl's heart rises to her throat. It is an effort to say,

And?

Mom's fine, Christine says, they'll be home for dinner. You be here?

And just like that, the girl's anger melts away. She watches as Christine's scissors turn a picture of a car into little slips of blue. She is silent for so long that Christine looks up at her.

No, she says then. Justin's mom is roasting a chicken tonight. I gotta get back. She resists the urge to add the word *home*.

Christine turns back to the page in front of her. She and Carly's scissors make a sound like water as they cut through paper. After a moment Carly looks up, blowing her bangs off her forehead with a puckered lower lip.

What?

Nothing, the girl says. I'm gonna do the dishes.

She hasn't exactly forgotten the men, not yet, but she's not exactly thinking about them either. Instead she feels a warmth across her cheeks, her shoulders: that's how she's remembering them. Later, over dinner, she'll tell Justin and his family about them, and she won't be conscious of the distance her words put between her and the afternoon, the men, the physical memory of their presence on her cheeks, her shoulders. Her mother will call after dinner, thank her for cooking lunch, quiz her about the two strangers she invited into her house, and the girl will find herself defending them slightly. They were nice guys, Mom. And anyway, the dad was old and the son was gay.

Certainly she's not conscious of the residence she's taken up in both the father's and son's lives. That she has confirmed the father's faith in good country people, that the son thinks of her as the one positive experience he's shared with his father as an adult. It would never occur to her that weeks, months later she'll be the person they remember from this trip. Not Donnie, not the father's brother Jimmy dying in Florida, not his mother sitting in the chair in her brother Herb's kitchen because of her arthritis and refusing even to move to a chair on the patio with the rest of the family. Not even the reunion—the union, really, the first meeting—with the father's long-lost half brother, his namesake whose name was changed, and who as a result disappeared for sixty years. Dale Peck who became Dale Gorman. Who lost his name along with his father, lost it to a brother who in his imagination stepped into it like a pair of handed-down shoes.

Almost as soon as they leave Hull Farm the father begins pulling cinnamon candies from a big bag on the center console of the Lincoln and sucking them down one after another. He puts the red cellophane wrappers in his empty coffee cup in the cup holder that sticks out from the dash. The cup holder can slide flush with the dash when not in use, but the son has never seen it empty of cups and candy and cigarettes in all his times in the car.

The son pilots the Lincoln along 81 through Oak Hill until he reaches the intersection of 81 and 32 in Greenville. The Thruway is dead ahead, the farm to their left.

Want to take one more look at the place?

Yeah sure, the father says, and the son can't tell if his voice is wistful or just quiet. He sucks on his candy. Why not.

Thirty-two to 38. Past what used to be the high school—it's the middle school now—past what used to be Shepherd's Bush—now it's called Pine View—then right toward what used to be Uncle Wallace's farm.

Used to run this every day, Dale. Yes, son, your old man was a cross-country star in his day.

How is your foot?

Last night, when he'd carried their luggage up to their motel room, the son had been surprised to find a pair of crutches in the trunk, even more surprised to find out they were his father's.

My foot's all right, thank you Dale. Last week I couldn't hardly walk it hurt so bad. But that's the thing about gout, it comes and goes of its own accord.

As the Lincoln ascends the last hill toward the farm the son feels a little thrill in his chest. It's not just his father's presence in the passenger's seat. He first discovered the farm two years earlier, and he's driven by it several times since then, and every time he crests the hill he feels that same sense of what if? in his gut. It's hard to frame the feeling more specifically than that because so much seems to hang off his father's decision to leave the farm when he was fourteen. If he had stayed, the son thinks, he would have been a different person.

Not the same man with different qualities, but someone else entirely. He would have had a different wife, different children. He—the son—would be different too.

First there's the abandoned house north of the farm. The Flacks own it now, Flip plans to renovate it for his daughter and her fiancé. Then there's the Flacks' own house, a stately white Greek Revival backed by a cluster of pristine green-roofed barns, divided by a gleaming asphalt parking lot the size of a minimall's. Then the farmhouse.

It seems naked without any trees in its front yard, just the row of six stumps cut flush to the ground like a row of checkers. This time the first thing the son notices is that the house doesn't have a porch. He remembers standing on the Hulls' front porch in the shade of the two well-grown sugar maples that flank the front walk, but the Pecks' farmhouse—formerly the Millers', as the historical marker next to the driveway still proclaims, and now someone else's—has neither a formal front porch nor a side porch for outside meals and sunsets. It does have a few extra feet of eave over the front door, but it is hardly a porch. It is barely as wide as a grown man's shoulders, just enough to shelter strangers—friends would come around to the kitchen—as they wait for someone to answer their knock. It is a compact Federal-style house. A contemporary viewer might call its simplicity elegant, but no one would ever mistake it for what weekenders call a country house. The Hulls and Flacks live in country houses; the Pecks lived in a farmhouse. A house that has only what it needs. Whose plainness isn't aesthetic, but economic. The fieldstone foundation was extracted from the yard; the rectangular dentals aren't decoration, but rather the tips of the roof joists extending beyond the asphalt-shingled eaves to provide a secure base for the gutters. The bay window on the east wall of the kitchen wing was added by the most recent tenants, and if you look closely at the mullions in their other new windows you'll see that they're just strips of tape applied in a cosmetic grid. By contrast the tongue-and-groove ceiling of the side porch on the Flacks' house is painted light blue—Tiffany blue, Prussian blue, sky blue. When the man's son tells him that it is a country custom to paint a porch's ceiling the color of the sky the man says, I didn't know that. That's very interesting. It certainly is the color of the sky, he adds, though he is still sucking ruminatively on a candy and staring at what used to be his uncle's house.

Those stumps used to be trees, he says.

They were elms, his son says, a little fact the son pushes forward like a novice chess player advancing all his pawns to get them out of the way. Flip said they had to cut them down in the early seventies.

Elms? the father says absently. Yes, Dale, I think they were elms. But his voice is so vacant he could as easily have said oak, ash, redwood, banyan.

It's a beautiful house, the son says now, though by then the slow-moving car has passed it. They're in front of the field now, what used to be the north pasture. It's freshly mowed, and a long black serpentine drive leads to a stately white neocolonial at the top of the hill. It's only a few months old, its corners so crisp against the empty sky it could be a billboard rather than a building.

Ah, now that's a house Dale. Look at that, right up there on that hill where I always wanted to build a house. If you'd only come up here a year sooner, that'd be my house up there on that hill.

The son hears his father say *house* three times, but none of the words seem to refer to the building on the hill.

You wouldn't want to live in Uncle Wallace's house?

Aw hell Dale, that place is a step above a shack. There wasn't a plumb line in the whole house forty-five years ago, who can say what kind of shape it's in now. Lead pipes, oil burner in the basement, some rusted-out cast iron tub with hot and cold water coming out of two different faucets.

There are some people who like that sort of thing.

I know it, the father says. They keep me in business.

He and the son laugh.

No, Dale, if I wanted to live there I'd have to gut the thing, rebuild it from the inside out just to make it livable. Be better off tearing it down and starting over. And the view's better up there on that hill.

Yeah, no, I guess you're right. He taps the steering wheel. Well, I guess we should head back then.

The son says he thinks he knows a shortcut back to the Thruway but as it turns out he doesn't know the area as well as he thinks he does, or would like to. He spends an hour piloting them through the twists and turns and hills of Greene and Albany County back roads, and the whole time the father admonishes him to slow down, you're gonna get us killed Dale, Jesus Christ, be careful, I want to get to the reunion but not on a stretcher.

Look, Dad, the speed limit's forty-five. He taps the digital speedometer. I'm driving forty-three.

Well there's no law that says you have to drive *at* the speed limit, Dale. Keep both hands on the wheel. You have to pay attention to road conditions.

It's a sunny day, Dad, road conditions are perfect. They wouldn't make the speed limit forty-five if it wasn't safe to drive forty-five.

The father reaches nervously for another candy.

Well just take it easy for your dad's sake then.

The boy slows down to forty, thirty-nine, sets the cruise control. Happy?

The father laughs. Father and son is a game the two have only recently begun playing, and both enjoy it.

This was a very nice trip, Dale, thank you very much for suggesting it.

It was my pleasure.

It was good to see the farm again. And Flip and Donnie. And of course Gloria Hull.

She was sweet.

Prettiest girl in Greenville, New York.

Actually, she lived in Oak Hill.

Prettiest, nicest girl in Oak Hill, the father says, untroubled. Oak Hill, Greenville, they're all the same. Hell, there's a Greenville in every state of the country, but you'd be lucky to find a girl half as pretty or as nice as Gloria Hull in any one of them.

That's true.

By the time they've reached Rochester she's become the prettiest, nicest girl in Upstate New York, and by the time the bulk of the family shows up Friday afternoon she's become the prettiest, nicest girl the father has ever met—except my daughter, of course, he says if his youngest child is in earshot. By the time Dale Peck Gorman shows up Saturday morning, thirty-six hours after the two men have returned from Hull Farm, the father has told everyone who passes through his Uncle Herb's house about the prettiest, nicest girl you could ever hope to meet—told many of them more than once, in between telling them about his rebuilt '31 Chevy street rod and the advantages of trenchless sewer pipe replacement over traditional methods, which in the father's eyes seem as backbreakingly labor intensive as Roman aqueducts. When he talks about his car he talks about how Donnie Badget messed this up or did that wrong (he calls him Donnie Sutton sometimes, and every time he does he curses his son for confusing him), and when he talks about trenchless sewer pipe replacement he talks about the four hundred thousand dollars he has invested in it and the downturn in Kansas's aerospace-driven economy, but when he talks about Gloria Hull his voice lightens, slows down. If his digital camera is handy he calls up her picture on the square-inch screen and points with his blunt index finger at the orange blob on the right, smaller than his nail. There she is. The prettiest, nicest girl in Greenville, New York.

The night before Dale Peck Gorman arrives the son dreams that he has awakened in his great-uncle's dairy barn, and as he runs down the milking alley the cows follow him with their dark eyes and wet mouths. When he wakes up he is standing in front of the washer and dryer outside the basement room where he had been sleeping on a row of twin beds with his father, stepmother, sister, sister's boyfriend, and his cousin Misty, daughter of his father's youngest sister, Priscilla. It is the first time in his life he has ever walked in his sleep, and he stands next to the washer and dryer for a long time, heart pounding half from fear, half from exhilaration. He has slept-walked! He has walked in his sleep! The cows' faces come back to him, their blank stares less menacing now. He wonders if the images come from Hull Farm, or his Great-Uncle Wallace's, which he visited when he was four or five. There is something vaguely pleading in the cows' direct gazes, but he will not think of it again until he sees his father's half brother the following day.

A few hours later the morning dawns humid but cool. The son can see fog through a window in Uncle Herb's basement, where the rest of his family still sleeps on their barrackslike row of single beds— except for his father, he sees, who wakes with the dawn. The son gets out of bed quietly, slips into a pair of shorts and a T-shirt and to kill time walks a mile or so down the road his Great-Uncle Herb lives on, a mile back. As he approaches the house he sees an extra car in the driveway. Florida plates. To distinguish the three Dales from each other, they are referred to jokingly by the family as Florida Dale, Kansas Dale, and New York Dale, and now the son—New York Dale—examines the short man in a short-sleeved plaid shirt and low-slung jeans who is only just now getting out of his car. He has a bit of a belly but he's still a lot thinner than Kansas Dale. Nearly bald on top, with a slightly blobby nose that fits right in with all the big Dundas noses surrounding him. The woman next to Florida Dale has a helmet of black curls sprinkled with gray. She is shorter than her husband, a slim woman in thick glasses. Her husband wears glasses too, and his eyes are wide and blank behind them, a little needy, a little scared.

The son thinks of the nicknames as signs like the one in front of Uncle Wallace's farm, alluding to history and yet excluding it as well, names like locked boxes that tell you what's inside without letting you touch the contents. All the Dales started out in New York, but it would take more than one book to tell you how they ended up in Kansas, Florida, down in the city, how they all came to be standing on a freshly mowed lawn in front of a tan brick ranch-style house outside of Rochester. Though there are six people on the lawn as the son cuts toward them—his father and his stepmother, Uncle Herb and his girlfriend, Dale Peck Gorman and his wife, Dot—the son still feels someone is absent, and he is surprised when he realizes the person he is missing is Gloria Hull.

It's like looking in a mirror, he hears Dot say as he comes up. Nobody seems to notice his approach.

The son's father and his father's half brother stand face to face. The father is a heavier man, more fat but a lot more muscle too, but their features *are* the same. Not identical, but filial. The son watches as the two men look at each other through nearly identical square-framed silver glasses.

Been waiting a long time for this, Dale Peck finally says.

Been waiting my whole life, Dale Peck Gorman says, and on the last word his voice cracks and he throws his arms around Dale Peck's shoulders.

The son watches as Dale Peck lets himself be held by Dale Peck Gorman. It's good to finally meet you brother, he says, his voice light, his words meaning no more than what they mean. He holds his brother for a moment, and then he lets go.